The Heart-Shaped Tin

The Heart-Shaped Tin

Love, Loss and Kitchen Objects

BEE WILSON

FOURTH ESTATE • *London*

4th Estate
An imprint of HarperCollins*Publishers*
1 London Bridge Street
London SE1 9GF

www.4thestate.co.uk

HarperCollins*Publishers*
Macken House, 39/40 Mayor Street Upper,
Dublin 1, DO1 C9W8, Ireland

First published in Great Britain in 2025 by 4th Estate

1

A catalogue record for this book is available from the British Library

ISBN 978-0-00-868563-8

Typeset in Adobe Garamond Pro by Jouve (UK), Milton Keynes

For Tom

Contents

Preface: The Heart-shaped Tin

'Objects can have about them a glow of significance,
sending sparks of their own into the imagination of the
beholder . . .'

Susan M. Pearce, 1995

I have long felt that kitchen objects can have a life of their own.
Even so, I found this eerie. One August day in 2020, I was going
to fetch clothes out of the washing machine when suddenly a cake
tin fell at my feet with a loud clang. It wasn't just any cake tin. It
was the heart-shaped tin I had used to bake my own wedding cake.
I wouldn't have thought much of it except that it was only two
months since my husband had left me, out of the blue.

Nearly twenty-three years ago, this giant metal heart had been
brand-new. My husband-to-be told me he liked fruit cake but
hated glacé cherries. For our wedding, I decided to bake him a
rich, dark fruit cake with no cherries and chopped-up dried apricots to take their place. There are photos of us cutting the cake
together looking blissfully happy. We would soon be on our way to
Venice for our honeymoon.

All these years, I kept the tin. We had three children and sometimes I used it to bake their birthday cakes: shiny brown hearts of
chocolate cake smothered in ganache. We stored it tucked away on
the bottom of a dresser in my hallway, where it was slowly rusting.
I kept it there because it was too vast to fit in any of the kitchen

cupboards. To give it away would have been unthinkable. It was a keepsake of our love.

At the back of my mind, I'd imagined that one day I would use the tin to bake an anniversary cake. In one of her books the food writer Ruth Reichl gives a recipe for the giant chocolate cake she made to celebrate her husband Michael's birthday the first year that she knew him, a cake so colossal it took four men to help her lift it to the car. Reichl calls it simply 'Big Chocolate Cake'. I had a vague idea that this would be the cake I'd bake for our twenty-fifth anniversary. We were getting closer to this moment. After we'd been married for about ten years, he made the same joke every year on our anniversary. 'Eleven *long* years!', he would say in an affectionate way. 'Twelve *long* years!' It made me feel safe when he joked like this, because surely no one would make that remark if they really thought the years *were* long. I told people how lucky we were and how *we never argued*.

As symbols go, a heart-shaped cake tin, bought for a wedding, is not exactly subtle. It's Disneyfied romance, fashioned into a shiny object. I was only nineteen when we met and twenty-three when we married. He was seven years older and was one of my college teachers, which didn't seem to matter at the time.

One morning in June 2020, sitting on an ordinary park bench, drinking a cup of coffee, he said he didn't love me anymore, not 'like that'. He never elaborated what 'like that' meant. It didn't seem real. I thought that divorce was something that happened to other people – my parents, for example, who split up when I was fourteen. At the time, this was the biggest shock of my life. One New Year's Day, my father announced over lunch that his resolution was not to live with our mother anymore. I was the one who had casually asked whether anyone had any resolutions. For years, I felt I had caused him to leave with my question.

My purchase of the heart-shaped tin suggests that I was

urgently searching for a happy-ever-after: a sweet and unbroken heart. Of all my ex-husband's excellent qualities, one of his greatest was – or so it seemed to me – that he was so steadfast. He never gave me a moment's doubt about his loyalty. The morning of the day he left he brought me a cup of tea in bed, just as he always did, and I thanked him with real gratitude, just as I always did. When the tin clattered loudly to the ground, it echoed my own shock.

Certain kitchen objects become loaded with meaning in a way that we are not fully in control of. You can't predict which will be the utensils you get attached to – the favourite mug, the spoon that feels just right in your hand – and which belongings decline over time into clutter. And then there are the objects that – even if they were made in some anonymous factory and bought in some anonymous shop – seem to carry with them a kind of magic. There is the plate that makes everything you put on it taste better, or the bowl you keep but can't actually bear to use because it reminds you too strongly of the person who gave it to you.

What should I do with the tin heart now that its original meaning was ruptured? When I told the story of it falling on the floor to friends, they all, without exception, made the same suggestion: I should invest the tin with new associations! I should bake a cake for myself in it, the richest cake imaginable, and throw myself a giant separation party. I was comforted by the kindness of the suggestion, but didn't feel quite ready for this yet. Instead, I left the tin where it was. I walked past it multiple times a day and sometimes winced slightly when I remembered it was there – a clanging metal symbol of rejection.

To cheer myself up (or at least to stop feeling so sad), I started reading books about Buddhism. I read that our suffering was linked to our attachment to things. These books told me that the ground beneath our feet is never as permanent or solid as we might hope and that the tighter we cling to our comforts, the more we hide the truth from ourselves that we can never really hold on to anything. One of the books – by an American Buddhist nun called Pema Chödrön – said that 'Abandon Hope' would be a good slogan to stick on your fridge. It says something about how low I was feeling that I found this a consoling message. All these years I had been holding on to my marriage as the support that would keep me safe in a dark world. But perhaps it was better to stop searching for something or someone to save me.

Sometimes you can't see what is right in front of you. However often I might have toyed with the idea of using the tin to make an anniversary cake, I had never actually done it. This metal heart became a piece of furniture my husband and I both rushed past each day on the way to work. Maybe the calm of our marriage, which I had taken such pride in, was little more than conflict avoidance or a sign that neither of us cared quite enough to voice our true feelings, including the negative ones. If the tin was a symbol of our love, why had we both neglected it to the point that it had become so rusty?

Once something has ended, when you look back all you can see are clues that it was always doomed. Tiny moments of dissatisfaction get inflated into portents. The past itself becomes contaminated. You forget all the good weeks and years and your mind crowds with memories of the times when you felt lonely or resentful, or the moments when you could see that the other person was somehow unhappy but you couldn't find the way or the words to reach out and help. I started to wonder whether the tin itself – and the cake I originally baked in it – was a powerful indication that it was doomed from the start. Maybe a man who was so fussy about cherries was not the man for me.

But when I picked it up, trying to decide what to do with it, the tin felt as solid as it did twenty-three years ago, as if it were still waiting to be used.

Charms

The Best China

'A china cup preserved over a generation is a victory of human purpose over chaos, an accomplishment to be quietly cherished.'

Mihaly Csikszentmihalyi and Eugene Rochberg-Halton, 1981

I started looking for examples of other people, past or present, who had invested objects in their kitchens with strong meanings or emotions. The more I asked around, the more I saw that feeling emotional about kitchen objects was the rule rather than the exception, even for people who were not especially interested in cooking. I wasn't alone in having intense and even magical feelings about the things I cooked and ate with.

Many people told me that they could still feel the presence of a lost parent or partner in their china cupboard. I met a woman who told me that she had recently burst into tears on opening a drawer and finding an old apple corer in it because it brought back the memory of her mother – long dead – making apple pie. Another person told me that she had a very powerful sense of one of her ancestors, whom she had never met, because she had inherited her rolling pin. A friend told me that the only thing she now had left from her French grandmother was a rusty old herb chopper which had belonged to her long ago in Paris, where her family ran a brasserie. My friend never used this chopper herself, but every time she looked at it she could see her grandmother's hands, alive and cooking.

Some of the people I spoke to said that they were not at all sentimental about kitchen objects, but then when they thought harder there was always at least one exception. One man told me that kitchen objects did not interest him, only to go on to reveal that after his mother's death he had held on to some special teatowels and placemats because they seemed to carry the 'texture' of her.

When people described their favourite objects, I noticed certain common themes emerging. Many of the most treasured objects were ones that they or people close to them had held in their hands and used every day – a grandmother's wooden spoon, a mother-in-law's butter dish decorated with a cow, a salt shaker inherited from a parent. Like pets or loved ones, these objects were cherished through daily touch. An excellent cook told me that when she walked past her Gaggia ice cream maker – which happened every day – she would smile and sometimes even pat it because she had owned it for so long that it felt like one of the family.

On the other hand, people also described as special the kitchen objects which they hardly used at all: a fragile porcelain bowl, some precious crystal glasses passed down through the generations, a linen tablecloth which only came out once a year. Some of these belongings had become so special – so hallowed – that almost no meal was good enough to justify their use. Like religious relics, they were venerated from a distance.

There is more than one way of demonstrating that an object is special, just as there is more than one way to show a person that you love them. One way to love an object is to use it as much as possible: to give it life through daily use; to stroke it, hold it, touch it to your lips. Another way is to worship it at a distance: to lock it away in a cabinet or cupboard, admire it, preserve it and use it as little as possible, for fear of damaging it or reducing its value.

To touch an object or not to touch it – that is the question. But you can also learn to relate to old objects in new ways. One of the people who helped me to start making sense of all this was Roopa Gulati, a chef and food writer who decided to start using her parents' precious best china after her husband Dan was diagnosed with a brain tumour. Having spent nearly five decades feeling that this beautiful dinner service was too good to use – she stored it in the attic for years – Roopa suddenly decided that life was too short not to use the good china while she could. Faced with the imminent threat of Dan's death, her diffidence about using the best china melted away. 'If it smashes, it smashes' became her new mantra.

Roopa's parents came from Punjab in northern India. She grew up in the north of England in rural Cumbria with her brother and sister: the only Asian family in the village. Her father was an eye doctor. The clinic where he worked on Saturdays was next to a very expensive china shop and Roopa remembers that when she was about eleven, he and her mother spent weeks looking at different sets of china before deciding. It was 1975 and the whole set was 'a huge outlay', maybe £500.

A generation ago, buying a whole dinner service was a weighty decision, perhaps all the more so for immigrants who were acutely aware of the judgement of others. It might seem strange now, but for a long time in Britain it felt almost obligatory to purchase a high-quality dinner service if you could afford it. A woman who worked in the north of England selling Royal Doulton and Wedgwood during the post-war decades in a big department store recalled a time up until the late twentieth century when 'everyone aspired to have a dinner set. Everyone seemed to have friends round.' Many of this woman's customers in the china department came in monthly, buying a precious piece or two at a time – a couple of cups and saucers one month, a dinner plate the next – until the set was finally complete.

To those who owned them, laying out a special dinner service was not just a way to honour your guests but to demonstrate what 'best' looked like in your home. Roopa's mother felt such pressure to get dinner just so for her guests that she laid the table two days before they arrived. Her beautiful dishes were a kind of armour with which, as a foreigner in this cold northern village, she shielded herself from the judgement of others.

As time slips by, the patterns on our plates become part of the mood music of our lives. The dinner service which Roopa's father eventually chose was called Braemar by Royal Doulton (not to be confused with a very different and later Royal Doulton pattern also called Braemar, with a splashy tartan pattern). When Roopa showed me one of the plates I instantly saw why her parents would have fallen in love with this particular set, which included vegetable tureens and bowls and platters along with plates. It was an elegant ceramic with a rare delicacy both in colour and design: white in the middle, with a rim of silver followed by an olive-green ring and then two different geometric patterns. Roopa thinks that – consciously or unconsciously – the look must have reminded her parents of the Mughal designs of northern India.

We were talking about the plates over lunch at Roopa's house in Pinner, where she has lived for the last twenty years. She generously cooked me lunch, a feast of dishes from a book she had been working on about the regional cooking of India, a country where she lived for twenty years after leaving school. She worked in Delhi as a chef, before returning to England. It was in Delhi that she and Dan met, after the sudden death of her first husband. Dan joined us for the first course, a translucent broth of lamb scented with two kinds of cardamom and royal cumin with fried onions and mint on top. It was only three months since Dan's last stem cell transplant to treat his brain tumour and he was still very weak, though it felt like a miracle that he was home from hospital and in humorous spirits, despite his ordeal.

As the three of us sipped the broth, Roopa described the pit she

used to feel in her stomach at the idea of breaking one of the Braemar pieces. The fear remained even after her mother died and she took possession of the whole dinner service. Then her father died, but still she kept the whole dinner service in the attic because the thought of breaking any of it was too awful to bear. 'It would be a bit of my mum and dad gone.' She explained that in childhood, the Royal Doulton set was considered so special that she and her siblings were never allowed to help wash it up. Her father was the only one permitted to wash it, and her mother always dried. When Dan heard Roopa saying this, he commented drolly that she should have asked her parents to buy more of the plates so that she could be excused washing-up duties altogether.

After the lamb broth, Dan went back upstairs to rest and Roopa brought out some of her beloved Braemar plates on which she served a deep-green *saag* of spinach and mustard greens cooked in copious amounts of butter, with flatbreads made from corn and finely sliced raw red onions on the side. The *saag* was a Punjabi winter dish: full of green minerally goodness. 'This is my heritage,' she said. It was a bright January day and the sunlight hit the silver edges of the plates and made them even shinier.

It was a joy to be able to use the dishes so freely, Roopa said. Her attitude to the dinner service changed immediately after Dan's diagnosis, just over a year before our lunch. In the midst of her grief, she started worrying about the unused plates up in the attic. She had a pressing feeling that by not being eaten off, the china had 'a life half-lived'. She wanted it to hold different foods and witness the conversations of another generation: her daughters' children. I noticed that she was talking about her tableware as if it were alive. It was impossible to know whether she and Dan would have another year together. But the plates, at least, could have a second life.

As a child, we may be taught that certain possessions are only for best, but what if today is all we have? 'Best' doesn't have to be saved for feast days or honoured guests. Each morning that Dan was alive was now a special occasion for Roopa. Using these shiny plates also became a daily treat that reminded her of her own worth: a way to celebrate her own existence even when she felt she had done little except visit Dan in hospital. She found herself using the Braemar to brighten her ordinary solitary breakfast of toast and marmalade – something her parents would never have done.

So many of us spend our whole lives denying ourselves the best things because the time is not right or we feel we haven't earned them yet, or we fear that someone – probably our parents – will disapprove of us if we drop them. This attitude to objects some-times goes along with a wider impulse of self-denial. This may be the legacy of hunger and rationing, or a religious childhood (both the Koran and the Bible contain prohibitions against touching holy objects without the right preparations), or simply of the social attitudes of earlier generations in which visitors were treated like royalty whereas close family members were unworthy of the 'good china' except in company. Some of us have memories of an older generation who kept beautiful cabinets of china and crystal locked away, waiting for the right occasion to dignify it. It feels sad that they spent so long choosing lovely things and so little time enjoy-ing them. It's like the idea of 'jam tomorrow' in *Through the Looking-Glass* by Lewis Carroll (1871). The Queen tells Alice that she can't have jam: 'The rule is, jam tomorrow and jam yesterday – but never jam today.'

If you don't use the best china now, you may never use it. 'Life is so precious,' Roopa said, offering me a bowl of figs cooked in rum and spices. The day we met, Dan was better than he had been for a long time, but she was still on edge with panic that he could have another seizure at any moment. I asked her whether the reason she was now brave enough to use the precious china was because the most fragile thing in her life was Dan and the plates seemed far less precious by comparison? The thought hadn't occurred to her before, but as soon as I said it she agreed that it was true. 'When I talk about Dan now, I sound like Dad with his china.'

Thinking about Roopa and her dinner service made me see that it was possible to change the way in which we relate to the objects that mean the most to us. We can learn to touch the things which we once loved only from afar. And when we do, we unlock different emotions about them. For nearly fifty years Roopa had believed that her family's beautiful china was to be venerated in public, not handled in private. 'We had to worship it,' she said. The plates carried an undercurrent of fear along with their beauty. But now she could love them in a less rarefied way, as a lovely but normal part of mealtimes. 'If it smashes, it smashes,' she said once again, as if trying to convince herself.

Roopa said that she still missed her parents' dinner parties and the excitement of standing in the living room, watching as her father put out bowls of pistachio nuts for the guests to have with drinks, while her mother, after all those hours of cooking and tidying, finally took a shower upstairs before dressing in a gorgeously bright sari of turquoise or pink. People in the village called her 'the peacock' because of her clothes, which embarrassed Roopa at the time but now she feels proud that her mother was so 'defiant in her colour'. Meanwhile, the plates shone on the table like sacred vessels. Roopa realised that the best way to honour the momentous and costly decision her parents made in the china shop all those years ago was to stop treating the plates as museum pieces. She might as well enjoy them, because now could be the best and only time. 'Dad's no longer there and Mum is not either. This is life.'

Our Kitchen Table

'How is it that a kitchen table we once admired in a shop window can later become the stable, silent foundation of family meals and conversations with friends?'

Jager, 1983

When you are very sad, your mind plays tricks on you. It can be hard to know which of your thoughts to trust and which to try to shake out of your head like a bad dream. While Roopa saw her china collection as a series of charmed objects, I was starting to look at some of the possessions in my own kitchen as tokens of bad luck, like a broken mirror or a horseshoe hung the wrong way up.

The business with the heart-shaped tin had unsettled me. Until now, I had not thought of myself as particularly superstitious. I walk under ladders without trembling and when a black cat crosses my path I hardly notice. I have had various friends who passionately believed in horoscopes or Tarot cards, but when they told me vital things about my fortune I did not feel it was anything more than a fun diversion.

Yet here I was, looking at a slightly rusty cake tin and believing that it was sending me messages. Who had I become? The tin wasn't even the only household item which I felt was talking to me. In the wake of my husband leaving, I was developing feverishly strong feelings about all kinds of inanimate objects, especially in the kitchen. I felt his presence – or rather, his absence – in the row of mugs on the dresser and in the arrangement of the frying pans in the drawer underneath the hob; in our shiny blue pepper grinder and in the white salt pig on the kitchen counter. When I opened the drawer where I kept the tea towels, I found the novelty apron one of his sisters had given him featuring the naked torso and penis of the statue of David by Michelangelo.

In truth, I wasn't doing so well. *How are you?* texted a friend. *A bit up and down*, I texted back. It felt shocking to hear my ex-husband speak of a new 'we'. Sometimes, when I needed to drive my youngest son somewhere, I put a Sharpie pen in my mouth to hold it in the shape of a smile, which was the only way I could reliably stop myself from crying while we were on the road.

In an attempt to purge some of the memories of my husband from the house and regain a little of my own sanity, I started to rearrange things. I emptied out the frying pan drawer and put the pans back in a slightly different order. I removed a grill pan which he had favoured but which I never used. I took it out of the kitchen and stuffed it into a little-used cupboard, which briefly gave me a sense of calm. But then I found that I actually wanted to chargrill some vegetables so the grill pan came back.

Next, I turned to a set of glass 'keep cups' for drinking coffee, branded with logos from his work printed on silicone bands. They sometimes made me cry just to look at them. I had the illusion that they, too, were rejecting me. But they were good-quality glasses; it would have felt a waste to get rid of them. They were made from shatterproof reinforced glass, which in a household of clumsy people (my children dropped or knocked glasses all the time, but then so did I) made them extra valuable. I removed the silicone bands and lo! – the keep cups had become perfectly neutral drinking glasses, good for hot or cold drinks, with no associations of him.

Yet no matter how many things in the kitchen I reshuffled or altered, there were still dozens more items that screamed to me that he was gone. Months after his departure, he was more present than ever.

There was a large iron knife which, for unknown reasons, he favoured for cutting home-made pizza. Neither of us used the knife for anything else, partly because I had allowed it to get blunt and it wasn't an easy knife to sharpen; but in the distant past, when it had actually been sharp, it was the best knife we owned. He had learned to make pizza dough using our electric breadmaker, and although it was one of only a handful of meals that he cooked he made it so many times that his pizzas became much better than mine. He took great care over the little details, slicing the mozzarella and leaving it to dry between sheets of kitchen paper so that the moisture would not make the pizza soggy. He rolled each piece out twice because he found that he could get the crust thinner if it had a rest in between the rollings.

Over the past few years we had developed a ritual whereby I would go to a yoga class on a Sunday night and he would make pizza for the children, giving me one night off from cooking. Those evenings were blissful. I came home and sat by myself with a book, eating whatever slices of cold pizza remained with a big salad. If there was no pizza left, I boiled some eggs. On the countertop I would find the big cast-iron knife, coated in little strings of mozzarella and dabs of tomato sauce. Now I could hardly look at this knife, let alone pick it up, because to touch its smooth handle would have felt like holding his hand.

Most of all, I felt his presence at our kitchen table: to be precise, in the left-hand corner of it, which was where he always sat. The very wood seemed to be full of him, as if his hands had left traces on the grain. I noticed for the first time that there were four dark knots in the timber exactly where his elbows used to rest as he ate.

Right from the beginning, this table was the place where we shared all of our meals. In the early years of our relationship I was an elaborate cook and we sat there together in our old house and ate such dishes as asparagus with walnut crostini or crab and saffron tart. Almost without fail we lit candles for dinner, a habit we adopted from his mother.

As wooden tables go, it's not a very special one. It's made of nondescript pine with an unappealing orangey colour on the legs and paler wood on top which became even paler over the years from all the times it was scrubbed. The surface was big enough for rolling sheets of fresh pasta on; big enough to have friends over; and later, in our new house, big enough for family card games or for the children to sit and draw pictures or do their homework. The best thing about the table was that it was *ours*.

In the daily life of a family, one of the most important rituals is the question of where everyone habitually sits to eat. My place was always at the end of the table. This was because I cooked and needed to be able to jump up and get food from the oven or the hob; but now that I come to think of it, I had made myself the head of the table. On my right was my youngest son, and one along from him was my daughter (who sometimes gently pointed out that his place had once been hers). On my immediate left was my husband, a place he adopted after our oldest son, who used to sit there, left home to study in another city. When our son first left home, I felt the ghost of his presence at the table for months and kept forgetting he was gone and laying a place for him. Now my husband was another ghost at the table.

Without him there the furniture itself felt unstable, like Van Gogh's painting of his chair in which all the angles are strange. When I came into the kitchen in the morning the ground under the table's legs was no longer as solid as it had once been. At dinnertime it felt as if the rest of us were actors who had turned up to perform a play in which one of the lead characters was missing. It helped when my daughter kindly moved to sit in his place, so at least it was no longer vacant. I could not have sat there myself. It would have felt like trespassing.

The table still felt so strongly his, even though he never asked to reclaim it or anything else from the kitchen. He left it all behind, although one of the children told me that he had bought a bread-maker just like the old one so that he could still make his pizza dough at a new table with his new person across town.

Drinking Glasses and Other Magical Objects

'The grasshopper hops on the glass, and falls in the glass. He falls to the bottom. How much would you like to drink the milk?'

April Fallon, Paul Rozin and Patricia Pliner, 1984

People are there in our lives and then they are not. But objects remain. So perhaps it's no wonder that we sometimes feel that the ones we have lost have found their way into our plates and bowls and spoons. Magical thinking is a much bigger feature of modern human life than most of us usually allow for, and not least when it comes to food and drink. Someone who has proved that this is so is a psychologist called Paul Rozin.

Paul Rozin is a scholar – a hugely influential one – of the strange and twisted ways in which humans sometimes behave around food. Among other things, Rozin is the person who coined the phrase 'The Omnivore's Dilemma', which the food writer Michael Pollan then used as the title of one of his bestselling books. I first came across Rozin's research a few years ago when I was writing a book (*First Bite*, 2015) about how humans learn to eat. No matter which aspect of the subject I was trying to research, all my avenues of enquiry seemed to lead me back to Rozin, a professor of psychology at the University of Pennsylvania in Philadelphia. This man was an expert on everything, from why (some) humans learn to enjoy chilli peppers to why Westerners are so squeamish about eating insects. Rozin is one of the leading theorists of disgust and why we find certain foods disgusting, even when they will do us no physical harm.

When I finally met Rozin at a food conference in 2016, he was as charismatic as his writing had led me to believe. Rozin was a humorous man with a gravelly New York accent – he was born and raised in Brooklyn – and an intense appreciation of food. Over dinner he explained to me that if chefs had any sense, they would pay far more attention to the dessert course. Because of the way memory works, Rozin found that diners have a tendency to attach the greatest importance to whatever they ate last. This means that a spectacular dessert can almost trick us into forgetting a mediocre main course, something I often think of when I am baking something sweet.

One of Rozin's most foundational ideas is that magical thinking is a basic aspect of 'everyday, healthy, human functioning' in the modern Western world. Behaving as if you believe in magic around certain objects is not incompatible with being a rational person in other areas of your life. This is certainly true when it comes to sports. I have known highly logical people who genuinely convinced themselves that their presence or absence in front of the TV could affect whether their favourite team would win. Rozin has proved that all of us are susceptible to magical thinking.

It is quite easy to make someone feel so repulsed by an ordinary drinking glass that it is as if it has a curse upon it. Rozin's most famous experiments involved seeing how people reacted to various receptacles into which dead sterilised cockroaches had been dropped. Almost all the participants (forty-six out of forty-nine people) found the idea of 'roached' apple or grape juice disgusting, even though they had been assured by a scientist that the juice would do them no harm.

One by one, the participants came into a room where an experimenter with a 'clean appearance' sat at a table covered with a tablecloth. The experimenter, who sat next to the participant, unwrapped two fresh disposable drinking glasses and filled them with a little apple juice (in one) and grape juice (in the other) and asked the participant to take a sip of each juice and say which one they preferred. The experimenter then revealed a roach in a small plastic cup and said the words, 'Now, I'm going to take this sterilised, dead cockroach, it's perfectly safe, and drop it into this juice glass.' The roach was swirled around in the person's preferred flavour of juice for five seconds with forceps before being removed with a plastic spoon. The second glass of juice, by contrast, was stirred with a plastic birthday candle holder. Unsurprisingly, when asked to rate the juices again, the cockroach juice had become undrinkable to almost everyone, regardless of the fact that the insect was harmlessly sterile. By contrast, people were willing to drink juice which had been stirred with the candle holder. When participants were offered a totally fresh batch of apple juice in a fresh glass, unrelated to the first, they now liked the juice less, as if the cockroach had tainted all apple juice from now on.

Thinking again about the cockroach experiment, I no longer felt so stupid for crying at the very sight of my husband's keep cups. Rozin's work shows that almost everyone can get spooked by certain vessels, although he has also shown that people vary greatly in how sensitive they are to eating or drinking something from the 'wrong' bowl or glass. As Rozin noted in another of his papers (co-written with April Fallon): 'Some people would still like a bowl of soup after a grasshopper fell in and was removed, whereas others would not consume soup from this bowl even after this bowl was washed three times and refilled with fresh soup.'

Me? I wouldn't mind eating soup from a bowl in which a grasshopper had fallen, though I'd like the bowl to be washed first.

But the traces of my husband in the kitchen were not so easy to wash away.

The belief that another being – whether an insect or a husband – can leave a semi-permanent trace on a piece of kitchenware is a form of 'sympathetic magic', according to Rozin. This kind of magic is a universal form of superstition all over the world, though the forms it takes vary hugely from place to place. The basic premise is that things can create magical effects (good or bad) on people because of the sympathetic connections between them. For example, the Kei Islanders of Indonesia traditionally regarded the umbilical cord as the brother or sister of a child after they were born. The navel-string would be put in a pot with ashes and set high up in a tree to keep a protective watch over the child. This might sound odd, but Rozin would say it's no weirder than feeling that a shirt worn by someone we love is preferable to the same shirt straight off the peg – a common belief. (Interestingly, he found that a loved one's used toothbrush did not carry the same special aura; most people would rather have a factory-fresh toothbrush than a soiled one, even if the person who has soiled the toothbrush is our beloved.)

Supposedly we live in a rational, secular age. We feel far removed from the ancient American tribes who built up whole mythologies around the pots they cooked with, believing, for example, that certain vessels would instantly crack if they were used to cook meat instead of vegetables, or insisting that pots would break during firing if the women who made them spoke a single word. Yet we still have odd reactions to the inanimate objects in our lives that cannot be accounted for purely by reason, even if we suppress the strength of these feelings because they feel too private or weird to air publicly. A prop stylist called Maeve Sheridan told me that she has 'almost a gag reflex' for certain utensils such as a fork that looks the wrong way to her; she starts to wonder if she is going crazy and wonders if 'someone hit me with the fork in a previous life?'.

The laws of sympathetic magic were first laid out by Sir James Frazer in his 1890 book *The Golden Bough*. Frazer found that across all the traditional cultures of the world, magical beliefs followed two basic rules. The first was the law of similarity: the idea that things that look like each other will automatically share similar properties. This law explains why, in Malay custom, clay figures of enemies were burned in order to cause burning pain to the enemy themselves. Rozin did a series of experiments to show that the law of similarity was alive and well in modern America. For example, his researchers made a batch of high-quality chocolate fudge. They found – which may not surprise you – that people did not want to eat the brown fudge when it was shaped like very realistic dog poo.

The second law of sympathetic magic is that of contagion. The basic idea is 'once in contact, always in contact', or, as Frazer put it, that 'things which have once been conjoined must remain ever afterwards . . . in such a sympathetic relation that whatever is done to the one must similarly affect the other'. This is the law, in Rozin's view, which explains why we find a drinking glass disgusting after it has been in contact with a cockroach. Magical contagion can be positive – as in Rozin's example of the shirt worn by a loved one – or it can be negative. Once apple juice has become linked with a cockroach, it's not easy to discard the association.

In 1890 Frazer collected many bizarre examples of contagious magic in action. A lot of the customs had to do with hair or fingernails. There was a widespread fear that if your enemy could get hold of some of your hair or nail clippings, they could do you harm from a distance using the debris from your body. There was also paranoia about teeth falling into the wrong hands. In Germany, when a child lost a milk tooth, the tradition was to go behind the kitchen stove and throw it backwards over your head to protect all the child's other teeth.

It made me feel a little less mad to realise that, as Frazer wrote, magical thinking was a universal aspect of human cultures. There was a comforting solidarity in thinking about other people who let this kind of magic creep into their thinking. Maybe it was not actually so strange or unusual for me to feel that my husband's spirit still inhabited his corner of the kitchen table after all of those years of him sitting there. When I brushed against the table accidentally I seemed to be bumping into *him*, and it was a sensation that made me curiously shy, even in my own kitchen. What was it that Frazer had written? '[T]hings which have once been conjoined must remain ever afterwards.'

The Ukrainian Kitchen Cabinet

'The house is a symbolic body for the family.'

Russell Belk, 1988

Objects can't have feelings – of course they can't. But if ever there was a tenacious and brave kitchen cabinet, it was the one that clung to the side of a building for dear life in Ukraine in the spring of 2022, oblivious to the Russian bombardment.

'Be Strong Like This Kitchen Cabinet' was a meme which went viral on social media in April 2022, a little over a month into the Russian invasion. In the Kyiv suburb of Borodianka an apartment block was bombed out by Russian shells on the second day of the Russian invasion, February 25th. The building was wrecked to the point where the whole outer wall on one side was ripped off and the inner wall that remained was scorched by the bombs. The floors and ceilings had been blown away. Yet amid the ruins photographer Elizaveta Servatynska noticed an extraordinary detail. Somehow, hanging on to the side of a wall, there was an intact wooden kitchen cabinet, with plates still neatly stacked on the plate rack and mugs lined up on a shelf underneath.

In lives marked by uncertainty and grief, maybe we all need magic charms to make us feel stronger, like Roopa getting out her best china to help her through the hardest times. In or out of the kitchen, almost all of us have objects which we use to shield ourselves. In ancient Egypt there were amulets. These were the spiritual equivalent of armour: little tokens similar to jewellery that you kept on your person for protection. The most valuable ones were made of gold or gemstones, or beautiful turquoise faience. They might be shaped like powerful gods or animals with special qualities. There were fierce crocodile amulets to repel danger, scarab beetle amulets to bring good luck (the beetle was believed by the Egypytians to symbolise rebirth) and hippo amulets for their strong and protective qualities.

Most of us still use charms of some kind to protect us, whether in the form of trinkets or lucky underpants or socks. I lost my engagement ring many years ago; it fell off my finger while I was shopping for tomatoes before we were even married. As soon as I realised, moments later, we went back to look for it but it was gone. I sometimes wonder what happened to the person who found a small diamond in their bag of tomatoes.

My wedding ring, on the other hand, a plain, cheap, gold-plated band, was a constant on my hand for more than two decades. When feeling nervous, I would fidget with it as if it were worry beads. After my husband was gone I took off the ring and put it in a bowl in my bedroom. My finger felt naked without it and I had nothing to fiddle with. It felt impossible to give it away; yet looking at it made me shiver. My feelings about the ring changed after I found a Syrian recipe for lentils which involved cutting out tiny croutons using a wedding ring. I cut out dozens and dozens of doll-sized circles of dough and deep-fried them until they were crisp and golden-brown. It was a comfort to use the ring as a kitchen implement. It was no longer a sad item of jewellery belonging to a cast-away person but a very tiny pastry cutter.

As for my naked finger, a friend who was also divorced told me that I must buy myself a new ring and put it on my right hand instead of my left. She said I would feel better. I didn't believe her, but she was right. The new ring – a silvery one in a zig-zag shape – gave me something shiny to play with again, which fooled me into feeling stronger.

Kitchens, too, are full of shiny treasures that can trick us into feeling that we have magical powers. The food writer Mark Bittman has observed that 'like cookbooks, kitchen equipment is a talisman; people believe that buying the right kind will make them good cooks'. Certain articles of kitchen equipment can also make us feel safe and at home when in reality we are neither.

In times of war, whole countries may need charms to help them to carry on believing in a home that is being destroyed before their eyes. The photo of the Ukrainian kitchen cabinet was first shared with the caption 'How are you, little kitchen cabinet? – Holding on.' Another variant was 'Hold on, like this kitchen cabinet!' and finally, 'Be strong like this kitchen cabinet.' The cabinet became one of the most potent symbols of Ukrainian resistance and resilience in the face of the Russian onslaught. Its sheer homeliness made a mockery of the brutal Russian offensive. 'See!' it seemed to say. 'Your weapons are so pathetic that they can't even destroy the humblest wooden cabinet.'

This was a moment when Ukrainians needed miracles, and the survival of the kitchen cabinet looked truly miraculous. The most extraordinary detail of all was that on top of it, still intact, was a ceramic rooster, an example of Ukrainian folk art which many people in the country have in their homes. Along with the cabinet itself, this rooster became a useful piece of propaganda. President Zelenskyy gave one of them to the British Prime Minister, Boris Johnson, when he visited the city.

A kitchen cupboard hanging off the side of a building has the air of being impossible, like Spiderman crawling up walls. The longer you look at the photographs, the more details you notice. On one side of the cabinet there were two glass doors and I started to wonder what was inside: glasses or cups or bowls? Underneath it there were some humble kitchen tiles, in a similar colour to the wood of the cabinet. Whoever fixed those tiles to the wall did an extraordinarily good job. They did not stint on the adhesive.

The owner of the kitchen cabinet – and the destroyed apartment to which it belonged – turned out to be Mrs Nadiia Svatko. Her husband had been one of the 'liquidators' called on to deal with the fall-out from the Chernobyl nuclear disaster in 1986. Like thousands of other liquidators enlisted by the Soviet state, he died of radiation exposure. By the time of the Russian invasion, Nadiia Svatko had been widowed for twenty-six years. The day of the shelling, she was in the middle of making soup. When she heard what was happening, she fled to the basement of a nearby building with sixty other people, taking only a few possessions. She walks with a stick on account of a sore leg and thinks she wouldn't have made it out alive without the help of some children, who gave her a hand.

After her cabinet became famous across Ukraine, Svatko returned to the bombed-out remains of her apartment to be interviewed about it. In the video on the website of the Museum of Civilian Voices, her short hair was dyed burgundy and she wore a T-shirt decorated with roses. She said fondly that it was her younger son who had installed the cabinet – an 'ordinary' one that happened to stick very well, she said. The fact that it had survived the Russian bombing was clearly a source of pride to her. 'It is a sign that victory will be ours,' she insisted.

Sometimes we treat inanimate objects as if they were human beings, because to focus on people directly is too painful and too complicated. When my husband came to the door now, his once-beloved face seemed to burn my eyes in their sockets. My dog, who until so recently had been *our* dog, started to bark when he appeared. It was easier to deal with my sadness when it came in the form of a tin or a table.

When we look at the valiant wooden cabinet, it represents the brave Ukrainians who chose to stay in Kyiv despite the war, huddling in the subway at night. But thinking of the cabinet is more comforting. Even if it should fall and get smashed to smithereens, it is still only an assemblage of wood and glass. It can't *feel*, unlike the millions of Ukrainians who were forced to flee their homes, not through any lack of courage but because it was the only way they could survive.

The idea of an indestructible everyday object is a powerful symbol, especially in the context of a war which stripped millions of people of their kitchens and homes. Alisa Sopova – a Ukrainian anthropologist who observed the war from afar in the United States – noticed that increasing numbers of Ukrainians seemed to be taking comfort in 'material objects that stubbornly persist'. In the context of war, homely possessions could become almost sacred because they symbolised the old Ukraine that existed before the Russians invaded.

Days after the war started, an initiative sprang up called 'Cook for Ukraine'. All over the world, cooks staged dinner parties and other gatherings at which they shared Ukrainian dishes such as dumplings, stuffed cabbage leaves, Ukrainian garlic bread and borscht. These community gatherings served many different functions at once. They were a way to raise money for some of the thousands of children and families affected by the conflict. They were also an act of solidarity with Ukrainians. For Ukrainians themselves in other countries, cooking the familiar dishes of long ago was a way to keep the dream of home alive.

The kitchen cabinet was a perfect symbol, because behind its tenacity there is a truth: cooking is a more enduring activity than war. How many homes – how many kitchens – how many cooks – have been destroyed by Putin's bombs? But whatever happens, long after the bombing has ended and the slow task of rebuilding is underway, there will still be cooks who chop vegetables for soup and stir them in pots and wash dishes and, at the end of a meal, place them neatly in a rack to dry, restoring order. Nadiia Svatko said she hoped that maybe one day she would be able to return to the place where her apartment once stood.

Even for us lucky ones who have never lived through war, who take the roof over our head for granted, kitchens can feel like places of enchantment. On a hard day, you may reach for certain items that help you pretend that life is OK; and then it is. Perhaps you have a favourite casserole dish or a beloved mug that seems to act as a counter-charm against bad luck. One of my kitchen amulets is a little stainless-steel pot for frothing milk for coffee. My mother K gave it to me years ago, and when I use it I still feel her protection and remember that she always wanted the best for me. This pot is pleasingly low-tech and has survived being dropped multiple times. You heat the milk on the hob and then push the plunger up and down until you have a pan of airy white foam. The process resembles alchemy. And why not? Cooking pots have never been very far from magic cauldrons.

The Chocolate Bottle

> 'Pots, with perpetual fire and secret, burned.
> The enchanter breaks them . . .'
>
> Ludovico Ariosto, *Orlando Furioso*, 1516

One of the most stunning artifacts I have ever seen – I say 'seen', but I've only ever seen a photo of it – is a 5,000-year-old vessel for drinking chocolate. In the early 2000s, a team of archaeologists led by Francisco Valdez discovered some pots, mortars and other relics which would show that chocolate was far older than anyone had realised. This vessel – a pottery bottle – was one of them. It came from Ecuador and it was decorated with a very realistic man's face. Looking at the photo gave me the strangest feeling because the bottle seemed to have a power of its own. I felt that whoever made it must have believed very strongly that objects could be charmed.

The standard story told about chocolate is that it was first cultivated and consumed on the site of modern Mexico and its neighbours (Mesoamerica) by the Mayas and others. But Valdez's work would lead to the discovery that cocoa beans were actually being consumed in liquid form 1,500 years earlier than had previously been claimed. Even more surprising was the discovery that the origins of cacao were not in Mexico but in South America, 4,000 miles away.

Valdez and his team were working in Ecuador in the Upper Amazon near the modern town of Palanda when they made the kind of discovery that most archaeologists can only dream of: the traces of an entire forgotten civilisation. Valdez discovered the site – Santa Ana-La Florida (SALF) – in 2002. It was a challenging area to work in, which perhaps explains why no archaeologists had ever attempted it before. The Upper Amazon is extremely hot and humid, and to get to the site Valdez had to navigate complex terrain by foot, avoiding dangerous animals and insects along the way.

All that was left of the people who had once been here were the vestiges of a small settlement of about twenty buildings on a river terrace organised around a central public space. Valdez named the civilisation – which dates back more than 5,000 years – the Mayo Chinchipe. To the east of the site there was an artificial mound, which stood around 4 metres above the river terrace and seemed to be a kind of temple. At the centre of this temple were a hearth and some tombs containing funerary objects of an amazing splendour and delicacy, considering their age. There were beads made from Pacific Ocean seashells and jewellery made from crystals; polished stone bowls and mortars, some of which were shaped like birds and other creatures; and well-made ceramics which ranged in colour from light brown to black.

The 'most spectacular object' of all, in Valdez's words, which he first excavated in November 2003, was a ceramic spouted bottle with a ring-shaped 'stirrup' handle and the effigy of a man's face on both sides. Judging from photographs, it is a vessel of breathtaking sophistication. If someone told you that this bottle was a Picasso sculpture from the 1930s, you might believe them.

This pot (or bottle) has so much personality that it seems to be a real person rather than a lump of clay. One on side the pottery man looks angry, or at least mildly irritated, with puffed-out cheeks. On the other side he looks happier. Whoever made this bottle – which is 14 centimetres wide, twice the diameter of a

modern wine bottle – was a master ceramicist. When I first saw a photograph of it I thought the man was bearded, but his face is actually emerging from a bobbly-textured spondylus shell, which was a common decoration on stirrup-spout vessels. The shell has been rendered in pleasingly textured detail, contrasting with the fine-grained smoothness of the stirrup handle.

To consider ancient ceramics of such intricate design is to doubt whether 'progress' really exists. This bottle is a far more thrilling and idiosyncratic object than the mugs from which we sip coffee-shop cocoa today. When Sonia Zarrillo – another archaeologist who was doing research on ancient farming in Ecuador – first saw this bottle, she wrote that she was 'stunned' by its 'beauty and sophistication'. Here was by far the earliest ceramic stirrup bottle found anywhere in the Americas. And yet it looked like an artwork made by people at the height of their craft. As Zarrillo told me via email, the bottle indicates that there must have been earlier ceramic cultures in this part of Ecuador. 'These are not the fumbling beginnings of ceramic use,' she explained.

But what was the purpose of this extraordinary bottle? Zarrillo's research at the time consisted of analysing fragments of ancient vessels – whether stone or ceramics – for traces of various grains such as maize. Valdez agreed that she should come to the Santa Ana site and look for sample grain residues in the artefacts he had found. About a year into this work, at a conference Zarillo met Michael Blake, an expert on Mayan chocolate. Blake commented that the stirrup bottle at SALF reminded him of the ancient spouted containers he had seen in Mexico for chocolate drinks. He asked Zarrillo whether she had considered testing the Mayo Chinchipe ceramics for a substance called *Theobroma cacao* – a starch found in domesticated chocolate. Zarrillo felt all of her 'brain synapses' firing 'in all directions' at his question, because she realised that this could change the whole timeline of ancient chocolate consumption.

Sure enough, when Zarrillo and the rest of the team in Ecuador started testing for cacao at the SALF site in 2010 they found traces in no fewer than forty-six samples: twenty-one stone artefacts and twenty-five ceramic ones. Chocolate was detected in stone mortars and stone bowls, in charred ceramic shards and also in the spectacular effigy bottle. The archaeologists were helped by the fact that the SALF ceramics were low-fired, at temperatures below 850 degrees Celsius, so they were porous: ideal for absorbing traces of whatever foods had once been cooked or contained in them. It took Zarrillo, Valdez and colleagues many years of painstaking work to confirm that the traces they had found were from domesticated cacao rather than wild plants, but eventually they obtained the proof (wild cacao has a different DNA). They could now say with certainty that Ecuador, not Mexico, was the birthplace of cacao-farming (until anyone unearths an even older chocolate bottle somewhere else).

Now that we know that the people of this Ecuadorean civilisation were the first on record to consume chocolate drinks, it would be fascinating to find out what this heady substance actually meant to them. Judging from the fact that it was found in a bottle, it seems that the cacao was enjoyed as a frothy drink, just as it was in Mexico. But was this drink a treat? A stimulant? A religious offering? Or all of the above? It is hard to come by definitive answers because, in contrast to the Mayans of Mesoamerica, who developed an elaborate system of hieroglyphs, the cultures of South America lacked any systems of writing until their first encounters with Europeans in the 1630s.

Without the evidence of the written word, all we have to go on are the objects themselves. But that is not nothing. A pot or a bottle can speak in ways that words cannot. From the fact that the Mayo Chinchipe people considered it worthwhile creating such a beautiful bottle for a dead person to take to the afterlife, we can be certain that cacao was considered a precious and spiritual substance. That the pot bears the form of a man – likely the face of the person in the tomb – makes it all the more meaningful. When Valdez first looked at this stirrup pot, he recognised that it was 'loaded with typically Andean symbolism'. The two faces evoked the character of a South American shaman 'who transforms into a jaguar after a rite, having consumed hallucinogenic substances'. You can tell that the man has become a jaguar because there is a line under his mouth which in the symbolism of the Andes stands for a cat.

I emailed Valdez to ask him more about who might have been in the tomb along with the chocolate bottle and he replied:

> As to who might have been in the tomb, we have indirect evidence that it could have been a shaman . . . We found at least two objects used by shamans to induce visions that are needed in their practice. One was a stone mortar used to grind seeds of a plant of the *Anandenanthera ssp* and a container used to mix lime with coca leaves as to extract the alkaloids proper to that plant through the practice of coca-chewing.

Zarrillo adds that the man's puffed-out cheeks on the first side of the bottle look like someone chewing coca leaves and that his heavily lidded eyes suggest someone under the influence of hallucinogenic drugs. All the indications are that the original cacao was more of a drug than a food. In addition to cacao, the bottle also contained traces of chilli peppers, maize and manioc. All of these may have been combined to make a kind of ritual beer. By bringing this charmed bottle with him as he passed into the afterlife, the shaman in the tomb in Ecuador was trying to use powerful magic to protect himself from harm. The bottle is like a mini-me: pottery as talisman.

Most pottery that has ever been made is far less ornate than this spectacular chocolate bottle from Ecuador. But it is eloquent proof that, from the earliest civilisations, culinary objects have been treated as vessels for human emotions as well as for foods. After I found out about the chocolate bottle, I felt less weird about the way I was reacting to various receptacles in my kitchen. If I had been living in ancient Ecuador, it would have been normal to see pots as potent carriers of feeling.

In 1988, the archaeologists Nicholas David, Judy Sterner and Kodzo Gavua published an article with a disarmingly simple title: 'Why Are Pots Decorated?'. Their answer was that in traditional communities patterns on pots are far from being 'mere decoration' or 'art for art's sake'. Rather, the decoration is a sign that pots are actually regarded as people in their own right. In many cultures, pots are described as having mouths and necks, bellies and bottoms, arms and legs. Like clothing on the human body, decoration on a pot is a form of protection, an insulation against the dangers of the outside world and a way – or so it is hoped – to protect the weak from the strong.

Pots are not just *like* people – they *are* people is the argument set forth by David, Sterner and Gavua. Among the Mafa and Bulahay groups of northern Cameroon there are all manner of different pots for different people, each of which comes with its own shape and decoration. After someone is born in these Cameroonian communities they are given their own special pot, to represent their soul. Twins share a single 'twin pot' with two bulges in it. When one twin dies, his or her spirit will wait in the pot until the other is ready to join them. Many of the patterns on jars echo those a person might wear on their body in the form of clothes or jewellery. There are specially decorated pots for men and pots for women (although an 'old or barren woman living by herself' is relegated to using undecorated pots, a sign that she is treated as less than a person).

In Europe, too, there are long traditions of treating pottery containers as charmed in such powerful ways that it is as if they have become people. Well into the twentieth century there were vessels in England called 'witch-bottles' which were used as powerful counter-measures against witchcraft. If it was believed that a witch had placed a curse on someone's cattle or horses, one way to stop her evil magic from working was to take some of the animal's urine and place it in a bottle with nail or hair clippings, water and other ingredients. Sometimes these witch-bottles – like the 'Bellarmine jugs' popular in Germany – were decorated with human faces. Another superstition common across Europe was that of burying pots under the threshold of a house. The pots were crammed with bones, oats, eggshells or other substances, and it was believed that these measures could protect a building from harm. In the popular sixteenth-century Italian play *Orlando Furioso* an enchanter breaks the pots underneath the doorstep of a castle and the result is that the castle is instantly destroyed.

Whether a table or a plate or a cup can *really* have special powers is the wrong question to be asking. The interesting thing is how universal these beliefs have been for thousands of years.

I could now see that treating kitchen objects as if they were charmed or cursed – strange though it might seem – was far from abnormal. Biologist Erol Akçay, who studies superstitions and how they spread, has commented that 'we are all basically superstitious', no matter what we tell ourselves. Psychologists have found that superstitious behaviour has an extra appeal during times of high stress. This might explain why, at a moment of heartbreak, I had started to believe that my cake tin had a life of its own. Treating certain possessions as if they were charms is a way of gaining some semblance of control in uncertain situations. Maybe this is why we feel the need of them all the more at those times when our own sanity is in question.

Mementos

The Mystery of the Silver-plated Toast Rack

'When to the sessions of sweet silent thought
I summon up remembrance of things past,
I sigh the lack of many a thing I sought . . .'

Shakespeare, Sonnet 30, 1609

One day in 2017, my mother informed me that someone had stolen her toast rack. It was a valuable silver-plated one which had once belonged to her own mother. The strangest part was that the thief had left everything else in her house untouched. My mother had a strong hunch about how the crime had been committed. She had accidentally left her back door open and felt sure that a strapping young man had scrambled over the fence into the tiny courtyard at the back of her house, then taken the valuable toast rack and done a runner. She phoned the police, who listened politely and wrote down what she said, but alas they had not yet apprehended anyone.

For a while now, my sister and I had noticed that our mother, a brilliant Shakespeare scholar, wasn't quite her normal self, but it was hard to say exactly what was the matter. All the little demands of life made her anxious and she no longer ventured out so much, except to do grocery-shopping or go to the cinema one block from her house, often seeing the same film several times in a week. The reason given was always that it was such a splendid film, *it was worth rewatching.* One of her cousins, who lived nearby and to whom she was very close, told me that she regularly phoned to say how sad and lonely she was, which made me feel guilty. But when I called and asked her how she was, she would assure me that she was on marvellous form. *There was nothing to worry about.*

She would come and stay with my family for a few days – her house was a three-hour train ride away from mine – and then only a week later would email to say she hadn't seen us for ages and ask when she could next see us. On one of her visits I took her swimming at my gym and, as I had done many times before, I went off to do a workout while she swam. But this time she appeared in the gym, dripping-wet, in her swimming costume, saying she couldn't find the changing rooms. She still carried books around in her bag, but no longer seemed to read them beyond the first page. Her circle of friends narrowed. Some of her academic friends didn't visit as much as they did before, although her friends from church remained as faithful as ever. For decades, her daily routine had involved doing research in the library and breaking off mid-morning to see a group of friends for coffee, but now she didn't go to the library anymore and so the sociable coffee meetings stopped too. She was often at a loose end. Her cousin urged her to get out of the house more and meet new people. *Why don't you try yoga?*

When she told me and my youngest son – we were staying with her at the time – about the toast rack, I realised that this was something more than anxiety and depression (although she did also seem to be both anxious and depressed, underneath her declarations of how well she was). I asked whether she was absolutely sure the toast rack was gone and she became indignant that I should doubt her. My son and I searched all over for it. We looked in every cupboard and drawer, but it was nowhere to be found.

One of the early signs of dementia may be a paranoia that someone – usually a family member – is stealing from the person. My mother's paranoia was slightly different in that the locus of her fear was outside the family. Looking back now, I feel a kind of consolation in the fact that she didn't suspect me or any of my children of being the toast rack thief.

Whether we have dementia or not, our favoured objects can be vessels for preserving memories. The things we surround ourselves with at home are a way to curate the past into a version of it that we can bear. When our memory fades, we may find ourselves clinging more tightly to our possessions, just so that we can keep hold of something. The Soviet psychologist Lev Vygotsky once wrote that 'the very essence of civilisation consists of purposively building monuments so as not to forget'. As individuals, we have our own private monuments and museums too: the objects that connect us with our past and the person we have always believed or wanted ourselves to be. One of my mother's most prized personal monuments was her toast rack.

My mother was always fond of toast racks. Thinking back, I can't remember a single day – except on holiday – when she didn't have toast for breakfast, along with plenty of strong coffee. Occasionally, the toast might be accompanied by something more substantial such as fried mushrooms. But mostly it was just toast and butter, always with some cucumber and usually with a few slices of cheese (she loved cheese for breakfast). Sometimes she would have marmalade instead of the cheese. After the toast, she always ate a pear.

There are many cultures in the world where toasted bread is a comfort food – the *pan con tomate* of Spain or the *bruschetta* of Italy, for example – but the British have a particularly deep and democratic relationship with toast. When I watched Peter Jackson's *Get Back* documentary about The Beatles (2021) I was struck that so much of the band's time in the studio was spent eating white sliced toast and marmalade. My mother's fondness for toast went back to her student days in the 1960s when, she sometimes told me, there was a café she loved to go to with her friends in the covered market in Oxford where you could order any kind of toast you wanted. You could have kidneys on toast or anchovies on toast, but sometimes when she didn't have much money she just ordered toast and dripping, the cheapest item on the menu: toast spread with solidified beef fat. She adored this and would go misty-eyed at the memory of it.

Toast racks – little metal constructions with vertical partitions to hold the slices – are not exactly standard-issue possessions these days, even for people who love to eat toast. The point of a toast rack is to keep the toast crisp as it cools. When you pile slices of hot toast on top of each other they become steamy and the inside pieces go soggy. The toast rack prevents the sogginess by maintaining gaps between each slice, allowing the steam to escape. But apart from hotels almost no one bothers with such formality. In my experience, most people who want to ensure that their toast stays crisp will simply lean two slices of toast against one another.

My mother, however, was a stickler for toast racks. She also preferred to make her toast on an old-fashioned grilling plate on the AGA cooker instead of in an electric toaster and she ate it from a Spode blue and white plate. All of this might have been a throwback to her own mother, whose parents ran a small post office in Devon. She was the first in her family to go to university. Fearing the judgement of others, my grandmother worked tirelessly to hide her roots and come across as more posh than she was. Sometimes she took this too far. When referring to Marmite (the salty yeast extract spread which so many British people love), my grandmother would adopt a French accent and ask if someone could pass her the 'Mar-meet', an affectation my sister and I found hilarious.

Despite her strict insistence on toast racks, my mother was not so fussy about which bread she used for the toast, buying any old loaf which was wholemeal and vaguely seeded from the supermarket. (After she developed dementia, I started reading gloomy articles about how the emulsifiers in industrial bread may be one of the many possible causes of Alzheimer's and I felt retrospectively worried about her bread choices.) But whatever the bread, to her a toast rack was one of the essentials of life, like a coat or a kettle. She couldn't imagine eating toast without it, and for this reason she believed it must be a highly covetable item for another person to steal.

Each time she told the story of the toast rack she embellished it slightly. Even though he had stolen one of her prized possessions, she almost seemed to have a crush on the thief. At first the thief was simply a strapping young man, but later he became *a strapping and very strong young man*. He was so strong, she said, that he probably managed to leap over her fence in one bound. All this exertion had made the young man hungry, she said, so he was most likely planning to have a picnic in a nearby nature reserve which had beautiful meadows. This was why he needed the silver toast rack – for the picnic! She had always been fond of these meadows herself, and in the retelling the thief became more like a handsome companion than a criminal – a little like Peter O'Toole in *How to Steal a Million* (1966). In any case, the thief clearly had flawless manners (thieving aside) and high standards. He understood that you couldn't eat a snack in a field without a silver toast rack. Much as she regretted the loss of her lovely toast rack, she seemed to respect his motives for the theft.

As her memory fell away, fragment by fragment, my sister and I struggled to find activities she could still enjoy doing. Once, she had been a fiendishly competitive Scrabble player, but it became too painful for her to try and fail to remember words such as

'A_N_D' or 'T_H_E'. Sometimes we read some of Shakespeare's sonnets out loud to her. At the height of her career she had spent years working on a scholarly edition of the sonnets, but now she could not even summon up Shakespeare's name. Still, her love of his words remained so deep and true that when we got to the end of one of the sonnets she would say how tremendous it was and ask, 'I wonder if we know who it is by?' Occasionally she would mouth some of the words as we read, showing that they were still there in her brain, somewhere.

One of the many awful aspects of dementia is that no matter how bad each stage of decline may seem, you will one day look back on it as a golden age compared to what is next. By the time we moved my mother to the care home in the city where I live a couple of years later, she had forgotten all about the silver toast rack.

For over a year, she had stopped making breakfast at home, preferring to go to a nearby café for mushrooms on toast or sometimes for eggs (she had forgotten that she didn't like eggs much and was disappointed when they arrived). She said the reason was that their coffee was better than hers, and she almost fooled me until I realised that she just didn't know how to boil the kettle anymore, let alone how to make toast.

At first she hated her bland new room in the care home and kept packing her bags to leave, but over time she seemed to have forgotten that her old house ever existed, just as she eventually forgot the names of her daughters and grandchildren and even of the poets and playwrights (including Shakespeare) to whom she had devoted a lifetime of scholarship. She started to refer to the care home as 'my place'. They gave her white toast and marmalade for breakfast and she never asked for the cheese and the pear without which for so many years her breakfast had been incomplete. She did not seem to mind that they served it without a toast rack.

She was still delighted to eat a pear when I visited and brightened as she ate it. Why did I not send her baskets of pears in the care home to have with her toast every day? If I could, I would send them to her now – the juiciest, most fragrant Comice, peeled with a blunt knife, just the way she liked them.

About a year before she died, my sister and I went to clear her house and sell it to pay for the care home fees. My sister was the one who found the toast rack at the very back of a cupboard.

Subha's Rice Pan

'Possessions are a convenient means of storing . . . memories and feelings.'

Russell Belk, 1988

My friend Subha Mukherji has a pan for cooking rice unlike any I've ever seen. It is made of flimsy-looking aluminium with a little wooden handle and looks no bigger than a doll's pan. But thanks to a small vent hole in the lid, this pan can cook a generous quantity – two to three hearty portions – of the most perfect fluffy white rice. This pan has been in Subha's life for nearly four decades, a daily reminder of Kolkata, where she grew up. A household companion, it has created the rice for dozens and dozens of meals and, through all the joys and disappointments of the years, it has never let her down.

I only got to know Subha recently, though we have both lived in the same town for years. Life sometimes has a strange way of allowing you to encounter exactly the person you need at that precise moment. Subha is a university teacher and researcher, a distinguished expert on tragicomedy and Shakespeare among many other subjects. The first time I went to dinner at Subha's house my mother had just died and I was feeling so flat I wasn't sure if I would make it through the meal, yet I came away energised. I realised later that Subha's kindness and knowledgeable passion for literature reminded me of my mother, even though she was decades younger and very different in personality.

We met at a party for a mutual friend to which Subha had brought one of the most delicious cauliflower dishes I have ever eaten. The cauliflower tasted so savoury and deep, it was as if it had been smothered in slow-cooked onions; but Subha assured me that it contained no onion at all, only *asafoetida* (or '*hing*'), a remarkable and strong-smelling seasoning which can mimic the taste of onion. She had also seasoned the cauliflower with oil, a few tomatoes and a little turmeric, salt and sugar, plus curry leaves. It was a Bengali dish from her childhood. Usually, she explained, she would have prepared it on the stovetop but she was exhausted at the moment and she had made it in the oven instead, which felt like a compromise to her (to me it tasted nothing like a compromise).

After I had known Subha for a few months, I saw that her pointing out the imagined flaws in her superb cauliflower dish was very characteristic. Every time she cooks for me she produces exquisite dishes and then outlines ways in which they might have been better with different ingredients or more time. This isn't false modesty; it's a sign of how acutely sensitive she is to the taste and texture of food.

Subha invited me over to show me her rice pan in action. Into this tiny vessel she measured out a cup of white Basmati rice and two cups of water. She rinsed the rice, but only a little. The rice she buys in Britain 'doesn't really need washing', she said. It looked like way too much rice for the pan but Subha seemed relaxed. I asked her how long it would take to cook, but she said, 'I can tell from the look, actually, not so much the time.' Sure enough, while we were chatting and drinking Riesling, she seemed to have a sixth sense for how the rice was doing on the stove and at one point elegantly glided across the room to rescue it seconds before it was going to boil over. She skimmed off the scum with a wooden spoon, clamping on the lid and turning the heat down. Very, very quietly, she whispered, 'It will be fine,' like an incantation. I felt at that moment that she was speaking not to me but to the pot.

The pan came from a little market in Kolkata; Subha can't recall exactly where. What she can remember is that it was one of the crucial vessels with which she first taught herself to cook in her twenties. A few years ago, Subha's ex-husband, who was also from India, was visiting her in England. They had remained close friends long after the divorce. When he saw the little rice pan, he exclaimed with disbelief. 'He said, "It's that one?" and I said, "Yeah." I said, "It survived our marriage and ten thousand [house] moves," and he said, "Oh my God, I will drink to that." ' He died not long afterwards, a death which hit her hard. But the pan lives on.

Growing up in an educated family in Kolkata, Subha was never expected to cook. She wasn't even allowed in the kitchen to boil an egg because her grandfather was convinced that 'I would burn to death'. Both her parents were academics and she was encouraged to study rather than do household tasks. As she stirs cubes of turmeric-marinated aubergine in hot mustard oil with red chillis and a whole-spice mix called *panch phoran*, Subha remarks that 'There is no gainsaying the fact that it's a cuisine destined for a society that was patriarchal and feudal.' Her family, like the other families they knew, had cooks who produced most of what they ate. Her mother was an excellent cook when she wanted to, but as a working woman she spent very little day-to-day time in the kitchen, saving herself for some 'fancy stirring' now and again.

When she left India for graduate studies in Oxford, Subha had no idea how to cook and the overdone English food on offer in college repulsed her. For the whole of that year, almost every day, she went to a nearby takeaway shop and bought herself a chicken and mushroom pie, a can of Coke and a packet of crisps. That was often all she ate in the course of the day. After a few months of this she was suffering from acute stomach pain and nausea, but when she went to the GP they told her that she must be homesick and put her on antidepressants, which made her stomach complaints even worse. It was only after one of her tutors gently suggested that she might have gastric ulcers that she got the medication she needed, which made her feel better in a month. This made Subha realise that for the sake of her stomach she must learn how to cook.

There's a deep-rooted idea that the most meaningful cooking is done by those who learned it at their mother's side, as a child. But cooking can be even more significant for those who learn it later in life. Without any prior cooking knowledge to fall back on, Subha set out to reverse-engineer the food of her childhood from memory. She cooked *moong dal* and delectable chickpea and potato salads seasoned with sharp tamarind chutney and cumin with crunchy *chaat* on top. One of her best-loved dishes in those days was a potato dish which was christened '*Aloo* Lulu' by her ex-husband. ('*Aloo* means potato, and he would always triplicate the last syllable of anything he liked.') 'I literally worked my way back to remembered tastes and smells and recreated them.' She is proud to say that her very first published writing was a handful of recipes for her college community cookbook.

The consumer scientist Russell Belk has written that the value of personal mementos (family snapshots, say) is that they make our past a treasure that can be 'savoured, handled . . . and kept safe from loss'. Belk adds that 'without these objects our memories may be as ephemeral as flowers'. A rice pot is a different and less purely nostalgic kind of memento than a photo album. When Subha picks up the pot, it is still the same utensil chosen by her younger self who didn't know the first thing about cooking. But, unlike an old photo, it has also developed with time, becoming a weightier and more significant object with each batch of perfect rice that it cooks.

This little pot has travelled with Subha from India to England to Italy and back to England. It has been a perpetual link with home, a source of certainty in a country that will never completely supplant the Kolkata of her childhood. Her latest academic project is about migrants and the knowledge they carry with them across oceans and continents. She quotes the philosopher Simone Weil, who once said that 'We must take the feeling of being at home into exile. We must be rooted in the absence of a place.' One of the most effective ways to root yourself is through objects which can act as comforting remnants and props of the place that was left behind.

While we were talking, the rice finished cooking. At exactly the right moment, without any timer to remind her, Subha lifted the lid and noticed that it was fluffy and had risen almost all the way to the top. She switched the heat off to let it steam and rest a bit more in the pot. 'A little less rice would be good but this is just about OK.' She quickly finished preparing the other dishes, which included a sumptuous *dal* and her famous cauliflower dish as well as the cubes of fried aubergine. She told me she was thinking of writing a cook-book about Bengali food – 'it's such a flavour-based cuisine'.

Subha was not sure, however, how well the nuances of her food would translate onto the page (apart from the fact that at the time she was exhausted, busy with teaching and various research projects – and also acutely worried about her ageing father back in Kolkata, who was very unwell; he died a few months later). Cooking, for her, was so rooted in the senses that it could hardly be written down. 'It's not a knowledge that can be carried in coffee spoons,' she said. 'You carry it with you.'

The Happy Hands

'things are perhaps the most faithful witnesses of all,
and in their fidelity to us they function as extensions
of ourselves . . .'

Robert Romanyshyn, 1989

Pie maker and teacher Kate McDermott says that her favourite kitchen tools are her own fingers. She uses them to rub butter and lard into flour for the pastry, lifting her hands high up so that it becomes airy. A metal pastry blender is a poor substitute, in her view, because the butter gets stuck between the blades.

Kate is widely regarded as one of the greatest pie experts in America, which is all the more remarkable considering she is coeliac and can't eat most of her own creations. What makes Kate's recipes so great (in her books *Art of the Pie*, 2016, and *Pie Camp*, 2020) is that she talks you through each step as if she were there with you. She writes of the 'sizzle-whump': the music a perfectly baked fruit pie makes when it comes out of the oven. This sounds far-fetched until you start to listen to your own pies and hear for yourself the quiet sizzle of the crust and the juicy 'whump' of the apples or peaches or cherries bubbling away beneath.

'I can actually hear it!' said my youngest son when he made his first apple pie from *Art of the Pie*. By now, he and I were the only ones left at the table (unless you count the dog hovering in the background, angling for crumbs) – my daughter had left for her studies.

The phrase 'and then there were none' sometimes came into my head. But the two of us settled into new companionable routines, including making pie for ourselves, not for any special occasion, just for the heck of it.

While so much else in our lives has altered, Kate's pie recipes and the ceramic dish we make them in have been a cheerful constant. One of the last times my mother seemed mostly her old self, though already confused, was at a Thanksgiving dinner. My sister, her partner and her girls were visiting from the US and my nieces and I spent all afternoon making three different pies: pumpkin, pecan and a lattice-topped apple pie in its red ceramic dish. My mother eagerly accepted a large slice of all three, as did my ex-husband. She had a greedy gene, which I inherited. It was a legacy of her wartime childhood; having known the deprivations of rationing, she loved to see a laden table. That Thanksgiving dinner (the second in a row at my house) was the last time we would all eat pie together. When I look at the jolly red pie dish, I feel it still carries an afterglow of that night. It remembers when our mother still knew apple from pumpkin.

I had a hunch that Kate McDermott would be someone with deep feelings about utensils and we arranged a video call. When I first asked her to describe her most cherished object, I was sure she would choose something pie-related. Sure enough, she was excited to show me her favourite rolling pin: an elegant long one with which she estimated she had rolled out the pastry for 10,000 pies. She tried many other pins in the shop before she found the one that felt perfect in her hand, as a musician chooses their instrument (her first career was as a piano player and teacher).

But technical perfection is not the only quality we prize in a tool. As excellent as it was, Kate explained that the rolling pin was nothing like as irreplaceable to her as another kitchen item: some very old tongs shaped like a pair of clapping hands. These tongs were a souvenir of a once-happy childhood that she lost quite suddenly at the age of ten.

Assuming it isn't made of precious metals, nothing gives an object more personal value than the memories it carries. When Kate's mother died in 1982, she told her stepfather that she wanted only one thing from the house: the Happy Hands. She didn't have to explain what she meant. 'Happy Hands', as everyone in the family knew, was Kate's nickname for the stainless-steel salad tongs with a pair of cupped hands on the end which her mother had been given as part of her bridal shower before she got married in 1943. The only identifying mark on them is the word 'Hand-server'. When Kate showed me these tongs via computer from her cottage in the Olympic Mountains in Washington State, her face was beaming with happiness.

Kitchen objects have their own particular moods. Some are homely, some are high-tech, some are stylish and some are as amusing as a toy. Kate said that she loved her Happy Hands partly because they are so 'playful' and 'whimsical', which she found remarkable considering that they were made in 1943, the middle of the Second World War, a time when you might expect kitchenware to be dull and utilitarian. As she clapped the Happy Hands over the Zoom screen, I could see why she loved them so much. When you squeeze the handles, the hands come together and they make a very satisfying clapping sound, like castanets. These tongs were a rare gem: a hand-shaped utensil that wasn't creepy.

What makes one pair of tongs more worthy of holding on to than another? As with any tool, part of the appeal is down to how well they work. Kate emphasised that her metal hands were 'extremely well made'. After eighty-one years, they are as solid and shiny as ever. In contrast to the standard spring-loaded tongs sold in kitchenware shops today, which consist of two simple metal arms hinged with a single joint at the end, these

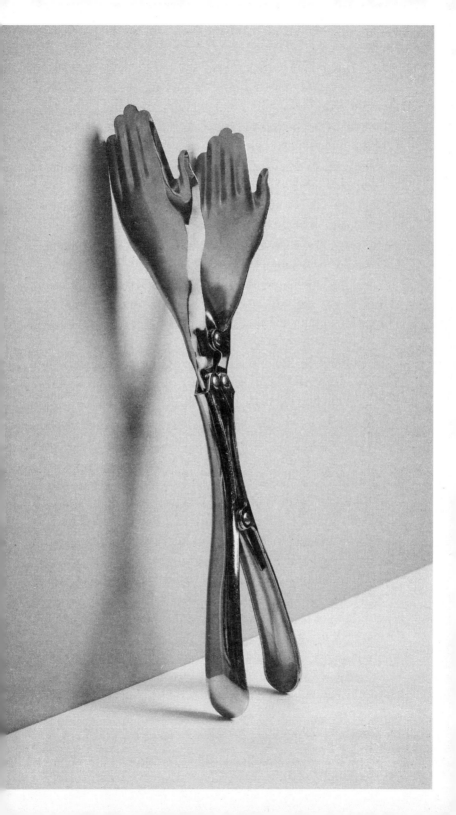

Happy Hands have their joint in the middle, like garden seca-teurs. The joint looks more like something you would see on a marionette than a utensil (indeed, Kate says that the hands feel 'doll-like' to her).

When we decide that a particular utensil is 'happy', it may reflect the darker side of life. Like all mementos, Kate's attachment to the Happy Hands is a form of selective memory: a way to pre-serve and celebrate a particular version of the past and to overlook the stresses and distresses with which every human life is also threaded. Mementos are props we use to edit our lives and tell a particular story about our own past.

Just as my pie dish enables me to remember my mother before the worst of the dementia took her away, Kate's tongs help her to leap over years of sadness to more straightforwardly joyous times. She was around ten when she first christened them the Happy Hands. In *Art of the Pie* she writes of two other events that happened that year. One, she was forced by her mother to go on her first diet; and two, her father suffered a terrible accident from which he never recovered. She writes in *Art of the Pie* that 'overnight I felt the magic of my protected childhood wrenched away'.

It is a depressing truth that for many of us – women especially – our pleasure in eating will never again be as unconstrained as it was when we were prepubescent children. During her very early years, Kate spent masses of time in the kitchen baking with her grand-mother Geeg and no one questioned whether or not she should be eating pie. But when Kate was ten, her mother decided that she was too fat and asked the family doctor to prescribe her a diet pill which she was made to take every morning with orange juice. Her mother had the idea that Kate should have the same slender ankles that she did. Given that Kate was adopted, this was probably never going to happen. Her mother signed her up for a 'reducing salon' along with a group of middle-aged housewives, something which Kate found humiliating.

The second change that happened when Kate was ten was that the family, who lived in Santa Barbara, moved from the small white house next to her father's mortuary business to 'the house of my parents' dreams'. A few months later her father had a bad fall, resulting in a blood clot lodging in his lung. He never recovered and died six years later of a rare kind of leukemia.

When I asked Kate what memories she associated with the Happy Hands, she reached for a moment when she was around six, long before her father's fall and years before anyone had tried to put her on a diet. Her mother – a busy piano teacher who wasn't an enthusiastic cook – decided that the two of them would make doughnuts using a recipe from *Joy of Cooking* (1931). Kate remembers that they had to buy nutmeg specially from the neighbourhood market because they had never cooked with this spice before (her grandmother only used cinnamon in her pies). She watched as her mother slipped the doughnuts one by one into a vat of hot bubbling oil, using the Happy Hands. 'She used them to lift the hot doughnuts, dripping with fat, out of the pot and onto a newspaper-covered rack to drain and cool' before rolling them in sugar.

Kate and her mother never made doughnuts together again. I hadn't realised it from Kate's upbeat tone at the start of our conversation, but the Happy Hands are a memento of a single afternoon of family baking, never to be repeated except in Kate's mind.

By the time Kate was twelve, her mother – by now having to deal with the ongoing strain of her husband's ill-health – would regularly say to her daughter, 'We have company coming, can you make the dinner?' Preparing food for grown-ups from such a young age made Kate a resourceful cook, but it was no substitute for cooking alongside her mother or her grandmother Geeg (who stopped baking after she suffered a stroke).

As someone who spent many lonely hours in the kitchen as a child when everyone else was working or out, hours which became much lonelier after my parents' divorce, I sometimes wonder whether some of us become so attached to our kitchenware because it is something to play with when no one else is willing or able to play. During those long years after her father got sick, Kate recalls a new family atmosphere of 'hushed voices' and hospital visits. The only hands in the house which were always clapping in celebration were the Happy Hands.

Familiar tools can help us to build better memories, even through complicated times. This was a skill that Kate passed on early to her son, Duncan. When Duncan was growing up she gave him his own little child-sized rolling pin. The two of them moved to the house where she now lives – which she calls Pie Cottage – after Duncan's father unexpectedly left. Even as a small boy, Duncan shared his mother's enthusiasm for the Happy Hands and for cooking in general. He is now in his late thirties and he and his wife live next door to Kate (Duncan, she says, is a 'fabulous baker and cook').

One of the differences between an object and a living being is that the object never changes. While generations of humans live and die, it remains its own constant self. An object may rust or crumble or fade in the dishwasher or get smashed, but it can never change its fundamental personality. This is its limitation but also its power. A pair of tongs cannot fall out of love with its owner or ask us to leave. It cannot question our food choices or tell us we would look better if we slimmed down. Whether we are in the mood for dough-nuts or broccoli, it is always there for us. The psychologist Robert Romanyshyn writes of the 'dumb faithfulness' of things, a great phrase which explains the succour so many of us derive from our old trusted possessions. Romanyshyn discusses the way in which the belongings a person leaves behind after death can be the most poignant reminders of our loss. 'The pipe he smoked in the evening found now beneath the chair, or the necklace which was always her favorite, attest in their patient waiting to the depth of the loss.' In Romany-shyn's reading, things do not move on.

There is another way of looking at the question, however. A utensil only takes its meaning from the person who uses it. It can therefore change its meaning in an almost enchanted way when the life of its owner changes. There is nothing inherently happy about the Happy Hands. It was only Kate who decided that was what they were.

An implement which was a source of consolation in sad times can become suffused with new layers of magic and joy when new playmates join us at the stove. Smiling broadly, Kate tells me that she is already looking forward to passing the Happy Hands on to future generations in her family, if Duncan and his wife should 'bless her' with a grandchild. She claps the eighty-one-year-old metal hands again, demonstrating how much fun it would be to let a new child play with them. She wonders what things she and this new person – who doesn't yet exist – might pick up together.

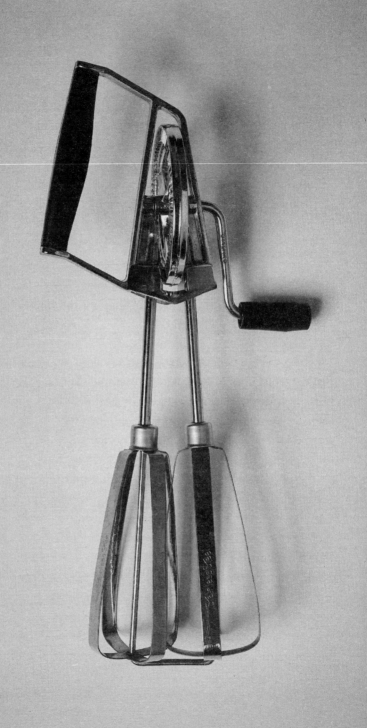

The Rotary Whisk

> 'When we say "How well I remember!" invariably we
> remember poorly. It is the emotion that is strong,
> not the details . . . Artifacts mystically quickened with
> sentiment await their reappearance in the imagination, a
> reenactment and a confirmation. Each time these tokens
> are handled, they give off sparks.'
>
> Wright Morris, 1989

I was at a friend's house having dinner when she got out a whisk to make whipped cream to go with dessert. It was one of those old-fashioned rotary whisks with a handle on the top and a crank on the side. As she turned the crank, the two interlocking beaters rotated in the cream. The whisk made a quiet splashing sound as she kept turning and turning the crank and eventually the cream thickened. The whisk had belonged to her mother, an excellent cook, who had died four years earlier. 'This is Mum,' she said.

Looking at my friend's rotary whisk provoked a range of conflicting emotions. My first reaction was nostalgia for a contraption that I recognised so well. Not this exact whisk; I never met my friend's mother. But in every respect it was like the rotary whisk my own mother used to beat eggs and cream and pancake batter with. When we were children, she used this whisk to teach me and my sister how to make cheese soufflé. One of us would be given the task of grating the cheese on a box grater while the other would whisk the egg whites. The whisk would slip and slide in the big ceramic mixing bowl as small bubbles started to form in the mucus-sticky egg. The moment when the transparent goo finally turned into white snow was one of triumph. Watching my friend whisk cream, I felt a stab of envy because she had been wise enough to keep her mother's rotary whisk whereas I – fool! – had given my own mother's away when my sister and I were clearing her house.

It was about a year after my separation when we started to sift through the stuff in our mother's house. My oldest son had lived there during the pandemic while studying at university, but now he was moving on and it didn't feel right to leave the place empty, aside from the fact that we needed to sell up because the money for our mother's care home had almost run out. It was startling to realise that she would never come back to this place where she had been – mostly – so happy. This house had been her own post-divorce fresh start.

During the process of clearing the house, there were hundreds of tiny decisions to make . I already felt strung out from making dozens of choices for my own life admin and was not sure I was equal to the task of addressing my mother's paraphernalia in addition to my own. Not now. My divorce came through in June 2021, just a year after my husband left. 'The marriage solemnised on 05 September 1997 at The Register Office . . . has legally ended', said the document. Solemnised!

When it came to making practical plans, my ex-husband had always been much more decisive and efficient than I was. For so many years, he had been the most reliable male presence in my mother's life, as in mine. In his low-key way he was unfailingly attentive, offering to drive her to places, carry heavy bags, replace lost keys, make cups of tea, play word games. But under the circumstances he was the last person I could ask for help in sorting out her house. He and his new love were already planning their wedding. *They seem to be in a hurry*, said a friend.

My sister and I took it in turns to do stints clearing the house, taking as much as we could to charity shops or to the recycling centre and trying to figure out which bits and pieces were worth saving. A lot of it fell to me because my sister lives in the States, but she flew over to do a few intensive days of putting stuff in boxes for me to store for her and trying to pull gems from the clutter, mostly old snapshots, plus a few things that, without having any monetary value, felt especially characteristic of our mother: a beaded necklace, some pretty blue plates, scraps of poems she had written as a child. We were confronted with the fact that most of the articles a person has carefully selected and accumulated across a lifetime are reduced to trash when they are no longer there to use them. What should you do with the not-especially-nice saucepan your mother used to warm milk for your children to drink? You have no reason to keep this pan when your own drawer of pans is so over-stuffed that it sometimes won't close. But how can you give such a thing away?

The hopefulness in some of the objects felt unbearable. There was a tiny and very expensive cot bed which she had bought because it had cleverly been marketed as suitable for grandparents. I remember her horror when she found out that, as expensive as it was, the price didn't include the mattress. None of her grandchildren ever slept in that cot because my children were too old and my sister's children were living a continent away.

I came back by myself to do one final sweep before the house clearers came to take the rest. A friend who lived nearby came round to help. My sister had said she didn't want anything else from the kitchen and I had already taken a handful of the objects I felt would remind me of our mother the most, including two of her trusty wooden spoons, a large white mug for drinking breakfast tea and some plates, bowls and platters. In my overwhelmed state, most of the objects felt like a burden I couldn't bear to take on and I became increasingly ruthless about chucking. If in doubt,

I gave it away. My attic was already crammed with suitcases of my mother's letters and papers and I couldn't face yet more boxes to sort through. I started having nightmares about getting trapped under mountains of papers and junk.

Having hired a skip, I started piling it up with belongings that were broken or otherwise unusable or simply unwanted. To my delight, a series of skip surfers started taking things out to salvage them. One man asked me if there were any pots and pans, and I ran back into the house to fetch her entire collection for him. A woman reacted with elation to find a spring-loaded ice cream scoop in the skip. She said it reminded her of the scoops of mashed potato the dinner ladies had served at school, and then I had the same memory and felt a little wave of regret. It might have been the same person who took the rotary whisk.

Getting rid of my mother's rotary whisk felt like an easy decision at the time for the simple reason that I have a long-held prejudice against them. I just don't think they are very good at whisking. When I first left home, I became a balloon whisk person and never looked back. Balloon whisks were what I had seen chefs using on TV, lifting the egg whites high in the air with a confident circular motion. With the treachery of youth I cast my mother's whisk aside. Whenever I wanted to whip even faster and more efficiently I used a hand-held electric whisk, something my mother never saw the point of, though I mentioned that they saved a lot of time. She was a deeply stubborn and determined person, and there was something about the elbow grease required to get egg whites stiff with her rotary whisk that appealed to her even though it sometimes exhausted her so much that she had to take a break halfway through. A rotary whisk wasn't flashy or modern and neither was she.

Now I see that, efficient or not, her rotary whisk was irreplaceable. I had looked at this utensil with cold eyes as if it were merely a tool, to be judged by what it could do for me. I didn't see that whether it whisked eggs quickly or not, it was really a memento which held within its black plastic handle the vestiges of my own mother's handprints.

In the late 1970s, a couple of social scientists embarked on a fascinating research project. They interviewed more than 300 people in eighty-two families in Chicago, asking them about the things in their homes and what they felt about them. What the scientists found was that domestic objects carried a huge weight of meaning, even belongings that seemed very mundane: a TV set, say, or a pot plant. People said they would not feel like themselves without their cherished stuff. Some objects were prized because of what they enabled someone to do, such as a child's football, a teen-ager's stereo system or an adult's power saw. Other objects were valued because of the memories they carried. For example, one father told the researchers that the most important things in his house were some pewter mugs which had been in his family since the 1700s, and a woman mentioned her Christmas tree ornaments and said that she would be 'very, very upset' not to have them because she had picked out each one specially, even though for most of the year she did not use them.

There were several ways in which household objects could acquire meaning, the scientists found. The two extremes were 'objects of action' and 'objects of contemplation'. The researchers found that children – and to some degree, men – were more likely to feel most positively about objects of action: things for *doing* stuff, like toys and tools (one man especially treasured a lathe for building model aeroplanes). One teenage boy said that the most special objects in his apartment were the dining table and chairs, 'cause I can sit on 'em, eat on 'em, play on 'em, do lots of things with the chair and table'. By contrast, older people – and to some degree, women – tended to place most value on more passive 'objects of contemplation' linked to memories and associations with other people. Among these

Chicago families, 59 per cent of the children's special objects fell into the 'action' category and only 16 per cent were suitable for contemplation. When it came to the grandparents, by contrast, a full 47 per cent of special objects were objects of contemplation such as photographs and silverware.

Our relationship with objects tends to change over the course of the human lifespan. The Chicago scientists noted that children have a powerful need to define themselves through 'direct kinetic control' – in other words, through movement and action. The key problems of identity at this age tend to be 'Who am I?' and 'What can I do?'. One boy told the researchers that he loved his family's new set of silver forks because they had 'jagged bottoms' and he could use them to 'make designs on the food'. By contrast, older people were more likely to keep their silverware in special chests or sideboards and to prize the objects that connected them with other people and the past. Twenty-five years after the death of her husband, one woman still kept his shaving kit in the bathroom cabinet, 'a relic she attended to each day'. Over time, the researchers found that people often took former objects of action – whether musical instruments or sports equipment – and started to treat them more as things to contemplate: symbols of youthful prowess or of blissful moments with loved ones.

My mistake, I now saw, was to judge my mother's rotary whisk by what it could *do* for me, rather than by the memories it evoked. She died only a year after we emptied her house. Grief hits you in waves. I wish I had understood that after a parent's death, the habits which you once mocked as quaint or old-fashioned become something you long for as a puppy wails for its litter. I might not need a rotary whisk to whip cream or stiffen egg whites (for this, my electric whisk really is a better and faster tool). What that old whisk offered was deeper: the chance, even after death, to summon up my mother's hands.

Barry's Pasta Bowl

> 'And I can't abear to part with anything I once lay hold
> of (or so my neighbours think, but what do they know?)'
>
> Krook in *Bleak House* by Charles Dickens, 1852

What to keep and what to let go of is one of the greatest questions
of existence, especially as it plays out in this strange late-capitalist
world of ours, flooded with so much stuff. Every time we let go of
a cherished object there is a sense of loss. Objects can keep us
company through the endless unasked-for upheavals of existence.
Then again, to hold on to every single memento would be to end
up swimming in so much clutter that you can't really do much
with those memories anyway.

 The ideal life involves a balance between keeping and discard-
ing, just as it involves a balance between remembering and forgetting.
But where to draw the line? We keep mementos to remind us who
we are, in the same way that we desperately try to ward off the loss
of memory itself. To live with dementia is to have one's past oblite-
rated by degrees until all that remains is blankness. It is as if someone
has gone through each room of a person's home and reduced it to
rubble. In her care home, my mother was surrounded by family
photos – of her father and mother and aunt, her children, her
grandchildren – but she stopped being able to say who any of these
people were. The mementos no longer served their purpose.

 Yet being able to remember everything would be another kind

of nightmare, as the Argentinian writer Jorge Luis Borges explored in his story 'Funes the Memorious' (from his collection *Labyrinths*, 1962). Funes is a man who is blinded in an accident, after which he finds that he can forget nothing. Funes recalls entire days in such hyper-intense detail that the act of remembering takes as long as the day itself. Without any effort, Funes teaches himself multiple languages. The downside is that he experiences his own memory as being 'like a garbage heap'. Remembering all the details of the universe becomes a kind of torture, depriving him of sleep and peace of mind.

The torment of being able to remember everything would be like living in a world of clutter. This, says writer Barry Yourgrau, was what he discovered when he began to research hoarding and hoarders for his book *Mess: One Man's Struggle to Clean Up His House and His Act* (2015), the funniest and most insightful book on the subject that I've come across. As the title suggests, Barry has skin in the game when it comes to hoarding (although he counts himself more as a 'clutterbug' or a 'pack rat' than an out-and-out hoarder). He decided to write about the subject as a way to deal with his own mess, which was affecting his relationship with his girlfriend, the food writer Anya von Bremzen (who appears in the book as 'Cosima'). When the book starts, Anya has not been inside his Jackson Heights apartment (which actually belongs to her) in five years because Barry feels such shame and sensitivity about his accumulation of stuff, including whole 'snowdrifts of plastic grocery bags', a dining table which can't be used because it is permanently covered in debris, many books and a set of half-broken opera glasses. Barry hasn't seen his kitchen counter in years. He eats all his evening meals in Anya's apartment.

Such problems are very common. Hoarding disorder – defined as an excessive saving of objects – is (as of 2013) a recognised mental health condition. It has been estimated that the overall prevalence in the United States and Europe is around 2.5 per cent of the adult population, or one in forty people. Sufferers develop strong sentimental attachments to objects, even broken ones. Dr Gail Steketee, a psychologist who works with hoarders, has treated people who make comments such as 'Getting rid of this [badly scratched] saucepan would mean I'm not a good cook.'

The love that a hoarder feels for their stuff looks from the outside more like torment, in that their homes often become almost uninhabitable. One study of elderly hoarders suggested that some of them were forced to climb or even 'swim' through mountains of dross – knee-deep or higher – to go from one room to another. Some hoarders sleep on the floor because their beds are so full of clutter. When one parent is a hoarder, the whole family may be forced to take turns eating meals at the only small portion of the dining table that is usable.

To free yourself of this stuff, you have to be prepared to let go of some of your memories too, or at least not to hold onto them quite so tightly. In order to change his long-standing inclination towards clutter, Barry set himself a series of challenges. He forced himself to discard not just items that meant relatively little to him – such as a hoard of empty coffee cans – but also objects of great personal significance. The first of these to go was a shallow serving bowl some 10 inches wide decorated with three red tomatoes. For several years, the bowl – which Barry mostly used for pasta – had been so cracked as to be unusable and 'not at all sanitary'. But to let it go was a wrench because the object immediately took him to a joyful time in his life.

I met Barry and Anya in the autumn when they were visiting London and we had a sumptuous dinner of Peking duck together. The following spring, I wrote to Barry to ask whether he would talk to me about his pasta plate. He kindly agreed. As soon as we began, he wanted to clarify something important. This had been a pasta *bowl*, he corrected me, not a plate. He wanted me to understand that it was an item with 'an element of generosity and sharing about it'. It was not a vessel designed for a single portion but to serve several people. The bowl's generosity was unmistakable even though he never, in fact, gave dinner parties and often ate from it alone. 'Bounty' was the word that came to mind when he looked at the decoration of red tomatoes and green basil leaves inside the bowl. From the moment he bought it – from a tourist shop in Little Italy – he had a feeling that it was precious, although he admitted it was a little kitschy.

As with other mementos, the main reason that Barry's bowl was precious was because of its personal associations. At the time he bought it, he had ended a long relationship and felt he was emerging into a happier phase of life. Five years or so after buying the bowl, when he was forty, it took on a new set of positive memories because he met Anya. The tourist shop where he bought the bowl was over the road from the salumeria where he bought Anya some excellent mozzarella, which he gave her on their first date. Sometimes, in those early days, he would cook Anya pasta and serve it from the bowl – his clutter was not so bad back then.

To throw away something that once meant so much is not straightforward, but Barry forced himself to yank the bowl in half, wrapping the pieces in plastic bags and tossing them down the garbage chute. He always felt an urge to wreck objects before he got rid of them. Apparently, this is a common trait among those with hoarding issues. Gail Steketee has found that people who hoard have a stronger than usual desire to control access to their possessions and may make statements such as 'No one has the right to touch my things.'

Falling down the garbage chute in fragments sounds a sad end for something he had loved so much, but Barry told me that actually it wasn't so difficult for him to discard it as it might have been

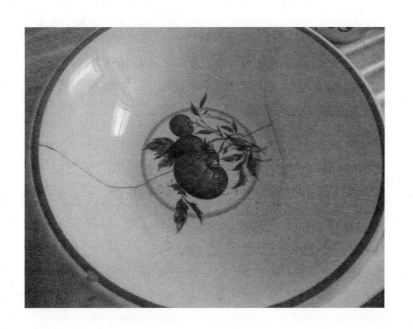

because of the crack, which had already spoiled it. By throwing the bowl away, Barry could return to the memories of what the intact tomato bowl had meant to him even if the thing itself was irreplaceable. He had looked for other pasta bowls in Little Italy but none of them compared, so he gave up.

How does someone become so attached to possessions? This is the great question raised by Barry's book and it isn't one that is simple to answer. Hoarding seems to be partly in a person's nature and partly the result of what they experienced as a child. Barry attended a few meetings of Clutterers Anonymous which gave him an even stronger sense of how many people's lives are blighted by clutter, although he realised that he was unusual among the group. Many hoarders are compulsive shoppers whereas Barry hates shopping. Some sufferers speak of their problem mostly in terms of quantity – a sea of belongings that forces them to walk in 'goat trails': narrow patches of floor between towers of junk. For Barry, by contrast, the problem as he saw it was the 'fetishistic spell' which certain objects cast over him. Some of his things meant so much to him that they actually seemed to give off vibrations.

For animals other than humans, hoarding is a survival mechanism. Birds and rodents hoard their food in two distinct ways: scatter-hoarding and larder-hoarding. Squirrels are scatter hoarders who collect small caches of food which are dispersed in a series of secret locations for retrieval at a later date. Chipmunks, by contrast, are generally 'larder hoarders' who store all of their food in a single burrow. In either case, the reason for the hoard is a very practical one: to avoid starvation. I once knew a lovely girl who was a classic scatter hoarder. Any house that she stayed in, she would leave small deposits of earrings, scarves, toiletries, scattered across many rooms. It seemed like a way for her to put down roots.

One of the theories about human hoarding is that it comes out of a chronic insecurity that gives people a twisted sense that stockpiling items is the only way they can survive, even if the net result is to make their lives worse. People who hoard – who in many cases have depression – say that their clutter makes them feel safe and cocooned, despite the fact that it causes them deep shame and inconvenience. Some sufferers have experienced poverty in the past, with or without some other kind of trauma, deprivation or loss. Research suggests that many severe hoarders come from families lacking warmth and/or childhoods in which they were not allowed to keep objects that they loved. When he was a young boy, Barry's father – in a grandiose gesture – gave away his teddy bear to the son of a colleague without asking if he minded, something which, he suspects, 'infected' how he felt about objects in general.

A cluttered home resembles a rodent's larder in so far as the person believes themselves to be storing valuable things up for various eventualities in the future. While trying to purge his apartment of excess stuff, Barry told Anya's mother that his large collection of plastic tubs was 'useful, no?' to which she replied, 'Not if you don't use them.'

Human beings are not squirrels, even if they sometimes behave like them. Barry feels that the strange and self-defeating ways in which humans hoard can only be understood in relation to psychoanalysis. After we speak, he emails to suggest that I research 'transitional objects'. According to the analyst D. W. Winnicott, a transitional object such as a teddy bear or security blanket is something that a child uses to provide physical comfort as a substitute for a mother's love when she is absent.

Any old thing can become a powerful comfort object to a child – even an empty disinfectant bottle, as Barry discovered during his early childhood in South Africa. His mother used to send him and his two brothers to school with a lunchbox including a drink of orange juice poured into an old rinsed-out Dettol disinfectant bottle. Barry's mother was a thrifty woman and had figured out that these flat glass bottles would fit nicely into a lunchbox. Once, he dropped the Dettol juice bottle on the way home. When he thinks of this now, he still experiences a 'stab of intimate loss'. That Dettol bottle – though worthless to the outside world – was to him 'an intimate talisman of my mother's love and concern, of the security and comfort of home in the alien universe of school'.

Hoarding also has a genetic element; it runs in families. Many hoarders are easily distracted and have problems with decision-making and attention. But don't we all? In addition, they may have what is called a 'hyper-sentimentality' towards objects in which they view their possessions as if they were people. Barry recognises this trait in himself. He writes that in contrast to others, he is hyper-sensitive to the 'resonances' of objects and their powers 'as bearers of memory and igniters of mood'. As a child, he collected marbles and relished their jewel-like colours and the 'weight and clink' of them in his hand.

For someone who views each object in their life as a potential memento, how does it feel to get rid of them? At the end of his book, Barry depicts himself reaping the benefits of having tidied up. For one thing, Anya can once again stay over in his apartment, which is a significant bonus. After my conversation with Barry, I started to feel better about having let go of the rotary whisk and some of my mother's other domestic things. He made me see that mementos are actually more powerful if we don't keep too many of them.

Barry is not cured, however, of his love of mementos, nor does he wish to be. He tells me that the small collection of objects he has allowed himself to keep are 'little companions of living': small, insignificant things that might seem kitsch or nondescript to others but which mean something deep to him. Many of them relate to the kitchen, such as a Moka pot which was a feature of his life in Los Angeles before he met Anya and which now lives on a shelf. He sees culinary objects as something to console himself with, whether he cooks with them or not.

Long after he discarded the pasta bowl, Barry says that there are still certain objects that bring back periods of his life in a way that nothing else could. They are not museum pieces. Over and above admiring, they are for using, and when he uses them his memories come alive again, he says. He told me he has a mug from a trip to Oaxaca in Mexico with Anya which was one of the happiest times he can remember. He could not bear to lose this mug because it 'radiates' with such memorable experiences. When the mug is not in use, Barry says it is as if the memories of that Mexican trip become 'dehydrated', like a dried flower. But when he pours coffee in it and holds the mug in his hand, 'it blooms again'.

Junk

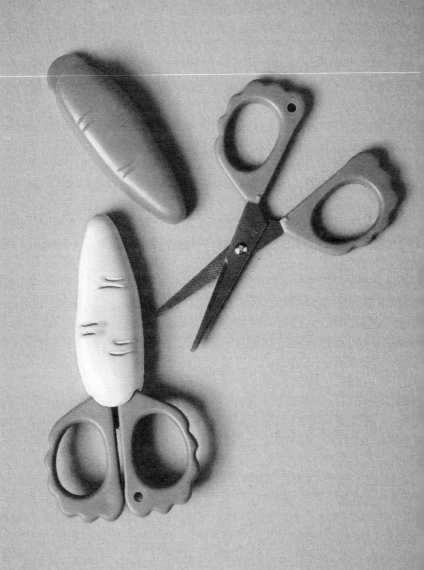

The Baby Food Scissors

'Old belongings are shed like a carapace,
  fostering the emergence of a new identity.'

Christian Jarrett, 2013

In a world flooded with cheap material goods, you do not have to be extravagant to end up with what feels like vastly too much stuff. Compare and contrast to the way people lived before the Industrial Revolution, when the household inventories that have survived suggest that even rich people in Europe simply had hardly any possessions. John Sadler was a gentleman of Stratford-upon-Avon who died in 1625, which made him a contemporary of Shakespeare. His inventory lists very few culinary things. Sadler's inventory included six jugs, two cups, two hogsheads (large casks), five brass candlesticks, one brass 'chaff dish' (a kind of brazier), one powdering tub (a container for pickles), one barrel for verjuice (a sour liquid made from grapes) and 'other odd implements'. There will certainly have been other kitchen stuff in Sadler's house not considered important enough to mention in an inventory, but even so, an economy in which five brass candlesticks and two cups are considered important assets after a person's death is a very different one from our own.

If you have children, the proliferation of clutter seems to increase tenfold. First come the baby clothes and the pushchair and cot; then the books and toys, which no sooner have you bought than they grow out of. In Japan, the problem of too much stuff is particularly acute thanks to a combination of cheap and well-produced consumer goods plus housing that is cramped compared to other industrialised countries. A 1994 study of housing standards in different countries by an economist found that when it came to newly constructed housing, the average Japanese person had access to only 21.4 square metres, compared to 36.8 square metres for a German and 56 square metres for an American.

Someone with direct experience of the consumerism of parenthood in Japan is Kay A., who writes about food, travel and parenting at her blog 'TinyTotinTokyo.com'. Kay (who doesn't use her real name to protect the identity of her daughter) lives in Osaka with her Japanese husband, after several years in Tokyo. She grew up in Canada and her mother is Indo-Fijian, so she experiences Japan both as an insider and an outsider.

Kay, I am hoping, will be the ideal person to explain to me a Japanese phenomenon I have just learned about: tiny scissors for cutting food for a baby. As Kay writes on her blog, during a baby's first year Japanese parents may use these scissors to 'cut noodles, meat or vegetables for your baby into smaller pieces right in the bowl or plate'. I am totally sold on the idea of these baby food scissors, which provide a much more elegant way to chop food than with a hand-held blender. Thanks in part to these scissors, Japanese babies can easily graduate away from the mush of baby food and on to the same real foods that the rest of the family eat, assuming they are soft enough to chew.

Customer reviews online speak of using the scissors to feed a baby slivers of rice ball or boiled vegetable. In Japanese baby shops the scissors are sold in myriad designs and colours: mint-green, baby-pink, sunshine-yellow. Some come in cases decorated with pictures of Curious George, Mickey Mouse, dinosaurs or Hello Kitty. My favourite example of baby food scissors looked like a carrot: the handles were green for the leaves and the blades were encased in an orange plastic carrot. When I heard about the baby food scissors, I imagined that they must be an object of great sentimental significance for the parents who use them, like the Christening mug my parents got for me with my name on it when I was a baby. What could be more special than a tool that enables your baby to enjoy their first taste of noodles?

When I manage to meet Kay on video call, she explains that she found these scissors most useful for cutting long, fat udon noodles for her daughter into smaller bits. She and her husband chose some plastic yellow-green scissors made by a brand called COMBI which cost about the same as a cup of coffee. Some baby food scissors are made of metal, but Kay explains that 'We felt plastic was a bit safer in case she wanted to hold it or something'. The scissors came with a little carry case, which meant that Kay could also bring the scissors with her to cut her daughter's food when eating out.

The very idea of baby food scissors is so novel and cute to me that I assume that Kay must still have her daughter's scissors stashed away somewhere as a precious keepsake, but she seems to find this a baffling notion. 'It's like any other kitchen tool,' she tells me, adding that she felt no emotional connection to the scissors after they had ceased to be useful to her and her daughter. Kay says – without a trace of unkindness – that she found the very idea of my book quite odd. She does not attach many emotions to possessions: 'You use it and you are done with it' is her attitude, though she does concede that back in Canada things were a little different. Kay's family had travelled from Fiji with a chopping knife, which they never stopped treating as special, and some very old plates which they referred to as 'Fiji plates', honouring the link with the country they had left behind.

Here in Osaka, however, Kay adopted a less sentimental attitude to possessions. Those cute little baby food scissors weren't needed much once Kay's daughter was nine months old so she got rid of them several years ago. She thinks she probably gave them to someone in a baby exchange group. Kay adds that in her experience, compared with Canadians, Japanese parents are 'surprisingly' unemotional about the apparatus of childhood. 'If it has no use then we don't need it any more' is her mother-in-law's attitude, Kay says. She explains that her daughter is now five and has been eating full-length noodles since at least the age of two. She has kept very few mementos of her daughter's early life. 'Japanese parents love getting rid of things,' she tells me.

Given how burdensome many of us find it to live with too many individual possessions, the mystery is why we keep acquiring so many of them. Russell Belk has spent his whole career studying our relationship with objects as an offshoot of what he calls 'materialism'. Belk tells me that many years ago, he and some colleagues studied people who had lost everything in a fire, a flood or another catastrophe. The big surprise was that, as traumatic as the experience was, most people do tend to 'get over' the loss of their personal effects, especially if they are relatively affluent. In the short term, the losses were a terrible shock but over time, many survivors found that having fewer things actually comes with benefits. One of the questions Belk keeps returning to in his work is why we don't acquire fewer things and share them more with others. He comments that in wartime, populations are generally very good at adapting to a model of sharing more with others.

Within families, sharing everything from food to various items of clothing is fully expected. As Belk has written, children are not sued by their parents for trespass when they sit on the family sofa, nor are they accused of theft if they take food from the fridge. Yet despite a few exceptions, such as public libraries and car-sharing schemes, sharing is very much underused in modern societies, even though it would benefit all of us if this could change. Belk takes hope from new schemes such as one in France in which neighbours can borrow large household machinery – lawnmowers and so on – for a small fee. The problem, as Belk sees it, is that values of individualism are so entrenched that most people still want their own versions of everything even if it quickly becomes clutter.

After the divorce, I started spending a lot of time at the recycling centre, where waste items are sorted into different categories, from old greetings cards to glass, from textiles to furniture. As with other mundane aspects of life during the pandemic, going to the recycling centre felt like a weird kind of treat. Because of social distancing you had to book a time slot, and for a while the spaces were so booked up that when you actually succeeded in getting one it was golden. And there was something cathartic in getting rid of stuff. I usually brought my dog with me, and after I had recycled everything I would drive us to a nearby nature reserve and walk round the lake. I would drive home feeling lighter.

Each time I went, I was shamed by how many *things* I had managed to accumulate. I had cupboards crammed with broken toasters and kettles, with old cardboard boxes, with piles of unread magazines, with torn duvet covers and curtains that were beyond repair, with remote controls for electronic toys which had not been played with in years, with spare tiles which builders had suggested we keep in case any of the tiles behind the sink should get cracked (but they never did), with dozens and dozens of metal coathangers, many of which had once held my ex-husband's shirts. There was a satisfaction in saying goodbye to all these things, though it was sometimes mingled with twinges of regret. The odds and ends we hold on to often represent buried dreams or delusions and this is why we find it so hard to toss them away, even when they serve no purpose in our lives. As I discarded the torn curtains I realised I would never be Maria in *The Sound of Music*, making beautiful children's play clothes out of drapes.

Gazing around the recycling centre, I would feel guilty that my presence in the world had given rise to so much waste. I would look at all the other people with their own bags and boxes of discarded belongings and marvel at the sheer volume of unwanted items at this one recycling centre in one town in one corner of England. Shiny mirrors in which a family's sleepy faces had once been reflected were now nothing more than shards of broken glass. Some of the things chucked away were broken but many of them were perfectly usable, like the baby food scissors which Kay had used for just three months or so. She felt good to have managed to find a new home for them. Apparently there is a big exchange culture for baby equipment on Facebook in Japan which dealt with at least some of the mountain of unwanted things. But even if you give things away as you go along, most of us still end up with more than we want or need, whether in Japan or elsewhere.

I was at the recycling centre getting rid of some old broken plant pots and garden rubbish on a cold March day when something caught my eye in the 'hardcore and rubble' skip. It was an earthenware mug decorated with polka dots with the letters 'MR' on it. It took me a moment to realise that these were not someone's initials but the shortened form of the word 'mister'. I wondered who the mug's owner was and why they had thrown it away.

I recognised the mister mug the moment I saw it. Not this exact mug, but I knew where it was made. It was a half-pint Emma Bridgewater mug. The Emma Bridgewater factory in Stoke-on-Trent is one of the very few remaining potteries in Staffordshire, a region which used to be one of England's great centres for ceramics. I visited the factory once and learned that these mugs – which, being on the pricey side, tend to be bought as gifts – are made with great care. In the manufacturing process, each one passes through thirty pairs of hands. First, workers take wet clay and mix it with a liquid called 'slip'. Then casters pour the wet clay into moulds and leave it to dry. Fettlers remove the tiny ridge which forms in the clay where the two halves of the mould join and hand the ceramic to spongers, who make the surface of the mug perfectly smooth. The mug is then fired before being decorated. Each polka dot on this mug will have been carefully applied by hand using a sponge before being glazed to a delicate sheen.

All of the labour that had created this mug was now reduced to nothing. It sat in hardcore and rubble with no more dignity than a smashed bathroom sink. It would probably end up being crushed and transformed into materials for construction or road-building. Of all the skips at the recycling centre, hardcore and rubble is the one that sets my teeth on edge. It feels noisy and slightly violent. There is a warning on the side not to put your hands in, lest you get cut on the many jagged edges. Whoever bought this pretty mug cannot have predicted that it would come to such an ignominious end. As it sat there in hardcore and rubble it was still pristine and unchipped.

Thinking about the mister mug made me sad. Who was the mister who owned it? These mugs are generally sold as a pair for a couple, along with a 'MRS' mug (or with a second mister mug, come to that). Was it a wedding present? If so, I wondered whether it was Mister himself who had discarded it or the person who shared his life. In my own rejected state, I started to paint the mister who owned this mug as someone who had cruelly abandoned his spouse, someone who did not appreciate how lucky he was to be drinking his morning coffee from this well-made vessel with a loving person by his side.

Or maybe the truth was less dramatic. Next to the mister mug in the hardcore and rubble skip I noticed a few perfectly nice blue earthenware mugs, which appeared to have been thrown away by the same person. Maybe Mister was just having a clear-out and he never really cared for this particular mug much anyway. Maybe the mug was an unwanted present and the polka dots clashed with the decor in his house. Or it could have made him cringe to be referred to as 'mister'.

For many ancient civilisations, shards of pottery are one of the few traces that remain: clues to explain who these people were and what mattered to them. Archaeologists often name communities after their pottery. In the third millennium BC, a set of people now known as the Beaker folk travelled across Europe, passing through what are now Spain, Germany and Britain. We know very little about them except that they liked to drink from bell-shaped clay drinking vessels, reddish-brown in colour. They were buried with one of these beakers at their feet.

If there is still life on earth a few hundred years from now, what will archaeologists deduce about us from our ceramics and our metals and our many, many plastics? They might notice that ours was a world filled with such a mad proliferation of stuff that scissors for cutting a baby's first food have a value as evanescent as mayflies, and a beautifully made mug which took thirty sets of hands to produce could be thrown away without so much as a second glance, along with all the other things we didn't want anymore.

The Paper Cup

> 'In much of Asia the tea cups are quite small and the beer bottles are quite large. For, in contrast to contemporary Western drinks, the beverages in these containers are meant to be shared.'

> Russell Belk, 2010

How can you love something when you are only going to use it for a few seconds and then chuck it away? And yet love is not too strong a word, I think, for how many people feel about disposable paper coffee cups. I have felt some of this love myself. I am old enough to remember when speciality coffee served in a branded paper cup (as opposed to a Styrofoam cup of instant coffee) was a novelty in the UK. In 1993, when I was nineteen, a company called AMT founded by three brothers opened its first branch at a street cart in central Oxford, where I grew up. I remember my sister coming home and saying she had bought a drink called a 'mocha' from this stall: a mix between a cappuccino and a hot chocolate. It sounded unbelievably glamorous. The specialness of the mocha seemed to transmit itself to the paper cup itself.

In the England of my youth, the coffee you bought outside of the home was usually stewy and dull-tasting. Sometimes, my mother took me with her to a little coffee shop in the market where she bought coffee beans and had the beans ground on the spot. As the shop owner poured them into the grinder through a funnel they made a gentle clattering sound. When she gave me the warm bag to hold it smelled like heaven.

The coffee my mother drank in cafés never smelled like this. It was bitter and gravy-ish and I had no idea how grown-ups could stomach it. The only good part – which none of us realised was special at the time – was that it was served in ceramic cups or mugs.

Cappuccino made with an espresso machine did exist, but it was generally only sold in restaurants or Italian cafés and the quality was far more variable than it is now. When I was a student in 1993, I would go with a boyfriend to sit in one of the few Italian cafés in town. We had met at the student film society. After the cinema he and I would go to a café called Clowns till late in the night to discuss whatever film we'd seen and drink frothy coffee in brown ceramic cups and saucers, the froth dusted with cocoa – there was no latte art back then.

For a long time, I thought of frothy milky coffee in a disposable paper cup as something you would only buy *in extremis* while on the move. My first son was born in 1999. He was a colicky baby and had trouble sleeping for his first year. I became even more caffeine-dependent than I had been before. My most important friendships from that period were all with mothers of other babies, and sometimes we drank coffee in takeaway cups while pushing prams. On train journeys, too, I developed a ritual of buying a disposable cup of coffee. The first few times I did this, with my American friend Lauren, it felt almost shockingly indulgent. 'I mean, Starbucks is not cheap,' said Lauren's mother, trying to understand why on earth so many people had started drinking it. Lauren's daughter, who was a couple of years older than my son, loved looking at the cute green mermaid on the cup.

It would be another few years before I consciously noticed just how many paper coffee cups with plastic lids were being used, even on occasions when people were sitting down at a table and had the option of ceramic cups. After our third child was born we joined a gym. I noticed that the people I got friendly with from various exercise classes often actively opted to have their foamy coffee in a disposable cup even when we were sitting down for ages inside at a table. It was as if the paper cup itself had become some kind of status symbol. These paper cups (the very name is a misnomer, because it fails to mention the plastic layer which makes them waterproof) were a connection with the celebrities in magazines, who were frequently snapped on their way to or from spin classes wearing leggings and dark glasses and clutching an oversized take-out coffee.

The key design feature of the new paper cups that Starbucks first launched in 1987 was not so much the paper itself as the plastic lid. Paper cups were not new. The modern paper cup goes back to 1908 with the invention of the Dixie cup, originally called the Health Kup because it flourished in the wake of public alarm about passing on germs through shared 'tin dippers' in schools and on trains. Another key moment in the history of paper cups was the Anthora in 1963, a blue and white cup with the slogan 'We Are Happy To Serve You', which was originally designed for use in Greek cafés but quickly spread throughout food carts and cafés in the USA, reaching peak sales of 500 million in 1994. What made the new Starbucks cup so different from the Anthora – apart from its much bigger size – was the lid, which was raised, allowing room for foam. There was also a hole for sipping, which enabled the consumer to return to the comforting state of being a toddler, drinking with a sippy cup, while feeling like a highly sophisti-cated cappuccino-drinking person.

Starbucks sold a new idea of coffee which – unlike the old watery diner coffee with its bottomless refills – was infinitely cus-tomisable. Ordering a paper cup of Starbucks coffee could make every customer feel special. How often in adult life are you ever handed something with your own name written on it? On a holiday to the West Coast, my ex-husband and I visited the original Starbucks in Seattle in 1996 when there was still a buzz about it. I drank so much coffee on that trip I thought my head would explode.

We like to think that love is a natural phenomenon that happens all by itself, springing directly from our hearts. But to live in the modern commercial world is to have thousands of desires and longings planted inside us without our say-so. You wake up with an urge to buy a giant coffee in a paper cup decorated with a green mermaid and you have no idea why. Maybe you saw the romcom *You've Got Mail* (1998), in which Meg Ryan walks through New York on a perfect Fall day – all orange leaves and crisp, bright air – clutching her Starbucks paper cup as The Cranberries' song 'Dreams' plays on the soundtrack. We see her placing her order with a dreamy look on her face – 'Tall skim caramel macchiato' – and smiling as only Meg Ryan can. What made this such an effective piece of marketing is that the whole plot line of the film hinges on Ryan being a tiny independent bookseller trying to fight Tom Hanks whose family owns Fox Books, a big corporate chain store. In real life, someone like Ryan's character would not be a Starbucks fan, let alone someone who orders coffee in a single-use cup. This is a woman who is such an opponent of wastefulness that she uses a cloth embroidered handkerchief to blow her nose!

The real question is how our love of paper cups can finally be dislodged and replaced with a new set of emotions which would drive us to different behaviour. To date, there have been only a few cafés that have taken a stand and ditched disposable cups altogether, giving customers the option to buy or borrow a cup instead. The first to do this in the UK was Boston Tea Party in Bristol in June 2018. They lost £250,000 in sales as a result, but calculated that they had prevented 100,000 cups from going to landfill in the space of a year.

Our love of paper cups cannot be driven out simply through information campaigns but by changing our ideas of what is normal and desirable. There is plenty of information out there on this subject. I could tell you what a crazy number of disposable cups are used, but I bet you have a good idea of that already. Exact numbers are hard to come by, but as of 2024 more than 500 billion beverage cups were being disposed of each year. I could tell you that only around 1 per cent of single-use coffee cups are recycled because the plastic lining makes them difficult to recycle (and that plastic also means that they leach microplastics into the environment). I could tell you that apart from being largely non-recyclable themselves, these cups contaminate other batches of recycling because people don't know that they can't be recycled and put them in the wrong bin. I could tell you that most of the very small gains made by people switching to reusable cups were wiped out during the pandemic when concerns about hygiene forced many cafés to adopt a disposables-only policy for a while.

It is possible, though, to redirect your love. The human heart can grow and shift. You may wake up and feel a surprising indifference or even alienation towards that which once claimed your affections and patterned your days. You may wonder why you ever felt you had room for it in your life. Are we still talking about coffee cups?

What makes our reliance on these cups so alarming is that they are just one piece in a whole universe of single-use throwaway utensils which includes chopsticks and plastic containers for sushi; hamburger boxes and sandwich cartons; plastic tubs for salads and cardboard cups with lids for soup; plastic spoons and forks and knives and sporks. And yet, as Russell Belk told me, there is now a movement towards minimalism in which increasing numbers of people are saying, 'I can do without these things.' Cultures of eating and drinking have changed many times before, Belk observes, and they can change again. It is conceivable that the West could return to a more communal vision of consumption in which the very idea of a person buying a huge individual paper cup of coffee and drinking it all by themselves would seem plain wrong. As Belk notes, in much of Asia it is generally 'unthinkable' that 'dinner companions would pour their own tea' without pouring it for others at the same time. Small ceramic cups are used because they are designed to be frequently replenished from a common pot. Then again, when I finally went to Japan in the summer of 2024 it was evident that the old, thoughtful Japanese culture of ceramics existed alongside a modern economy of 7/11s selling a vast array of food and drink, including coffee, in disposable packaging. To move away from paper cups, Belk told me, we would need to get to the point where the alternative – the keep cup – actually 'means more to us'. There are a few signs of this happening already with the current frenzy around reusable double-walled Stanley mugs for water among the youth of America, although the problem here is that the hype about certain limited-edition colours of the mugs becomes so great that people buy multiple mugs, thus keeping the cycle of overconsumption turning.

It is the *meaning* of paper cups that needs to change, more than anything. An Australian study of consumers and coffee shop owners found that, contrary to what economists might expect, people were not very sensitive to economic incentives such as offering a discount to those bringing in their own cup (other studies have suggested that a far more effective lever is making people pay a surcharge for a disposable cup rather than the other way round). The study also found that many people – even those who owned them – had a negative view of keep cups compared to paper cups. There is a certain responsibility in owning a keep cup, like any form of ownership, and many people seemed to feel weighed down by it. One woman who used a keep cup said it made her feel 'scabby' to be holding it because she was in a minority. Another woman said she did not want to be seen using a 'grotty' keep cup in an external meeting. A third person said that coffee tasted better in a disposable cup.

Habits around paper cups only changed among this small group of Australians when people started to doubt whether those disposable vessels were really so likeable. What most helped consumers change their behaviour was noticing other people around them doing the same. This is called 'mimetic' behaviour: humans have a natural desire to copy each other. One woman said she began using a keep cup because one of her staff members had started using one and she thought, 'Hmmm, that's very environmentally conscious of her.'

Like any utensil, a paper cup can change its significance. It can go from lovable to unlovable in a second. And it needs to. Here is what can happen, judging from my own experience. You have a fierce friend – fierce in her loyalty and fierce in her political views. She tells you she never, ever uses paper cups and this makes you – far too late in the day – feel you simply must change your ways. You buy yourself a nice reusable cup, so nice that you actually want to drink from it. It is clear and amber coloured, like the necklaces your mother wore when you were a child. After months of forgetting to bring it with you, finally it becomes an easy(ish) habit to put it in your bag. Sometimes you are slow to put the cup in the dishwasher and it gets a bit gross, but then you remember again and all is well. You drink enough delicious coffee from this cup for it to become associated in your mind with the toasty, milky taste of a flat white and the dark jolt of an Americano, not to mention all the AeroPress coffee you make at home. Although there can be slip-ups when you are travelling, paper cups start to look weird to you, just like the plastic straws you used to give your children without hesitating.

The Unused Platters

'All objects either scared or charmed her
With secret meanings they'd impart'.

Alexander Pushkin, *Eugene Onegin*, 1825–1832

Some of the most poignant objects I found in my mother's house when we were clearing it were two small platters made by Royal Doulton. They were in the bottom of one of the drawers where she kept her plates and bowls. These small oval-shaped platters were decorated in dark, inky blue and bright green with flower patterns done in fine lines using a delicate sepia brown, all against a creamy-white background. I never saw china with quite this colour scheme before. There was a curious atmosphere about them which delighted me. One of the platters was slightly chipped, and this made me like it even more. On the back of the platters it said 'Matsumai', with the Royal Doulton mark. Both platters still had tags attached to them with the words 'Gift Aid', suggesting that my mother had bought them from a charity shop and never used them.

I brought the platters home, along with various boxes of papers and bowls and books and other keepsakes to pass on to her friends and relatives. These platters were too distinctive and special to give away to a charity shop, even if this was where she had got them in the first place. But they didn't feel like something to give her friends as a keepsake because they had no real personal association with her. She had never served anything on them or even got round

to removing the tags and washing them. I have no idea when or why she bought them. They felt much less hers than other items in the house such as her books, many of which were scribbled with elaborate margin notes in her very distinctive handwriting.

Among some Maori tribes, one way to establish that you really owned something was to lick it. Animal behaviourists suggest that a cat licking its owner may be doing the same: once you have been licked by a cat, it owns you, not the other way round. Some of the same process happens anytime you bring a new utensil or dish into your home. 'You break it, you own it' has been the rule at some shops selling fragile goods. I would change this to: 'You buy it, you lick it, you own it.' Even after you have bought a plate, it is not entirely yours until you have washed it and eaten off it, and perhaps even licked it. In this way you make the item part of yourself. My mother's Matsumai platters had failed this test of ownership. They were in a limbo state, waiting to become hers but never passing the final hurdle. They remained unlicked.

For a long time, I forgot about the platters. It was only when we were distributing my mother's stuff that I looked at them again. My sister did not want them so I washed and dried them carefully and put them on a shelf with my other serving dishes. The first time I used one of the platters was to serve a *tabbouleh* – a Middle Eastern salad of bulgur wheat with masses of parsley, mint, lemon, onion and olive oil, decorated with chopped tomatoes. The green and red of the salad looked especially lovely against the dark blue – so dark it was almost black.

'Royal Doulton' sounds posh, but the company has a rags-to-riches story. Its founder, John Doulton, started off specialising in ceramic drainpipes rather than anything as rarefied as fine china. In the library I found a history of Royal Doulton from 1993 by Michael Doulton – the sixth generation of the Doulton family to be involved in the business. As a producer of bone china, the company was much later to get established than Wedgwood or Spode. Doulton began with John Doulton (1793–1873), who trained as a potter in London before investing his life savings (£100) in a small concern making simple functional stoneware such as beer bottles (plus sewage pipes) called Jones, Doulton and Watts. His son Henry, one of eight children, joined the firm in 1835 and greatly expanded the sanitary side of the business. Doulton became famous for the manufacture of toilets, sinks and drainage pipes and set up the first factory – in Lambeth – devoted to stoneware pipes. At the same time, however, Doulton was cultivating a more artistic kind of pottery through the Lambeth School of Art. At the Lambeth studios, he employed hundreds of female artists to generate his 'art pottery'. Finally, in the 1870s Doulton managed to buy a factory in Stoke and he moved away from sewage and into the refined world of bone china in 1884.

Some of Doulton's flashier china products in these early days included the 'Gibbon's Party Plate' consisting of a tray with a saucer and cup all in one, leaving 'an arm free to offer a lady'. Another Doulton gimmick was a self-pouring teapot of 1886 invented by John J. Royle. It worked through a pumping mechanism which generated pressure and the tea poured out of the spout without anyone needing to lift the pot. Henry Doulton produced thousands of these ingenious gadgets and supplied several of them to Queen Victoria. Doulton supplied water filters to all of Queen Victoria's residences and in 1887 was the first potter ever to receive a knighthood. In 1901 Doulton was given a royal warrant and the right to add the word 'Royal' to the name.

My mother's Matsumai platters were produced nine years later, in 1910. This was a time – before the First World War – when Britain was the most industrialised nation in the world. The fact that they were oval would have made them more difficult to make. As Michael Doulton explains, every Doulton oval piece was hand-made because of the difficulty of spreading the clay evenly: 'The dish maker uses a special tool operated by a shoulder press. Too much pressure and the clay becomes dented and useless.'

I became a bit obsessed with the Matsumai oval platters. I discovered that the design was rare but not as expensive as another, much more polished Doulton version of Matsumai which included red and orange and gold as well as the green and blue. When I saw this other version my mother's platters looked unfinished by comparison. But I preferred the slightly eccentric colour scheme that she had chosen. On eBay I managed to find a couple of dinner plates in the same design for £20 each – not cheap but less than half the price of a brand-new Wedgwood china dinner plate. (I mention Wedgwood rather than Doulton because the current Royal Doulton brand no longer does full dinner services.) Even though she had never so much as touched these particular plates, never mind licked them, they felt like a connection with her.

All my mother ever wanted was to be in the right; and to be loved. When her marriage was breaking down she regularly felt that she was neither. One summer, not long before the divorce, she spent ages choosing a new pale summer dress for herself in a cool linen which she hoped would be flattering, although she was self-conscious about her figure. She sometimes apologised for the fact that her waist was not what it had been when she was twenty-five. ('Why should she try to look younger?' my ex-husband said when I told him this story. I loved him so much for it.) The dress came from an expensive boutique. When she appeared wearing it my father said, 'Grey isn't really your colour.'

When I served and ate food from the Matsumai platters, I wanted to bring her back so that I could tell her that she was right to buy them and that I loved her. When I was talking in this vein over dinner one night, my oldest son said, 'You've forgotten how difficult you found Grandma', and it was true. She was a deeply anxious person. When some tiny detail went wrong – and in the normal run of life, tiny details are always going wrong – she would loudly exclaim, 'Oh no!', as if the thing simply could not be borne. My sister got a B in Art once and it was a day of mourning in our house. Much as I loved her, I often felt on edge in her company. She repressed many of her feelings (because her parents had taught her to do so) and made me feel that I must repress mine too. It was only after she developed dementia and some of her inhibitions had fallen away that she was able to tell me and my sister directly that she loved us. When I hold the Matsumai platters, I yearn to have her back – all of her, even the parts that drove me crazy.

Most of all, the platters make me feel how fleeting and sad life is. You buy these small treasures, hoping they will come in handy. You save them for something special. And then you die before the special event happens and they never get used. It's like the fine vintage wine that people keep stored away for the moment that never quite comes. My uncle, my mother's brother, loved champagne but usually felt that not enough people were present to justify opening it. He once uttered the words, 'Are we quorate for champagne?', as if it were a meeting. He died a year and a half after my mother and one of my first thoughts was that I wished he had seized the day and drunk more champagne.

Things can have a second life (and a third and fourth one), even if people can't. Roopa Gulati spoke of giving her family's Braemar dinner service another chance of living. I did the same with my mother's unused platters. The more I celebrated them and arranged beautiful food on them, the more I could justify her original purchase and stop them from being seen as junk, even if she would never know.

Bonnie's Salt Shaker

'Why should it be a matter of wonder that the dead
should come back? The wonder is that they do not.'

Margaret Oliphant, 1879

'Let me go get her,' said Bonnie Slotnik when I ask about her about
the 1930s salt shaker which she had already described to me as her
most prized kitchen possession. Bonnie reappeared on the video
call a moment later in her one-room rent-controlled apartment on
West 10th Street between 5th and 6th in New York City with what
looked like a bright-red tomato in her hand. She explained that it
was actually a ceramic salt shaker with the word 'Japan' on the
bottom which had once belonged to her mother.

If you want to create a piece of kitchenware with mass appeal,
making it look like a cheery red tomato is not a bad place to start.
Utensils of one kind or another shaped like tomatoes have been
popular for more than a century. Squeezy ketchup bottles. Timers.
Jam pots and cream jugs. In the America of the 1930s and 1940s,
tomatoes were most strongly associated with salt and pepper shakers. Bonnie remembers that her parents and all of her aunts had the
exact same cheap 'tomato ware' ceramic salt shaker. They probably
bought it from Woolworths or a similar low-cost shop. The word
'Japan' on Bonnie's one suggests that this particular little salt
shaker dates to sometime before the Second World War, because
versions of the same one made after the war say 'occupied Japan'

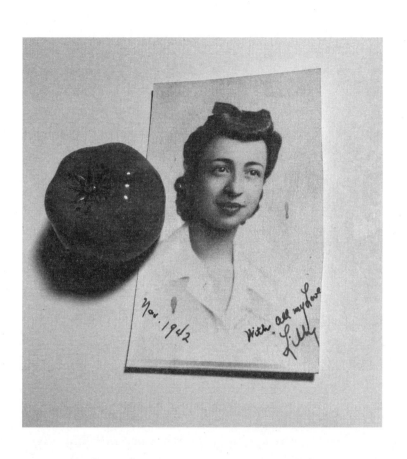

With all my Love

Lilly

Nov. 1942

instead. Bonnie thinks it originally cost about ten cents but to her it is a very precious possession. A 'plump little gem' is how she once described it, in *The Gourmand* magazine. 'If I break this, something is going to end,' she tells me.

Bonnie Slotnik has a much deeper feeling for obsolete kitchen trinkets than most people you meet. Her New York shop, on East 2nd Street, has a cult following. The store – which sells second-hand cookbooks and vintage kitchenalia, all chosen by Bonnie herself – has been going for twenty-five years although it only moved to its current location in 2014 after her previous landlord 'flatly refused' to renew her lease. Bonnie's new landlords are young people who happened to own a commercial space in a house and wanted to support her by renting it to her for a reasonable cost because they loved books so much. She describes this new rental arrangement as 'beyond anything' she imagined after she lost the old place.

It is hard to describe Bonnie Slotnik's store because it is not like others. If you search for it on Google, you will see a message from Bonnie herself saying '********NB IGNORE ANY HOURS THAT GOOGLE POSTS HERE! THEY'RE PROBABLY WRONG . . .' If you persevere and manage to go when it is open, you find yourself walking down some stairs off the street into what looks like the basement of a large brownstone house, because it is. The only way you know it is a shop from the outside is a swinging white sign saying 'COOK BOOKS' with an elegant silhouette of a female cook bearing a pie. When I got inside, it felt like stepping into a time capsule where electric whisks were still a novelty and cookbooks with colour photography were not the norm.

Everywhere I looked there were interesting old utensils, china and books, and yet somehow the small room did not feel cluttered because everything was arranged in such an orderly, purposeful way. Most of the books had been carefully wrapped in cellophane to protect their jackets. 'Please remove books by SIDES, not tops', read one of the notices on the bookshelves. My eye fell on some quaint orange and white teacups with a matching cakestand near some books on 'COOKING FOR MANY OR FEW': *Going Solo in the Kitchen, Cooking on the Go, The Newlywed Kitchen.* I found myself staring at an 'uncommon eggbeater' from the nineteenth century near some pamphlets that came free with old mixers and pressure cookers. And here was a large, rusting 'Dutch Cough Drop tin' for sale. The tin featured a picture of DR LOUQUETTE, a bearded man who presumably invented the cough drops. Outside, on the jostling streets of New York, people were still going about their business, talking into mobile phones and buying bags of snazzy new gadgets. But here in this basement was a different economy in which it was the old and the 'uncommon' things which were the ones worth cherishing.

The day I visited, in the spring of 2024, Bonnie wasn't there. Someone had collided with her in the street and she had broken her kneecap. Her friend Chris was in charge of the shop. I browsed for a while and talked to him about how Bonnie was before buying a charming little nutcracker, a spring-loaded ice cream scoop and some old cookery pamphlets.

Bonnie kindly agreed to talk to me about her salt shaker and other kitchenalia a month or so later when I was back home in England. She suggested doing a 'show and tell' via video so that she could show me some of her treasured items, including the salt shaker. I immediately saw that her kitchen was very similar to her shop. There was 'nothing twenty-first century' in her kitchen, she told me. When I asked whether she owned any gadgets, she said she had a wooden spoon and an apple corer and didn't feel the need for anything more.

In Bonnie's kitchen I could see assortments of vintage candy tins and cookie tins and baking powder tins, all beautifully arranged. The history of baking powder was one of her obsessions, she said. She has been in this apartment since 1976 when it was a rent-controlled unit, which is the only way she could afford to live there. It was built in 1892 and still has the original gas fittings and a fireplace that doesn't work, although the kind of people who now move into these buildings are 'millionaires and billionaires', according to Bonnie. She has only survived in this apartment for forty-eight years by being 'cheap', she says. Life as a second-hand cookbook seller is far from lucrative.

Although she had recovered enough to be back working in the shop, she was plainly still shaken and in pain after the injury to her knee. She showed me a tiny toy kitchen where she stored all of the medication she had to take. Having been very fit most of her life – she describes herself as a 'gym rat' who used to do aerobics every day and ate meat only once a year – it was a shock to find herself in poor health at the age of seventy. Before the accident with her kneecap she had suffered a scare over her heart. 'It's the schmaltz, there's schmaltz in my blood,' she said, referring to the chicken fat that is such a feature of Jewish-American cooking. Bonnie told me she remembered the smell of the schmaltz being made, the way the fat melted and the skin turned into 'these little crisp things' that she used to eat with rye bread as a child.

When people have an especially deep feeling for a certain artifact, it is never just about the thing itself. Russell Belk observes that our relationship with possessions is not two-way (person–object) but three-way (person–object–person). It is other people who make us desire or dislike a particular object. In early childhood, things may represent our rivalry with other children or our parents' love and care. As Barry Yourgrau had shown me, even something as seemingly meaningless as an old disinfectant bottle can become a talisman of home.

As we talked, I was wondering where Bonnie's devotion to old cookbooks and kitchen ornaments really came from. In the course of our conversation, Bonnie told me how she got into them in two different ways. The first version she gave me was very matter-of-fact, as if she were giving me her CV. She studied fashion illustration at university but she never practised it because it was a dying art form. So she went into publishing as an editorial assistant and ended up working on cookbooks, writing recipe headnotes and fact-checking. As a sideline, she started buying out-of-print cookbooks, mostly selling them to Kitchen Arts and Letters, a much-loved cookbook store a few blocks from the Upper East Side of Central Park. Eventually, she explained, it became too much to do both jobs at once and she took the plunge into being a full-time bookseller.

But then Bonnie told me her story again in a way that got closer to the heart of the matter. She had already mentioned that the tomato salt shaker reminded her of her mother. Her mother would not leave the house without red lipstick and dangling earrings and Bonnie felt that the gloriously bright salt shaker echoed her lipsticked mouth and petite figure. Now I understood why she referred to the salt shaker as 'her'. Bonnie's parents had both arrived in the USA in the 1930s from 'that part of land that was always changing its borders: Russia-Poland-Russia-Poland'. Her father and mother were the last children in their respective families to get out and leave the old country while there was still time; others were not so lucky. Several of her mother's siblings who were left behind ended up in concentration camps. Sometimes, when Bonnie was young, in the split-level house where they lived in New Jersey her mother would 'just lie on the couch and cry for no reason that I could discern'. Neither of Bonnie's parents ever spoke of the Holocaust, let alone of what had happened to their relatives.

Then something happened which has coloured the last fifty-six years of Bonnie's life. It was only late in our conversation that she told me that her mother died unexpectedly of a heart attack on a trip to Israel with her father when she was just fourteen and her sister was seventeen. 'That was such an abrupt interruption of my connection with her,' Bonnie says. For the next twenty years she dreamed that her mother had come back and that there was some kind of explanation for what had happened, only to wake up and find the loss as senseless and terrible as before. Her father was so grief-stricken after her mother's death that he said he understood why, in some cultures, a widow might throw herself on her husband's funeral pyre. He too died only a few years later.

After her mother's death, Bonnie became devoted to reading the one cookbook her mother had owned, which dated back to 1947. It was *The Settlement Cookbook* by Lizzie Black Kander, which was first published in 1901 as a fundraiser but remained in print continuously until 1955. As a profile of Bonnie by Hannah Goldfield in *The New Yorker* noted, the book was published by the Settlement House, 'an organization in Milwaukee, Wisconsin, that supported recent immigrants, many of them European Jews'. When her father was still alive, Bonnie would read *The Settlement Cookbook* lying under the dining room table near the air conditioner and feel close to her mother. 'That was a talisman for me.'

Bonnie also held on to scraps of handwritten recipes from her aunts. One of them was for Connecticut Chicken, which sounds odd, but Bonnie swears 'it tastes amazing': chicken cooked with dried onion soup, apricot jam and French, Russian or Thousand Island Dressing. Years later, when she went to flea markets and saw rows of old cookbooks, she realised that they spoke to her in a deep way. She had already inherited a liking for thrift shops and rummage sales from her mother, who had bought her clothes there because money was so tight. But now these old cookbooks had a deeper meaning. Reading them was a way to escape into the world that existed before her mother died.

In her shop, Bonnie always has multiple copies of *The Settlement Cookbook* and it moves her when people come in and ask for it. They almost always say that the reason they want it is because it reminds them of a family member. Sometimes, 'tears are shed'. Kitchenalia, she finds, can be equally emotional. She told me that just yesterday she had a young chef aged about thirty come in and buy a 'little garnishing knife' with a fluted blade for cutting fancy carrots or cucumber pickles. 'It had a wooden handle and the paint was almost worn away.' The man explained that his grandmother had one and she had lost it. Bonnie couldn't tell from what he said if his grandmother was alive or dead, but in either case she understood the urgency of this young man's need for an old, worn-out garnishing knife. She refers to old cookbooks and kitchenalia as a form of 'medicine': they take the mind to happier places.

Her mother 'hewed to a narrow course of cooking', Bonnie remarked. She 'didn't do a ton' of cooking but she 'fed her family very nicely'. Monday – hamburgers. Tuesday – roast beef. Friday – Sabbath dinner and roast chicken. Saturday – leftover roast chicken. 'It's amazing how far one chicken would go.'

Bonnie herself more or less stopped cooking and having people over during the pandemic (which was never easy, in any case, in a one-room apartment). But on the occasions she does prepare something simple, she still shakes salt from her tomato-shaped shaker, and scoops flour with her mother's old flour scoop and uses a set of plastic measuring spoons that reminds her of the clattering sound her mother made when measuring vanilla essence for cakes. She showed me a photograph of her parents on their wedding day. Her mother had a flower in her hair. 'I think she was inspired by Billie Holiday.'

No salt shaker in the whole of New York City could replace the little tomato one that Bonnie has kept safe for the nearly sixty years since her mother died. You can only put regular fine table salt in it – the holes in the top are too small for kosher salt or flaky sea salt. But regular salt is just fine for Bonnie because that is what her mother used.

My Grandfather's Teapot

'Strange the affection which clings to inanimate objects –
objects which cannot even know our love!'

Letitia Elizabeth Landon, 1831

The week my ex remarried, I painted my bedroom olive-green, replacing the nondescript magnolia it had always been. He hadn't been a fan of colour on walls but said that pure white was 'clinical', so we ended up with various shades of off-white. The work of painting the olive green was tiring, in a good way. Focusing on lining up the masking tape and counting the hours between layers of paint stopped my mind from brooding. My old jeans got splattered in green and the paint splashed through the rips to my skin beneath but I didn't mind. I scrubbed myself with dish soap and a scourer, relishing the slightly penitential feeling of the roughness against my legs. When I woke up on the day of the wedding, it felt like a new room, one I could bear to live in.

My next decorating task was to paint the hallway walls all the way up the stairs to the top of the house. We had neglected these walls for years and some of the plaster was falling out in chunks. It felt like too big a job to do myself. A friend recommended a decorator who was as calm and quiet as a lake (his great hobby was fishing). When he came to the house, his presence was so unruffled and still that my dog didn't bark once. I told him I had chosen the colour: a subtle shade of greyish blue that was pale but not too pale. It was like sky-blue, but with a pleasing coolness and not a trace of baby-blue sickliness. He said the blue would go well with white as a contrast on the ceiling and skirting boards. He was calmly painting away the week when my mother died and was unfazed when I rushed past him in tears on the way to the funeral.

My new blue hallway made me feel so serene that I started to wonder if I could find a teapot to match. I have always drunk a lot of tea. It was a habit, like many, that I got from my mother without exactly acknowledging to myself that she was the reason why. She believed in making her tea in a china teapot with loose-leaf tea and a tea strainer, maintaining that it tasted better that way. My own relationship with teapots was more erratic. Out of laziness, I got in the habit of mugs and teabags. I told my mother they were just as good. Another consideration was the fact that we were incapable of keeping our teapots intact. For several years, my youngest son considered the mantelpiece where I stored my teapots to be a football goal and practised repeatedly kicking a ball very hard against the cupboard underneath it. This led to several smashed teapots, until I conceded defeat and bought a couple of cheap metal ones from a supermarket which I didn't like much, but at least they couldn't be broken.

It's strange how someone's opinion can carry more weight with you when they are dead than when they are alive. Speaking about someone in the past tense gives you a new lens through which you can see the whole person at once for the first time. After her death, I felt the full force of my mother's kindness warming me like the hot water bottles she liked to put in my bed just in case I got cold, even at the height of summer. I knew that she would want me to have a ceramic teapot (we had given away her own teapots to her friends).

It didn't take me long to find my perfect teapot second-hand on eBay. It was an old 1950s Wedgwood design called 'Summer Sky' in the most beautiful pale pearlescent blue, a fraction of the price of a new Wedgwood teapot. The blue closely matched the blue of my hallway walls and the spout, handle and top of the teapot lid were creamy-white, echoing my hallway ceiling. The design was so simple. There were no willows or cranes to break up the expanse of colour. Even more than the colour I loved the shape, which had a 1950s jauntiness. The spout stuck out in a confident manner and the body of the teapot was cartoonishly curvaceous. This was a teapot with a sense of humour. It made me want to laugh just to look at it and every kind of tea seemed to taste extra-delicious poured from it. The most amazing aspect of all was that this teapot, which I felt could have been made specially for me, turned out to have been designed by my own grandfather.

My grandfather, Norman Wilson, was the production director at Wedgwood in the 1950s. I was only eleven when Norman died and I never knew him very well, whereas I have strong memories of my granny (Jean), who outlived him by fourteen years. They lived in a Welsh town in a house overlooking a beach. I have fleeting memories of a funny man with a very upright military posture and smart clothes – he had been a lieutenant-colonel in the army during the Second World War – who loved to tell rude jokes over dinner. He habitually recounted a story of some dignitary or other loudly farting when they visited the Wedgwood factory. He told me and my sister that if we ate beetroot our urine would turn purple. I wasn't sure whether he was hinting that we should eat extra beetroot or try to avoid it. Mainly, I think he just wanted to make us laugh, and he succeeded.

I was ignorant, though, of Norman's role in creating Summer Sky. Or rather, I knew about it without knowing. I now realise that I must have sometimes eaten off these pale-blue dishes in Wales when my granny cooked for us, but it was a detail which I did not consider important at the time. My father was forever telling me about Norman's work at Wedgwood but, with the arrogance of youth, I only half-listened. Now, I wonder whether I have buried memories of Summer Sky. I was reminded of the Agatha Christie novel *Sleeping Murder* (1976), in which the protagonist arrives in a house she believes she has never visited before and chooses a wallpaper that turns out to be identical to the one that was there years before. She has forgotten that she lived in this house as a child.

I wanted to find out more about Norman and how it was that he came to be involved in creating such a beautiful teapot. In the library, I found a book called *Wedgwood: The New Illustrated Dictionary* (1989) by Robin Reilly, a man who had himself worked at the firm and who knew Norman. Reilly wrote that Norman's contribution to the success of Wedgwood would be 'difficult to overestimate' and added that he must be considered among 'the most versatile, inventive and effective manufacturing potters of his generation'. Norman had a particular genius for inventing glazes, including a series of coloured matte ones which were used by Keith Murray, one of the great Wedgwood designers of the 1930s. Norman's matte glazes had poetic names such as Moonstone, April Green and Matte Straw. South Korea was the country that Norman revered the most for its ceramics and he tried to emulate the simplicity of Korean form in his own 'N. W. Unique Ware' pieces, some of which are now in design museums.

My father, the youngest of the family after his brother Steve and sister Jeannie, remembers that Norman's job was 'all-in-all' to him. When my father was a little boy, Norman drove him to the Wedgwood factory in his Bentley on a Saturday morning. My father describes the colour of Summer Sky as being two shades lighter than Norman's own blue eyes. But it was not actually Norman who invented that beautiful blue. It was an old Wedgwood colour for earthenware called Lavender which had been in production since 1858, although the exact recipe changed over the years. The blue was not painted on or applied as a glaze but baked into the body of the ceramic itself. By 1950, a notebook shows that the recipe for Wedgwood Lavender earthenware consisted of:

Ball Clay 36
China Clay 12
Stone 9
Flint 43
Whiting 2
Lavender Stain 1.8

I find this curiously moving: a recipe for a coloured teapot.

The two-tone blue and white Summer Sky range was originally launched by Wedgwood in the 1930s. There was another two-tone variant called 'Wintergreen' made from celadon earthenware (celadon being a subtle pale green) and in the 1950s a version in brown was added, named Havana. Colour aside, the original 1930s Summer Sky looked similar to dozens of other Wedgwood sets. It was made in the classic plain Queen's Ware shape which had been produced by Wedgwood since the eighteenth century. The knob on top of the teapot's lid was round, like a doorknob or a finial on a staircase, and the handle of the body sticks out at a right angle. The overall effect was elegant in a conventional way. Unlike Norman's version, there was nothing humorous about the original Summer Sky teapots.

It was only after the war that the version of Summer Sky which I know was launched, in 1955, when Norman was fifty-three. Summer Sky was part of a post-war flourishing in ceramics, equivalent to Dior's New Look for fashion. During the war, with resources diverted to the war effort, the only products that Wedgwood and other manufacturers were allowed to produce for the home market were 'Utility Ware', a dull set of flatware devoid of decoration, colour or flair. The first few new Wedgwood designs after the war were 'hesitant' and unimaginative, according to Robin Reilly. Designers fell back on the same old styles of the 1930s. 'A new tableware shape was urgently needed,' Reilly writes; and my grandfather was the person who supplied it.

The new shape was called 'Barlaston', named after the village in Staffordshire which was the site of the Wedgwood factory. It was designed by my grandfather and modelled into existence by a sculptor called Eric Owen. Barlaston wasn't just used for Summer Sky but for many other Wedgwood ranges. For a period of around twenty years, Reilly says, Barlaston largely replaced the Traditional ranges. Reilly marvels at the way that the Barlaston designs – which had a concave rim and exaggerated curves – managed to look both modern and yet recognisably true to the Wedgwood style. The Summer Sky toast rack, for example, which I have spent ages staring at online without ever buying it, has five oval cream-coloured dividers of which the middle one is raised. The base is lavender-blue. It brings to mind the confident curves of a 1950s sports car.

I was awestruck to think that Norman had created a whole new shape for ceramics; all the more so as I came to realise that it was a range that so many people had used and loved. Because it was made of earthenware and not bone china, Summer Sky was one of the most inexpensive Wedgwood ranges: much gifted to young couples. As ceramics expert Roland Head has written, in the 1950s the bridal market in ceramics was changing. Couples now 'wanted bold colours, modern styles and affordable, attractive tablewares they could actually use – not just store in a cupboard for special occasions as their parents might have done'.

The new 'Barlaston' shape designed by Norman comprised seventy different items. Norman himself wrote that the process of designing Barlaston was 'highly detailed work'. As he explained, each shape required 'meticulous full- or half-size drawings followed by 3D modifications in the clay state in the modelling shop'.

One morning, before starting work, I was sipping a cup of smoky lapsang souchong tea, brewed in the Summer Sky teapot, with a new friend. He was someone I had only recently met but we had already fallen into a tea ritual. Several days a week we shared a quick cup of tea when he was passing my house on his way to the train station. Like my mother, he preferred proper tea made from loose tea leaves in a proper teapot: Earl Grey, lapsang, oolong. No milk. For the first few months I knew him, I made him tea with my usual metal teapots. When he first saw it he very much approved of the Summer Sky teapot. 'Look how well it pours,' he said. We were talking about how bizarre and wonderful it was that, forty years after his death, I could find a piece of my own grandparent on eBay.

Thanks to online marketplaces, what was once irreplaceable can now be ordered with a click and a credit card. Whether this is an exciting thought or a depressing one depends a great deal on context. When I met Roopa Gulati, she became quite upset when she talked about eBay. Her parents' Braemar tableware was so special to her that she imagined it must only have gone up in value over the years since it was bought in 1975. 'I always thought', she told me, that if any of the pieces smashed, especially one of the more substantial items, it could be 'a thousand pounds to replace'. When she finally looked it up she found that she could actually buy one of her beloved Braemar vegetable dishes for just twenty pounds or so. 'How could it be?' Roopa felt outraged on her parents' behalf. It was as if their good taste had been undermined by the cheapness of the second-hand dishes. 'To know it's gone down in value!' she exclaimed, sadly.

I understood how Roopa felt. Above and beyond their beauty, it was the touch of Roopa's parents that made her plates so valuable. Roopa told me that she would not have the same feelings about a Braemar plate that had been purchased by any other family. Such a plate would never fully be hers. When Roopa looked for replacements online, she said she hesitated over the phrase 'previously used'. 'Used with what?', she asked me. The thought of other people's leftovers leaving a trace on the plates – as opposed to her mother's cooking – was slightly disgusting to her.

Yet I did not feel the same about the Summer Sky teapot. Maybe it reflects the relative distance of my relationship with my grandfather that it does not trouble me at all to think that I am not the first person to drink tea from it; nor that the particular teapot in my possession was not Norman's own but one of thousands churned out of the Wedgwood factory. On the contrary, I like the teapot all the more for being second-hand. The word 'used' tells me that, for once, I have not been wasteful and brought another new item into the world that didn't need to be made. I am assuming that the teapot's previous owner may have died; or that it belonged to someone downsizing or having a clear-out. And now I have the matching toast rack too. My father thoughtfully got one and posted it to me. My mother may have lost her toast rack, but I have found mine.

It gives me pleasure to know that the original design was my grandfather's; to think of him sketching out the shapes in his notebook and watching as they were modelled in clay for the first time. When I look at the teapot now I can see Norman, with his very straight military posture and his outrageous sense of humour, smiling back at me.

Tools

Paola's Pressure Cooker

'A tool or weapon allows us to do things of which
we would otherwise be incapable.'

Russell Belk, 1988

If you want to get a strong reaction from Paola White, ask her
whether she puts nutmeg in her *ragù*, the rich meat sauce Italians
eat with pasta. 'No!' was her unequivocal reply when I asked her
this question. She said it very firmly, to shut down the very notion
of it. 'I would never put nutmeg. I would never even *think* about it.'
Paola, who is eighty-six, is from Tuscany, although she has spent
most of her life in England, and she was explaining to me that a
Tuscan *ragù* is not the same as one from Bologna, the version I
learned to make from a book by Marcella Hazan, where nutmeg
may indeed be added. In Paola's family in Florence, nutmeg was
something added to rich dishes made with lots of dairy and certainly not a *ragù*, which, in her view, should be seasoned only with
basil and parsley plus wine (assuming she has any in the house).
She starts her *ragù* with the classic *soffritto* of onion, celery and
carrot softened in oil and a little butter and adds canned tomatoes
and tomato paste along with the wine after the meat has browned.

I met Paola through a friend in Cambridge, where we both
live, and was struck by the stylish hat she was wearing and her easy
laughter. A few weeks later, I cycled round to her house near the
river to talk to her about her pressure cooker, because I had heard

that she had been cooking with one for more than sixty years – sixty-six, to be precise. It turned out that the pressure cooker she now used was not the same as the original one, which broke. But it is still only the second pressure cooker Paola has owned in all those years and comes from the same brand as the first one: a 6-litre High Dome made by Prestige, an old-fashioned kind that sits on a hob (as opposed to the electric plug-in Instant Pot, which is the model I favour). The classic Tuscan meat *ragù* should simmer for at least an hour and a half, but thanks to this wondrous tool Paola is able to make hers in just fifteen minutes at high pressure. Sometimes she gives it a couple of minutes more if she thinks it needs it.

Certain domestic objects seem to give us superpowers. They make us feel stronger and more capable. Some of these tools enable us to speed up time or simply to cook when we might otherwise lack the energy. After my separation, I relied a lot on my electric pressure cooker to create good, quick meals for myself and my children on days when it took effort to force myself out of bed. I came to regard it as another body in my kitchen. It wasn't as talkative as my ex-husband, though it did make various beeps at the start and finish of cooking. As I opened the lid, I would sometimes stare in wonder at the stew or soup in the pot and think 'how did I make this?'.

For Paola White, the pressure cooker has been a tool that has consoled her through great personal loss and enabled her to eat the food of Tuscany no matter where in the world she found herself. When I asked Paola why she liked her trusty old pressure cooker so much, her first answer was that it allowed her to cook all kinds of dishes such as hearty minestrone which otherwise would be too time-consuming. 'I would miss it if I didn't have it.' For the past thirty-six years Paola has been living alone, but she still likes to batch-cook recipes such as *ragù* for herself and freeze them. She also uses it for beans. 'In Tuscany, we eat a lot of beans and chickpeas.' The pressure cooker was so much part of her family's lives that when her four sons left home one by one to go to university, they each took their own pressure cooker with them to replicate Paola's cooking. Her son Chris White later told me that he and his brothers were the chief cooks in each of their homes, something they attributed to their mother.

Through kitchen devices, humans extend their powers. We become mighty beings capable of slicing and dicing, even if all we are doing is making a salad. We freeze ingredients or transform them through fire. Of all the tools in the kitchen, perhaps the one with the most significant technology of them all is the cooking pot, though it lacks the gleam and violence of a knife. It was only with the adoption of cooking pots – which happened as long as 16,000 years ago in East Asia and 12,000, give or take, in North Africa – that what we think of as cooking emerged. For the first time, hunter-gatherers could nourish themselves with grains and a wide variety of plants which needed long cooking in water to make them digestible.

For Paola, the pressure cooker has been as transformative as those first cooking pots thousands of years ago. 'It enabled me to cook certain vegetables that take time' is how she summarised it when we met. She used this giant hissing pan to boil potatoes, soften cannellini beans, stew peppers to oily sweetness. More than that, it is a tool that has enabled her to eat deliciously and healthily in good times and in bad.

Despite spending most of her life far from Florence, this pan has blessed her with a lifetime of eating the Tuscan food that means so much to her. 'I come from a family of cooks,' she told me. For many years she worked at an import-export business in Huntingdon in the east of England, selling textiles. During those years she prided herself on the fact that she would arrive home from work at 5.30 and have dinner for her children cooked from scratch on the table by 6.30. All because of the pressure cooker. Was she never frightened of explosions, I asked? So many people seem to have bad memories of the pressure cookers of the 1950s and 1960s, viewing them as a short route to scalding yourself or splattering your ceiling with burning-hot food. Paola shook her head. 'I've never had a problem in sixty-six years. I am obviously a very courageous person,' she added, laughing.

Pressure cookers were not something Paola grew up with. Neither her mother nor her grandmother used one and she remembers her family in Italy being 'quite surprised' when she married her English husband at the age of twenty and asked for a pressure cooker as a wedding gift. It was 1958, and in contrast to some other European countries such as Spain, in Italy the pressure cooker would not take off until the 1960s, when it was launched in a sleek stainless-steel version from the Lagostina company. In the 1970s the Lagostina was boosted by a series of iconic blue and white 'La Linea' adverts depicting a funny man drawn with a single line.

It might have seemed like a novelty to her Italian relatives, but by the time Paola got her first pressure cooker the technology had actually been around for more than 300 years. 'Did you know it was invented by a Frenchman?' she asked me excitably when we met. 'I checked it because I knew you were coming!' The first pressure cooker was presented to the Royal Society in London in 1679 by Denis Papin, a French physician, who called it 'A New Digestor or Engine for Softening Bones'. In 1682 Papin cooked a famous dinner in London using a series of these 'digestors'. John Evelyn, the celebrated diarist and gardener, marvelled that the hardest bones had become 'as soft as cheese' in this machine. But it was not until the twentieth century that Papin's invention reached ordinary cooks. The first domestic pressure cooker was patented in the United States in 1902 – the 'Kook Kwick' – and the term 'pressure cooker' first entered the language in 1910. A cookery booklet boasted that daily use of the 'Kook Kwick' would 'banish tough meats from your table'.

The great innovation of pressure cooking was the realisation that if you make steam build up in a sealed vessel, you can increase the boiling point of water from 100 to 120 degrees Celsius. This means that food cooks much more quickly and with less fuel. Unlike Paola, I was quite a late adopter of the pressure cooker, but I remember my astonishment at being able to make fork-tender stews of lamb or perfectly soft lentils in a flash or even cook a risotto in just a few minutes with hardly any stirring.

In England, unlike in Italy, pressure cookers were already much used by the 1950s. In 1949 an article in the *British Medical Journal* extolled the virtues of a 'pressure pan' for cooking vegetables, observing that the Vitamin C content of, for example, cauliflower, winter cabbage, new carrots and broccoli was preserved more through pressure cooking than by the traditional British method of boiling them to death in a large volume of water. Pressure cookers were extremely popular in the USA too. By 1950, according to *The New York Times*, 37 per cent of American households owned at least one pressure cooker, although its popularity fell after the microwave oven came along: a pity. I agree with Paola that the wondrous time-saving qualities of pressure cooking have never been bettered. She told me that she had read somewhere that vegetables cooked in the pressure cooker lost their flavour, but in her decades of experience the opposite was true. 'I think that stuffed vegetables actually taste better . . . more concentrated.'

Her son Chris (who has spent forty years working in trade publications for the fruit and vegetable industry) told me that when he was growing up in the 1970s, Paola often made red or green peppers stuffed with peperonata: a rich jammy stew of peppers, onions and tomatoes which usually requires slow simmering. Thanks to the pressure cooker, she could have the peperonata for stuffing the peppers ready in minutes. An added perk was that if she removed the lid, the base of the pressure cooker was the only pan in the house tall enough to cook spaghetti for six people.

Paola can't be entirely sure where she first saw a pressure cooker but thinks she learned to use one from her English husband, who was ten years older. They met in London when she enrolled in an English-language course he was teaching near Oxford Street (she was visiting England as an au pair). One day, he asked the students whether any of them would like to go to the cinema with him that evening to see *War and Peace*. Paola was the only one who said yes. 'It's amazing how life works.'

After the wedding, Paola and her husband lived in Florence for a while. He worked at the British consulate and they had three boys in quick succession: in 1960, 1964 and 1965. Then her husband got a job back in England at the Foreign Office and they moved to a town – Amersham – where she knew no one and had a fourth boy. Her husband was away from seven in the morning until seven at night, but Paola doesn't remember it being 'a bad time'. The pressure cooker helped.

When her husband told her that he was going to be posted to Senegal, she knew she had to bring the pressure cooker with her. They were in Senegal from 1966 to 1970 and, thanks to the pressure cooker, she still cooked every day. It also accompanied her when he was posted to Sweden and then to Mumbai. India was the only place where Paola met people who were as enthusiastic about the pressure cooker as she was. There, the modern pressure cooker was first sold in 1959 under two competing brands (Hawkins and TT PvT Ltd) and soon had many fans, not least because *dal* of many kinds is so beloved in India. In an ordinary pan, certain lentils can take an hour to soften, depending on the variety. In a pressure cooker, as a 2021 article by journalist Diya Kohli explains, 'the thumb rule for *masoor, moong, toor* and other *dals* is three whistles on high heat and then the next five minutes on medium without the lid'.

Despite the joys of Indian food, Paola was finding life in Mumbai hard. Her older children were at boarding school in England and they were all missing each other dreadfully. So they decided that her husband would transfer out of the Foreign Office to the Home Office and they would return to England. They settled in a town called St Neots, eighteen miles west of Cambridge, and could finally all be together again around a table, eating her *ragù*. 'It was the best thing we ever did,' she said. 'We didn't know what was going to happen.'

When Paola's oldest son, Mark, was only twenty-six he died of cancer. Mark had gone to the doctor to ask them to look at a mole on his skin but they had reassured him it was all right. Nothing was done, and by the time the cancer was diagnosed, it was too late. He died in 1988. Paola and her husband had moved from St Neots to Cambridge a year earlier. Mark's death gnawed away at Paola's husband and he died the same year, without so much as a day's warning. He phoned her at work to say he wasn't feeling 'terribly well', and by the time she managed to get a neighbour to go round and check on him while she drove back from work he was dead.

'Even in tragedy, I was lucky,' Paola told me, returning to the sunny demeanour she has had throughout our conversation. 'Mark made it bearable. If Mark had not faced it, I don't know where I would be.' She told me he was a very sporty person and that he loved life. During his short life he cycled to Italy twice, all by himself. At university he had become an evangelical Christian. When he was dying in hospital his friends asked a vicar to visit him. Because of this Paola started regularly attending the vicar's church and ever since, for thirty-six years, it has been her 'extended family'. Once a week, a friend from her church comes to take her grocery shopping. Hearing Paola talking about how much the church meant to her reminded me of my own mother, who was likewise taken grocery shopping by two friends from her church during her last years in her own house.

The day after we met, Paola told me she was planning to go to a church brunch with other women from the congregation. But first she wanted to buy a replacement for her trusty little kitchen timer, shaped like a tomato, which had broken for no apparent reason after many years of use. Paola's love for this timer reminded me of Bonnie and her salt shaker. Paola told me she used the tomato timer to time the dishes for her pressure cooker and was puzzled to find that none of the shops she had looked in so far seem to sell timers anymore.

'I think it's because people use their phones,' I said. 'I have a phone!' Paola replied. 'I'm glad I mentioned it to you.' Then she looked thoughtful. 'I quite like my little timer.' We both realised in that moment that a phone would be no substitute for a cheery wind-up timer shaped like a tomato. I was glad to hear a few weeks later from our mutual friend that Paola had managed to find a new one.

Jacob's Spoon

> 'We can also see this . . . process at work in the small, illicit, talisman-like possessions that inmates use as symbolic devices for separating themselves from the position they are supposed to be in.'
>
> Erving Goffman, 1961

Jacob Chaim was supposed to be making weapons for the Nazis, but when none of the guards were looking he made a spoon for himself instead. Chaim, a Polish tailor in his early thirties, was imprisoned in a forced labour camp when he took a piece of tin and turned it into a little spoon with a flat handle and an oval bowl. This is the single most eloquent story I've come across about the power of utensils to give meaning to a life.

Gentler than a knife and less spiky than a fork or a chopstick, a spoon is the most universal of eating utensils. Spoons can play many roles for many people. They can be devices for measuring sugar or for stirring cream into coffee. They can be pieces of toylike plastic given to babies or big silver implements for eating pasta or serving salad. Eating wet food with spoons is one of the few universal benchmarks of being human (although chimpanzees make sort-of-spoons for themselves from blades of grass). As Margaret Visser writes in her book *The Rituals of Dinner* (1991), spoons are 'unthreatening, nurturing objects'. They are the most peaceful of all eating utensils. As Visser writes, 'A spoon is a bowl with an arm attached, the earliest spoon being a cupped human hand.' In various superstitions, spoons are seen as little people.

To eat with a spoon is to feed yourself as a parent feeds a baby. It's an undemanding way to have a meal but compared to using fingers, there is a sense of propriety about it. When my mother lacked the energy to cook for her children, she didn't cook Tuscan minestrone in a pressure cooker, as Paola White did for her children. She gave me and my sister bowls of white bread torn into pieces and soaked in milk with crunchy sugar sprinkled over the top. And spoons to eat it with. The spoons were what made it dinner.

Spoons are tools for ferrying food to the mouth, but for Jacob Chaim a spoon became a different kind of tool: a means of resistance. At the Dora-Mittelbau camp in Nordhausen in central Germany, prisoners were not given any cutlery with which to eat their rations of food. Even by the standards of other Nazi labour camps, the conditions in Dora-Mittelbau were brutal, with the highest death rates of any of them. The majority of the prisoners lived and worked underground in tunnels and saw no sunlight for weeks on end. These tunnels were so filthy that – according to a Czech survivor called Otakar Litomisky – some prisoners tried to do extra work in the hope of being given an additional portion of coffee, not to drink (the coffee was fake and disgusting) but to wash themselves with.

As hellish as the camp was, it is remarkable that Jacob Chaim (who was born in 1910) made it there alive. When he was just seven or eight, he had witnessed his father being killed in an anti-Jewish pogrom in the small town in Poland where he grew up. Then, in 1942, he and his family were rounded up in the Warsaw ghetto (where he had been doing tailoring work) and put on trains. His wife and child got off their train and were never seen again, something he never spoke of later in life. Jacob's train was headed for Treblinka (which would have meant certain death) but an instinct told him and his brother to get off and try another train, which was on the way to Majdanek: a concentration camp. After that, the Chaim brothers worked in various camps, always unobtrusively supporting each other (concealing the fact that they were brothers from the Germans, to avoid being separated) before finding themselves together in Dora.

Some of the prisoners referred to the camp – which was technically a subcamp of Buchenwald – as the 'Hell of Dora'. The network of underground tunnels in which they worked had been dug by prisoners transported from Buchenwald in the autumn of 1943. There was cold water dripping everywhere and the prisoners slept on wet straw, with a single damp blanket for every two people on top of bunks riddled with lice. The only toilets were barrels cut in half. Jean Michel, a French resistance leader who was sent to Dora-Mittelbau in October 1943, later described the horror of a fifteen-hour working day, being shouted at and hit by the Kapos (prison bosses) while the noise of their work 'bores into the brain and shears the nerves'. At the end of the first working day, Michel recalled that 'over a thousand despairing men' collapsed onto the rocks 'hoping for sleep which never comes' because the noises of explosions and shouting of the guards woke them even in the night.

The original objective of the camp at Dora-Mittelbau was to manufacture a new kind of rocket for the German war effort – the A-4 – although over time it diversified into the production of other weapons. Hans Kammler, who oversaw the construction of the camp, sent the instruction: 'Pay no attention to the human cost. The work must go ahead, and in the shortest possible time.' Albert Speer, the Nazi Minister of Armaments and War Production, wrote to Kammler to congratulate him for transforming the tunnels into a functioning weapons factory in just two months, noting that the achievement 'far exceeds anything ever done in Europe and is unsurpassed even by American standards'.

While the Nazis crowed about their technological achievements, the human slaves who laboured underground at Dora-Mittelbau were treated as worthless. On 22 June 1944, a secret report noted that the camp doctor had observed that detainees had been beaten by managers 'because of this or that offence, or even have been stabbed with sharp instruments'. The report reminded employees that all infractions should be reported to the SS, who would mete out the appropriate punishment. Thousands of men died of overwork and thousands more from starvation or disease (dysentery, tuberculosis and pneumonia were rife). In all, it has been estimated that 60,000 prisoners worked at Dora-Mittelbau, of whom more than 9,000 died of overwork and many more from starvation. Yet the Chaim brothers survived.

Just as I was longing to find out more about Jacob Chaim and his spoon, and thinking I had hit a dead end, I managed to make contact with Shoshana Chaim, who is married to Jacob's grandson. Through Shoshana, I arranged a video call with Jacob's daughter Gloria and her husband Mark, who live in Toronto. We were joined by their daughter, Avra, as well as Shoshana. Mark – who knew Jacob for the last twenty years of his life – told me that the single thing he found most extraordinary about the spoon was that Jacob risked his life to produce it. Gloria suspects her father made the spoon a little at a time, during snatched moments when he was unobserved. The main thing she wants me to notice about the photograph of the spoon – which is roughly the size of a teaspoon – is how meticulously crafted it is: a thing of beauty. Her father brought the same perfectionism to his work as a tailor in Canada after the war. He made coats and suits for ladies. 'Everything he made, it had to be perfect,' Gloria said.

At Dora-Mittelbau it was a deliberate and systematic policy to treat prisoners as less than human. There were daily humiliations, many of them centred around food or toileting arrangements. The goal was to make the prisoners feel like punished children. They had to ask permission to urinate or defecate and when the time came there was no privacy. Jean Michel recalled that the prisoners with dysentery would often foul their trousers. 'They no longer have the strength to sit over the barrels, even to get to them. The SS beat them. The blows are useless, they do not get up.' Through all of these humiliations, the officers would abuse the prisoners and tell them that they were *unerzogen*, a word that translates as 'badly brought up'. It was the scolding rebuke of a civilised adult to an uncivilised child. The SS took away almost all the trappings of human life and then taunted the prisoners for their lack of manners.

Such horrors are still with us. It has been estimated that over the past decade, the Chinese Communist Party has detained between 1 and 3 million Uyghurs – ethnic-minority Muslims – in prison camps known as 're-education centres'. The centres are designed to force Uyghurs to be indoctrinated into Chinese culture, and this is carried out by dehumanising and demoralising the inmates until, as one survivor of the camps recalled, they became so exhausted that they no longer fully knew what they believed anymore: 'We were ordered to deny who we were. To spit on our own traditions, our beliefs. To criticise our language. To insult our own people.' Among countless other indignities and abuses, Uyghurs living in these camps are tortured through food. A Uyghur woman who was employed in one of the camps between 2017 and 2018 to teach the Chinese language to prisoners described how inmates would be routinely underfed, except on Fridays when they were forced to eat pork, in violation of their Muslim faith.

In Dora-Mittelbau the rations of food were scarce and bad and sometimes there were not even any mess-tins, forcing the men to eat like animals. The standard rations in Nazi concentration camps consisted of a breakfast of bread or thin porridge with ersatz coffee, a lunch of watery vegetable soup with bread and a dinner of more soup and bread. But at Dora-Mittelbau the rations were more sparse than normal. A resident of Nordhausen wrote to the local newspaper to describe how men in the camp were so hungry that they stole cabbages and beets from the fields nearby. Gloria told me that her father's food in the camp was mostly 'water with something floating in it'.

For those not too weakened or beaten down, the obvious response to this grotesque brutality was sabotage. Dora-Mittelbau was known for being a place with a very active underground resistance movement in which prisoners deliberately sabotaged the weapons that they were supposed to produce or slowed down production. It is thought that this sabotage explains why many of the German missiles suffered from quality control issues. From 1943 until the end of the war in 1945, around 200 prisoners were put to death at Dora-Mittelbau on charges of sabotage. In January 1945 two of the directors of the missile factory wrote that 'Over and over again our installation has been consciously and maliciously damaged through intrusion, destruction and theft.'

When all of your own possessions have been forcibly removed from you, the most trivial personal scraps can become special because they are a way to claim something back, however small, from the system you find yourself in. In a 1951 study of the inside workings of the prison system in America, the authors noted that many prisoners had an 'urge to collect' which was taken to 'preposterous extents' as a counterbalance to the anonymity of prison clothing and furniture. Prisoners would collect: 'Rocks, string, knives – anything made by man and forbidden in man's institution – anything – a red comb, a different kind of toothbrush, a belt – these things are assiduously gathered, jealously hidden or triumphantly displayed.'

Jacob Chaim clearly had some of this urge to collect. Before he was at Dora, he spent time in the original Buchenwald camp where he found a coin and kept it safe on his person. After the war,

he took this coin to a jeweller and asked for it to be transformed into a star of David, with his initials on it. Gloria calls the coin a 'macabre souvenir': a way for Jacob to prove to himself that the camp had not succeeded in annihilating him. In the 1960s, the sociologist Erving Goffman noted that in both prisons and mental institutions it was common for inmates to engage in what he called 'make-dos': taking 'available artifacts' and using them 'in a manner and for an end not officially intended'. Examples of 'make-dos' would include making a knife 'hammered from a spoon' or extracting ink for drawing from the pages of a magazine.

The spoon made by Jacob Chaim was certainly not the greatest act of theft or sabotage that took place in Dora-Mittelbau. He only stole a little bit of metal, almost nothing in the context of the sheer volume of materials used in an arms factory. But what an act it was – what a beautiful, subversive and self-loving act. In an environment of horror, he had built himself a fine-looking possession: a quiet act of defiance.

Jacob Chaim is not the first or only person to have made a spoon out of the tools of war. The Syrian-British artist Issam Kourbaj – whose art draws on the idea of repurposing objects – has spoken of how in childhood he ate with a spoon which used to be a bomb. Kourbaj's uncle made a habit of dismantling bombs left by the French in Syria in the 1920s. He would then beat pieces of the metal into spoons. In an interview in the 2024 book *Crossings* (co-edited by my friend Subha Mukherji), Kourbaj recalled that 'My uncle was incredibly resourceful, thinking in the time of hardship how one could use whatever is available. To transform bombs to spoons is to turn a weapon of destruction into a tool of nurturing.'

By making a secret spoon for himself, Chaim claimed back his humanity from the SS guards. He proved that no matter how he was treated, when it came to eating he still had his own standards and his own values. Far from being 'badly brought up', he was much better brought up than his tormentors. The Nazis might serve him tiny rations of disgusting food, but with his spoon he kept his faith with a better way of living and eating.

Chaim's family told me he was always very particular about table manners. After the war, he and his brother married a pair of Polish sisters who had also endured several camps. They all relocated to Montreal, where Jacob once again worked as a tailor and where Gloria was born (her older brother had been born in Hanover). He never ate with his spoon in Canada, but he still kept it safe. Gloria said that he would never allow her to eat an ice cream walking down the street because it was 'not proper'. He did not say this in an overbearing way; it was simply a question of pride for him to eat an ice cream sitting down in a dignified fashion, without making a mess. He dressed immaculately in a suit and tie, even if he was just going to the grocery store. Gloria commented that Jacob would remark that the Nazis 'treated us like dogs and we had to find a way to be human'. This was what the spoon was about for him: being human.

After the war, Chaim donated his spoon to the Montreal Holocaust Museum, along with some ration tickets for meals in the camp which he had somehow managed to squirrel away. The museum's website says that Chaim 'created the spoon because Nazi guards, to dehumanize Jewish inmates, did not provide cutlery to eat their small food rations'. What it does not say is that in Hebrew the name Chaim means 'life'.

The Casserole Protests

'In Myanmar, if you want to drive evil from your home,
 you bang pots and pans.'

Lorcan Lovett, 2021

Just because a tool is made for one purpose does not mean that it can't be used for another. Three times in quick succession after my husband left, we had burst pipes and water gushed through at the top of the house. 'It feels as if the house is crying,' I said. By the third time it happened, my daughter and I knew the drill and would run as fast as we could to fetch every pot and pan we owned for catching the drips while we waited for the plumber to arrive.

Pans are designed for cooking with. But in most houses, that is far from the only task they get used for. The bottom of a pan can become a handy weight to press the liquid out of salted aubergines as they drain or to flatten chicken breasts into escalopes or crush whole coriander seeds into a powder. A giant pasta pot may be a vessel in which to soak stained shirts or sterilise water bottles. *In extremis*, a pan can be used as a noise maker to express sorrow or outrage at moments when the human voice feels too quiet.

For sixty evenings in a row in 2002, the Correa family – five sisters plus their mother and father – went out onto their balcony in Caracas and banged pots for an hour to protest the authoritarian policies of the Venezuelan leader, Hugo Chávez. All around the city, the Correas could hear other families on other balconies making the same noise. 'My mother would go crazy, hitting the pan out of sheer rage,' recalls Sasha, the oldest of the sisters, who was a student at the time. Sasha – who is now a food writer in her early forties and an adviser to many of the top chefs in Spain at the Basque Culinary Centre – remembers that her mother broke many wooden spoons because she hit her pan with such force. 'What about metal spoons?' I ask, but Sasha replies that the clang of metal would be 'unbearable' to the ears and much too hard on the hands. When 'casseroling', as Sasha calls it, there is a trade-off to be made between noise and comfort. These are details you only learn when you have devoted hundreds of hours to banging pots as a gesture of political protest.

A casserole protest – *cacerolazo* in Spanish – is a form of public rebellion which is especially popular in modern Latin America although its roots are medieval. Charivari, or 'rough music', was a series of European folk customs in which kitchenware was rattled with metal sticks to make loud noises. In medieval times, people expressed social disapproval of wrongdoers such as adulterers, wife beaters and thieves by banging pots and pans, usually on many consecutive days. Today, casserole protests have become more political and take place all over the world: in Burma and Hong Kong; in Lebanon and Turkey; in Chile, Brazil and Mexico; and in Iceland, where the so-called Kitchenware Revolution of 2009–11 was a protest against the government's handling of the country's financial crisis.

The first Venezuelan *cacerolazo* Sasha Correa remembers taking part in was during the first few years after Chávez assumed power in 1999. Chávez swept into office as an 'outside' candidate on the promise of a new kind of democracy, a new kind of socialism. For many it felt like a time of great hope, with Chávez pledging huge amounts of money to decrease poverty in the country. But it wasn't long before Chávez's version of socialism took on authoritarian overtones. He increasingly used emergency measures to give himself more power and moved to seize control of the petroleum industry – by far the largest source of Venezuela's wealth. In 2002, more than half a million people marched against him and violence broke out on the streets; nineteen marchers were shot dead and many more injured by thuggish '*chavistas*' (Chávez supporters). In April 2002, for two days, Chávez was ousted by a coup, only to return to power, after which he moved to shut down and threaten independent news channels.

According to Chávez himself, the casserole protesters who opposed him throughout his presidency were simply middle-class elitists who were out of touch with the lives of ordinary people. In 2012, a year before he died, on hearing some casserole protesters in the streets, he got out of his car and started mockingly dancing to the rhythm. But sometimes Sasha and her family would hear the banging of casseroles coming from the poorest part of the city, proof that despite what the government propaganda said there was opposition to Chávez among every class of society. 'That was very emotional,' Sasha remembers. Back in 2002 she was a journalism student, channelling the idealism of Lois Lane in *Superman*, still hoping there might be a way to improve her country by exposing corruption and wrongdoing.

Why would someone choose to bang a pot rather than engage in some other form of protest such as marching on the streets? Sasha says that it was 'cathartic – a way of not feeling alone, not feeling crazy'.

A pot is the one tool of protest that is owned by pretty much everyone. Ariel Ávila, a Colombian politician and peace campaigner, has said that the *cacerolazo* is a form of peaceful protest that allows normal people to join in without even leaving their homes. Some can't go out because they are caring for children. Others are understandably scared to march. In Venezuela, people are still haunted by February 1989, when 300 anti-government protesters were killed on the streets by official troops and police. On a balcony, with a pot and a spoon in their hands, people can show solidarity with the marchers without risking their lives.

What Sasha remembers most about the sixty days of casserole protest in 2002 was how her father refused to give up, returning to the balcony every single night at the allotted time. 'He would stand alone on the balcony, very proud. It was heartbreaking.' Mr Correa had grown up in poverty in one of Venezuela's largest slums. His mother was a seamstress and his father mended shoes, and he was the only one of seven children to go to university. He got a good job working in engineering in Brazil, which was where he met Sasha's mother. They decided to get married and start a family. At the time, Venezuela seemed a much more stable country than Brazil, so the couple took a gamble on moving to Caracas. Mr Correa had an 'amazing job' in engineering for many years, says Sasha, but then he lost everything after Chávez swept to power: one of tens of thousands of people to lose their jobs as Chávez seized control of industries and gave his own cronies the top positions.

Banging pots for a whole hour is 'exhausting', Sasha comments. 'Your hands would get blisters and I wore kitchen gloves to protect them.' A few days into the 2002 *cacerolazo*, she and her sisters got bored and tired and begged their father to come back inside, but he was determined to see it out. Sasha recalls that there was a quiet dignity to the consistency with which he stayed out there with his pan and his spoon.

How do you choose which pan to protest with? Sasha remembers that over the years, when she went to other people's houses in Caracas, she could gauge their attitude to the government by the state of their kitchen. 'There would often be a cemetery of misshapen pots and pans.' I had assumed that the pots used to protest with would be retired from cooking, but Sasha tells me that on the contrary, when 'casseroling' her family reached for their favourite cooking utensils. 'We would go to the pans that we liked, the pans that were light and comfortable in our hands. It's a practical decision.' One of Sasha's sisters had a baby girl and by the time she was three she came out on the balcony to protest with everyone else. The little girl was excited to see her grandmother banging on the very same pan she used to heat up her milk.

Over time, the connotations of 'casseroling' have changed in Venezuela. 'It stopped being political and started being about sheer hunger,' Sasha says. After Chávez died in 2013 and his successor, Nicolás Maduro, assumed power, pot-banging became an activity done as much out of sorrow as rage. That was the year when Sasha left Venezuela for a new life in Spain, and she remembers how 'tired' people were and how it felt as if the energy had seeped out of the protests. Under Maduro much of the country was plunged into outright hunger, with many basic necessities expensive or unavailable. To bang an empty pot was a way to signal that there was literally no food to cook. In 2016 a pot-banging protester told a reporter for Reuters: 'Now it feels completely different because there's no food, there's hunger, and this thug we have as president is scared of *cacerolazos*!'

There is clearly magical thinking in the casserole protest. No matter how many times you bang an empty pot, you can't make food appear out of thin air. The main result is you ruin your own kitchenware. Sasha remembers that even at the height of her family's longest casserole protest in 2002, when there was still a freshness and energy to their rage, she knew at some level that 'what you are doing is worthless'. As the years passed, casseroling started to give her 'a feeling of being silly'. After all the years of protest, the situation had gone from bad to catastrophic in the country. Chávez's great promise was to improve life for the masses, yet poverty is now so bad that since 2015 more than 7 million people have left in search of a better life. In 2019 a UN report stated that 94 per cent of the country was living in poverty. These days, when Sasha returns home to Venezuela and sees someone casseroling in the street, she feels pity for them. 'It reminds me that I had to leave my country,' she says.

Not long ago, Sasha was talking on a video call to her niece, who asked her whether any of the clever Basque chefs Sasha worked with in San Sebastián could help her to solve a cooking puzzle. It was this: 'How can you bake a birthday cake when you have no electricity?' So far, none of the chefs have come up with an answer.

Dave's Poetry Jars

'A man's self is the sum total of all that he can call his.'

William James, 1890

Some of the most valuable pots in the USA today were made by a nineteenth-century potter called 'Dave', aka David Drake. In 2021 one of Dave's pots – many of which are now in museums – sold at auction for $1.56 million, setting an all-time record for American pottery. What makes this so extraordinary is that Dave produced his pots in conditions of slavery. He used pottery as a tool of profound self-expression, despite the fact that he was born into a life in which he was denied the basic freedoms due to any human being.

Dave was an enslaved artisan potter who lived in South Carolina from around 1800 to sometime in the 1870s. He made a series of massive stoneware jars and pots on which he wrote short, elliptical poems in beautiful handwriting (usually cursive), along with his signature. By leaving his words and name on the surface of the clay, Dave ensured that despite his enslavement, more than 200 years after his birth, we would know who he was, long after the people who enslaved him have been forgotten.

For Dave's white 'owners' his pots were a tool for containing and transporting food – his biggest pots could hold colossal quantities of salted and pickled meats for feeding other slaves. But for Dave pottery became a different kind of tool. Gifted both with

words and pottery, he used the wet clay as a medium for expressing himself. Unlike my white British grandfather whose ceramics work for Wedgwood gave him a comfortable and well-paid job plus international recognition, Dave received little credit or reward for his astonishing pottery in his own lifetime. More than a hundred years before Norman joined Wedgwood, one of the pottery's most famous works (produced in 1787 by Josiah Wedgwood) was an anti-slavery medallion depicting a black slave with the words 'Am I Not A Man and A Brother?'. The Wedgwood cameo became so fashionable that it was reproduced on snuffboxes, bracelets and hairpins. While the British upper classes were using pottery in a paternalistic way to parade their anti-slave sentiments, Dave's pots were something more profound: a vivid denunciation of the entire system of slavery from within.

In all, there are more than forty surviving examples of Dave's poems (as well as over 100 other jars and pots with his signature on them). His verses – written across the shoulders of those vast stoneware storage jars and jugs – are by turns witty, boastful, personal, cryptic and poignant. Here are some examples, with their dates:

> Give me silver or; either Gold =
> Though they are dangerous ; to our Soul =
> 27 June 1840

> I made this jar = for cash-
> Though its called = lucre Trash
> 22 August 1857

> Whats better than kissing –
> While we are both at fishing
> 10 February 1840

I saw a leppard, & a lions face,
Then I felt the need of ---- Grace.
3 November 1858

The fouth of July – is surely come –
To blow the fife = and beat the drum//
4 July 1859

Of all the mysteries raised by Dave's poetry pots, one of the greatest is how he managed to learn to write at a time when slave literacy was illegal in many parts of the South. We know from estate documents that he was a 'country born' slave, meaning that he was born in the United States, not Africa, and that he was 'about 17 years old' in 1818, placing his birth date at 1801. We know nothing of his mother or father. His surname – Drake – came from his first owner, a man called Harvey Drake, who ran a pottery factory. During his lifetime, Dave was one of about seventy-six Black enslaved people working in the potteries of Edgefield in South Carolina, an area so dominated by pot-making that it was known as Pottersville. The riddle is how Dave learned to write messages on his pots when the other Black potters of Edgefield didn't. The best explanation seems to be that Harvey Drake had a sideline as the proprietor of a local newspaper called *The Edgefield Hive* where Dave is known to have worked. Being surrounded by so much newsprint may have helped him to learn to read and write all by himself, or perhaps he was given lessons by someone working at the newspaper. Lacking pens and paper, Dave practised his writing on bricks: one found in Pottersville bears the date 'April 18' in his handwriting.

Knowing how to write was one thing. Daring to do it in public and actually signing his name to it was a whole other level of audacity. It is astonishing that he got away with it. In 1834, the year of Dave's first known inscription on a jar, South Carolina passed a harsh new anti-literacy law stating that any white person convicted of teaching a slave to read or write would be fined up to $100 (thousands of dollars in today's money) and sent to jail for up to six months. A slave convicted of teaching another slave to read would be given fifty lashes.

Two years after this law was passed Dave made a 14-inch storage jar with two slab handles on which he carved a single word, 'catination', meaning the state of being chained or yoked. In the context of his times, to write this particular word on a pot that would be sold and bought by white men was a fierce act of rebellion. Perhaps Dave was banking on the fact that most of the white men who beheld the pot would have no idea what the word meant. Someone in Edgefield who knew Dave in the 1830s remembered him as a 'grandiloquent' man. Instead of asking 'How are you?' he would greet people with 'How does your corporosity seem to sagatiate?' As scholar Michael Chaney has written, 'Dave seems to have hidden revolutionary self-expressions in plain sight.' He used the surface of the wet clay jars on which he worked as something between a billboard and a diary.

Aside from his writing, Dave was a remarkable potter whose talents were recognised as unusual by those around him. In his lifetime he was famed not so much for the words on his pots as for the sheer size of them. His largest storage jars stood more than 2 feet tall and could hold 40 gallons, with twice the capacity of the largest jars made by competing potteries in Edgefield. To handle such a colossal weight of clay required strength as well as skill, an even greater achievement considering that Dave had lost one of his legs sometime in the 1830s, possibly by getting run over on the railroad tracks.

Even though he was working in conditions of servitude and reaped none of the profits, Dave took an artisan's pride in his work, carving the words 'Great & Noble jar' on a particularly giant one. The power of words on stoneware is that they have a permanence. One of Dave's pots, from 1858, is inscribed with the lines: 'I made this for our, sott/it will never – never rott'. Sott may refer to a kind of fermented mash used when making beer, or it may be a misspelling of 'Scott', a fellow pottery worker whom he refers to in another poem as trying to 'get a piece' of pork or beef from a jar.

Dave's pots are thick-walled and solid, but according to one of Dave's biographers, Leonard Todd, they 'give the impression of being almost casually made'. To make his very largest pots he would have used a combination of coiling and turning. First the bottom half of the pot was turned on the wheel and then the top half was built up from coil after coil of roped clay until the pot was the dimensions required. Finally, it would be dipped in an alkaline glaze and fired. Art curator Jill Koverman has described the distinctive 'lopsided style' of Dave's pots, with a glaze that was 'light olive-green to oatmeal-beige in colour with a drippy appearance and a glassy surface on which there is some crackling or crazing'. Someone called Arthur Simkins, who knew Dave in the 1830s, wrote a reminiscence in 1859 in which he remembered how 'the boys and girls used to think it a fine Saturday frolic to walk to old Pottersville and . . . watch old Dave as the clay assumed beneath his magic touch the desired shape of jug, or jar, or crock, or pitcher, as the case might be'.

His magic touch may explain how Dave got away with writing poems on his pots. He had skills which his masters lacked. But that didn't change the fact that he was not free. One of Dave's jars – a storage jar with two slab handles dated 31 July 1840 – reads:

> Dave belongs to Mr. Miles/
> where the oven bakes & the pot biles//

It is shocking to hear a person describing themselves as being owned by another, but Dave was indeed the property of Lewis Miles at the time, having passed to Miles on loan from his current owner, the Reverend John Landrum (his first owner, Harvey Drake, had died in 1832). In 1847, after John Landrum died, Dave was once more put up for sale – advertised as 'an excellent Stone Ware Turner'. He was sold alongside other Black slaves as well as items of Landrum's including a piano, a carriage, mules, cattle and hogs.

This sale gave rise to one of the worst tragedies of Dave's life. Historians surmise that one of the female slaves put up for sale alongside Dave – listed as 'Woman Louisa' – was Dave's wife and that several of the children in the sale, including two called Nicey and Tucker, seem to have been his children with Louisa. Nicey, Tucker and Louisa were sold to a plantation ten miles away from Edgefield, while Dave went – for $800, a vast amount – to Franklin Landrum, the son of Dave's previous owner. Franklin Landrum was known to whip his workers. For the two years he was owned by him, Dave carved neither poems nor his own name on any pots. Dave's poetry only resumed in 1849 when he found himself once more in the employ of Lewis Miles, whose pottery, Stony Bluff, was where Dave spent his most productive years. Productive but lonely.

We can get some sense of the sadness Dave must have felt at being ripped apart from his family from a pot he made years later, in 1857. The inscription reads:

> I wonder where is all my relation
> friendship to all – and, every nation

'I wonder where is all my relation' is a tragic cry. It suggests the loss not just of Dave's wife and children in 1847 but of his parents and all of his extended family in Africa, whose names could never be retrieved.

Dave's last known poem dates from the time of the Civil War. As a one-legged man in his sixties he was not called upon to fight but spent the war living at Stony Bluff, continuing to do his work. The poem is written on a storage jar 20 inches tall, which Jill Koverman describes as Dave's most 'perfectly formed vessel', and reads:

> I, made this jar, all of cross
> If, you don't repent, you will be, lost==

As with so many of Dave's poems, this is hard to interpret. It is a reference to the Bible (Acts 2: 14–42) when Peter calls upon the men of Judaea to repent. But who did Dave want to 'repent'? Was it a call for the South to atone for the evil of slavery?

Dave lived long enough to see and experience freedom. One former slave remembers the excitement in Edgefield in 1865 when all the slaves were finally set free. 'Everybody went wild. They was jes' crazy cause they was free.' We know that Dave was finally reunited with his wife and at least some of his children. An account book from Lewis Miles's business partner in 1866 shows that a man called Dave – who was apparently still working for Miles – bought one peck of meal 'for his wife'. How he felt about being with them again after nearly twenty years apart we cannot say, because there are no surviving Dave poems from the period after the Civil War.

My favourite of all Dave's inscriptions – on a jug made in 1854 – reads:

> Lm says this handle
> will crack

In these six words there is a lightness and humour, as well as something more: the confidence of someone who knows his worth in a world that treats him as less than human. No matter what nonsense or cruel words a white person might spout, slaves were never allowed to answer back. One of the hallmarks of Dave's jugs was a deep thumb or finger mark at the point where the handles met the body of the vessel. By 1854, after decades of pot-making, Dave's hands must have been exceedingly sure of what they were doing when they took the wet clay for the handle and joined it to the body, like a cook's fingers crimping the top crust of an apple pie.

The 'Lm' mentioned on the pot was Dave's supposed master, Lewis Miles. But who is the master now? Nearly 180 years on, the jug's handle still hasn't cracked.

The Cream-coloured Aga

> 'Our fragile sense of self needs support, and this we get
> by having and possessing things, because, to a large
> degree, we are what we have and possess.'
>
> Yu-Fi Tuan, 1980

In the winter of 2017, my mother, who was seventy-six at the time, announced excitedly that she was going to buy herself a cream-coloured AGA. When she first downsized into this house a few years after my father had left, one of the details she most loved about it was that the kitchen, though small, came with a red AGA. This was how she made her toast in the morning, placing the bread inside a flat grilling rack on the hotplate. But now the red AGA was broken and the idea of a new, elegant cream one excited her even more.

For the uninitiated, an AGA is an old-fashioned Swedish range cooker, much loved in certain circles in the UK, particularly among posh people who live in the countryside. It was invented by a Nobel Prize-winning Swedish physicist called Gustav Dalén, who had lost his sense of sight and wanted to find an easier way for his wife to cook. An AGA comes with a minimum of two hot-plates (one hotter and one cooler) and two ovens (again one hotter and one cooler). For those who are attached to them, there is no better tool for anything from drying clothes to baking scones to reheating casseroles in the low oven. The TV cook Mary Berry has described her duck-egg-blue AGA as the 'heart of the kitchen' and said that she would 'loathe' to live without it. The cosiness of a trad-itional AGA is not without its downsides, however. They are hugely wasteful of energy because they are hot all the time (although some newer models have more flexibility and can be turned down or off more easily). Unlike a conventional oven, the older models of AGA must be serviced once a year, and when they go wrong they may either be too hot to touch or lose heat altogether.

Becoming an AGA owner was part of my mother's new post-divorce persona. In some ways it felt like a step up in the world. A professor of literature, she was drawn to the picturesque. She pre-ferred rose-petal jam to strawberry and used a cloth handkerchief in preference to a paper tissue. To own such a pretty oven made her feel snug and capable, like the kind of person who could whip up a stew or a cake at a moment's notice, especially when grandchil-dren came to stay. Unlike an electric oven, the original AGA does not need to be preheated: it is a constant source of warmth and comfort. K's old red AGA was not only a cooking device; it con-tained a boiler for heating the whole house. This meant that when it began to malfunction and eventually could not be mended it urgently needed to be replaced, which was the rationale for the new cream-coloured one.

Almost everyone close to K – except for one of her friends, who went with her on the trip to buy it – thought that the new cream AGA was a bad idea. There was the expense for starters: even second-hand it would cost thousands of pounds to get the exact model she needed. Our main worry, though, was that she wouldn't be able to use it, especially when the weather changed and it needed to be turned on or off altogether. The thought of an AGA with an unfamil-iar set of controls and a new instruction manual seemed unwise.

We had realised by now that her worry about the silver toast rack getting stolen was far from a one-off. An appointment with an Alzheimer's specialist confirmed that she had 'mild cognitive impairment': problems with memory and thinking which in many cases develop into full-blown dementia.

Her closest cousin, the one who was like a sister to her, offered to help K buy a much simpler and more user-friendly cooker with a separate boiler. Meanwhile, my sister and I tried to persuade her of the ease of a microwave oven and an electric toaster. But she was adamant and when the new AGA arrived she gloried in its cream-coloured good looks. When I first visited her after it was installed, she told me proudly that she had bought a Mary Berry AGA cookbook and looked forward to cooking lots of recipes from it.

Over the following year my sister and I shared many emails, texts and phone calls between ourselves and with her other relatives about our mother and the declining state of her mind, and what kind of care she might now need (if only we could get her to accept it). Looking back on these messages, I am struck by how many of them focused on the cream AGA and what a mistake it had been. My sister reported that K had used the AGA to make some 'uneatable burnt toast' for her girls. K's cousin wrote to say that she couldn't even make toast anymore because she had dropped the toasting rack between the AGA and the new edge. Her brother emailed to complain about her forgetfulness, adding that 'maybe dependence on the AGA is part of the problem', and his wife reported during a visit that she suspected that 'cooking was not taking place'. When it came to my mother and the AGA, we all seemed to feel that we were right and she was wrong.

In practical terms, my mother's new cream-coloured AGA may indeed have been the 'wrong' oven. On one of my visits I discovered a dish of macaroni cheese in it which, judging from its dark colour and fossilised texture, had been cooking for several days. On another occasion, her cousin found her unable to go in the kitchen at all because the AGA was turned up full blast, making the room unbearably hot, and she had no idea how to turn it down again. It kept malfunctioining. One of the hotplates stopped working, which caused another mini-drama.

A tool can serve more than one function, however. K's AGA may not have been the most efficient device for cooking with, but it was an excellent tool for making her feel better about herself at a time when she must have been very frightened and uncertain. Its arrival was a way to shore up her fragile sense of self. One by one, words failed her; yet, as a competitive person, she *hated* anyone suggesting that her memory was not what it was. She started referring to wine – which she was now, uncharacteristically, drinking throughout the day – as 'red liquid' and 'white liquid'. To buy a splendid and expensive new oven was a way of signalling to herself and the outside world that she was still a person who cooked and who did so in a stylish manner: someone who could take care of themselves, whatever her bossy daughters might be suggesting.

Whether we have dementia or not, one of the main jobs of possessions is to change the way we feel about ourselves. The things we surround ourselves with give meaning to our lives. In 1988 Russell Belk published a groundbreaking article called 'Possessions and the Extended Self'. Belk argued that if we wanted to understand what possessions mean to people, it was crucial to start by recognising that every single one of us, intentionally or unintentionally, regards 'our possessions as part of ourselves'. When I interviewed him Belk told me that his work created 'a lot of anger' in the field, because most consumer scientists at the time were very invested in the idea that consumers should behave according to a rational model, as if they were computers. Belk's thesis – based on hours and hours of fieldwork, interviewing Americans about their belongings – was that people simply don't behave in such coldly rational ways in relation to the objects in their lives. We acquire or keep all sorts of stuff we don't technically need because of the emotions it helps us to generate.

A year and a half after K bought the AGA, she was officially diagnosed with dementia and I was still trying to persuade her to let me buy her a microwave oven. By now I had arranged for her to have drop-in carers every day who heated up ready-made dinners for her. There was a lovely carer called Amanda who understood that K needed to be treated as a friend rather than someone in need of help. Amanda sat with her at the dinner table and told her what beautiful blue eyes she had. Amanda told me she worried that K wasn't eating enough. I mentioned to K that a microwave could make it much easier for her or other people to heat up food quickly, but she replied by email saying: 'I'm not sure that I need a microwave – I can use the AGA v well.'

The Hungarian psychologist Mihaly Csikszentmihalyi – who is most famous for coining the concept of 'flow' – once wrote that possessions 'tell us things about ourselves that we need to hear in order to keep ourselves from falling apart'. He added that some household goods – such as a new car, good furniture or 'the latest appliances' – may give us external social recognition. But there is also 'the much more private feedback provided by special household items that objectify a person's past, present and future'. When I saw K during the era of the cream AGA she would usually admit she had no idea how to use it, but after I had returned home again she would text or email to say how excellent it was and how well it was meeting her needs.

The old red AGA had meant a huge amount to K. After my father left her for someone twenty years younger than her, the life went out of her cooking for a while. Overnight, she almost entirely stopped cooking meat. This made sense – my sister was already vegetarian. But there was a strong feeling that the meat had only been cooked for *him* and that without a man in the house to feed, the reason for meat, and indeed for celebration, had gone. She stopped baking as much, which made me sad. I had loved her breads and buns and cakes: her sticky almond macaroons, her pillowy-soft bread rolls. Her appetite seemed to have vanished and she lost an alarming amount of weight that year. The dinner she now cooked most frequently – sometimes several times a week – was ratatouille with brown rice on the side. My sister and I were each descending into different forms of disordered eating and gathering together for meals did not feel the same now that we were three, not four. The ratatouille had a watery, slightly dour feeling to it: heavy on the courgette, low on the olive oil and salt.

After K moved into the new house with the red AGA, joy returned to her eating life. In this new place she loved having friends round for dinner or drinks. Sometimes she bought a feast of Lebanese food from a nearby restaurant, but at other times she cooked exciting new versions of the old casseroles she had always made. I remember big dinners for which she cooked pigeon or pheasant stewed in red wine. After her grandchildren were born – my sister and I each have three children – it delighted her to feed them, something she did with generosity and an urge to please. My youngest child had a picky phase when he struggled with new foods, especially vegetables, but he would consent to eat red peppers when they were part of 'Grandma's chicken stir-fry', which she made in a flat-bottomed frying pan on the hotter of the two AGA hotplates.

I'm pretty sure she never made a stir-fry on the new cream AGA. Two years after she bought it, it didn't feel safe to let her stay at home anymore, even with live-in care, though she kept telling me she was on great form, never better. She fell over one night on some wet leaves and broke her arm. At that point we decided to move her to the care home in the town where I live, so that my ex-husband and I could see her more (this was six months before he left).

As a tool for preparing food, this AGA had been a near-total failure which had generated a whole lot of worry and very little cooking. Then again, as a tool for making her feel better about herself at a very vulnerable time, it was a superb device. Buying it was a stubbornly optimistic act. My granny – my mother's mother – always described K to me as someone who was fiercely determined. My mother was born with a cleft palate. In those days, in the UK, this meant having an operation at the age of two. The children were separated from their parents for several weeks while they were in hospital, supposedly for their own good. Both my granny and my mother repeatedly spoke of this experience as traumatic. My grandmother would add that she believed that the enforced separation made K deeply self-reliant. Whether this was true, I can't say. Another relative told me that the real reason for K's self-reliance was that her parents had left her alone so much when she was a child and that – like Kate McDermott – she was expected to cook dinner for the whole family from a young age. Whatever the reason, she was someone who valued her independence very highly, something that made the slow slide into dementia especially hard to bear.

Her possession of the smart new cream AGA contained within it the promise of a different future from the one she ended up with. In this version, she would not spend her time sitting in an overheated room, drinking milkshakes with other dementia sufferers. She would not lose her ability to swallow and her capacity to form sentences. She would not need other people to bathe her and dress her.

In the future foretold by the AGA, she is still standing in her own kitchen wearing an apron with classical music playing on the radio. She has spent the morning at the library, making discoveries in the archives. When she speaks her words still make sense, to herself and to others. She has many friends. There is a table full of hungry grandchildren waiting to be fed and she is the woman to do it.

Symbols

The Melon Baller

> 'Each clan has its totem, which belongs to it alone; two
> different tribes of the same clan cannot have the same.'
>
> Émile Durkheim, 1915

For reasons that are lost in the mists of time, both of my sons –
who are ten years apart – developed a fetish for the family's melon
baller. They don't use this utensil as it was originally intended – for
making a bowl of spherical pieces of melon to be shared out.
Rather, they want to be the person who has the prestige of eating
their own piece of melon with the only melon baller in the house.
It has become like a sacred fruit-chalice to them, even though my
older son once admitted that, in truth, it kind of hurts his mouth
to eat with it. Their love for the melon baller is both slightly ironic
and deadly serious.

A melon baller, if you don't have one, consists of a handle with
a sharp little scoop on the end. These implements were once much
used by fancy French restaurants, not just for creating balls of
melon but for turning any fruits or vegetables into tiny globes,
from potatoes to courgettes, from cucumber to papaya. In addition, you can use them for hulling strawberries and taking the
core out of apples. When I was younger, food writers used to look
down on melon ballers as a byword for over-garnished food – style
over substance – but their reputation is now reviving somewhat.
The 'Wirecutter' column in *The New York Times* remarks that just

a few 'little globes' of melon can 'top a salad, whimsy up a dessert or garnish a cocktail'. The authors of *The New Cooks' Catalogue* (2000) say that as well as balling melon, melon ballers are 'also surprisingly effective for shaping chilled ganache into chocolate truffles'.

My sons don't use the melon baller for any of that fancy cooking, though. They just want it for eating melon with. This doesn't happen all that often because I generally only buy melons in the summer when they are more likely to be sweet and ripe. I still have memories of eating luscious orange Charentais melons on holiday in France in June, and no melon I buy in England ever matches up. Maybe this explains why the boys are so crazy about the melon baller. Melon as a fruit has a certain rarity value in our house that doesn't extend to apples or oranges and both the boys say that melon is their top fruit. My younger son is so stubbornly pro-melon that he once spent an hour trying to convince me and his brother that the particular melon we were eating that night was delicious even though it was under-ripe and disappointing ('turnippy' was the word his brother used). If it's melon, it must be good, is his view. His sister, who has the tact and diplomacy of a middle child, largely stays out of these melon debates, which she finds tedious.

For the brothers, the melon baller has taken on the quality of a totem. It is a special item which binds them together in ways that no outsider could fully understand. Perhaps it is all the more important to them because of the large age gap between them; and latterly because of the divorce. When a nuclear family loses its nucleus, the shared rituals that remain feel all the more precious. My older son is only home from time to time these days. To return to the old fights over who gets to the drawer first to grab the melon baller is a way of restating their kinship with one another, albeit comically.

The year after the separation, my older son moved back near home to study, and for that year he came to have dinner with me and his brother at least once a week. It was especially joyous at this time to see them arguing over the melon baller. To me it was a sign that one detail, at least, hadn't changed in their lives. After dinner I would drive my older son back to his student rooms and we talked in the car about how the situation really was in the family, more earnestly and sombrely than we had at the dinner table. But I'm not sure whether there was more truth in these serious moments than there had been in the shared ebullience over the melon baller.

A strong feeling for a particular totem can be one of the most powerful ways of binding a group together. The French sociologist Émile Durkheim argued – in his 1912 book *The Elementary Forms of the Religious Life* – that totems were the kernel of primitive religion among the Aboriginal tribes of Australia as well as Native Americans. Durkheim noted that almost all totems consisted of plants or animals such as a kangaroo, a tea tree or a white crested cockatoo, although there were also clans in which the totem was a natural phenomenon such as 'clouds, rain, hail, frost, the moon, the sun, the wind, the autumn, the summer, the winter, certain stars, thunder, fire, smoke, water or the sea'.

Without a totem – and related special objects – there could be no clan. The daily life of a clan, Durkheim observed, was saturated with images of the totem: on helmets, on wigwams, on the inside of houses, on tattoos on the body, on canoes, on 'utensils of every sort' and on funeral pyres. The effect of all these images of the totem was to bind the community together (just as sports fans are united by wearing their team colours). When the totem was a bird, men would wear the feathers of the bird on their heads. Among the Turtle clan of the Omaha, men had their hair shaved off, except for six bunches, to resemble the legs, hair and tail of the turtle.

I can't in all honesty pretend that my sons' enthusiasm for the melon baller stretches to reproducing pictures of it on their clothing or bedroom walls, let alone getting their hair cut to resemble an orb of melon (the mind boggles). But what their passion for the melon baller does share with totemism is the fact that it is eminently social. It is an enthusiasm – and a rivalry – which they perform only in each other's company. When his siblings are not in the house, which is most of the time, my younger son and I can go for weeks without getting the melon baller out of the drawer.

I've noticed that different families have their own special kitchen totems: the utensils they hold sacred and the ones they refuse to go near. There are microwave clans and air fryer clans. There are households that use garlic presses and households that very much don't. When we first got together, my ex-husband couldn't have imagined making salad without a wooden salad bowl because it was what his mother always used, mixing the dressing in the bowl itself rather than in a separate jar. Her salad bowl took on a delightful garlicky scent and the wood was conditioned from all those years of being bathed in oily dressing – like a violin rubbed with linseed oil.

Salad from a ceramic bowl was tasteless to my ex because the bowl had no scent to add to the dressing. Maybe this was another moment when our relationship silently frayed. After our wooden salad bowl split in half, I started to make salads in ceramic bowls. This wasn't such a terrible development; we still mostly ate good salads. But perhaps it was a sign that we were no longer as united and clannish as we had once been. In very close families, it is unthinkable to depart too far from the clan's set way of doing things in the kitchen. Even after grown-up children have left home, they will replicate the colanders and graters they grew up with or maintain fidelity to a specific way of cooking rice.

Durkheim's great insight about religion was that the particular choice of totem was less important than the bond between the group it gave rise to. When the men of the clan believed that they were revering the totem, what they were actually worshipping was society itself, forged by a shared belief in the sacred. He wrote of a phenomenon he called 'collective effervescence': the feeling of being carried away by belonging to a group spirit greater than the sum of its parts. It is the kind of collective sentiment that happens when people dance round a totem by the light of a campfire – and suddenly anything could happen.

A much milder version of this collective effervescence occurs when two boys eat melon together while vying to be the person holding the one and only melon baller in the house. It isn't really the device itself that excites them so much. It is the feeling of being together, half fighting and half not, still caring madly about the same thing.

The Queen's Sieve

'A sceptre is one thing, and a ladle another.'

George Herbert, 1651

In the national art museum in Siena, there is an enigmatic and beautiful portrait of Queen Elizabeth I, ruler of England from 1558 to 1603. The painting was done by a Flemish artist called Quentin Metsys the Younger in 1583. One of the many striking details in it is that the queen is not holding a sceptre or an orb or any of the other more obvious symbols of monarchy. Rather, she is carrying a humble domestic tool: a large sieve made from brass-coloured metal. The mystery is *why* she is holding this sieve given that, as queen, she would never have set foot in a kitchen.

Sieves, I was charmed to learn, were the queen's favourite heraldic device. Elizabeth's penchant for them was so well known that she was once given a golden sieve-shaped pendant 'garnished' with diamonds as a New Year's present. The so-called Siena Sieve Portrait is just one of a whole series of paintings – created by a number of artists between 1570 and 1590 – in which the queen is depicted with a sieve in her hand.

When her father, Henry VIII, had his own most famous portrait painted by Hans Holbein, he was depicted with a dagger to symbolise his might (and a giant codpiece to allude to his virility). Elizabeth's sieve is a far less obvious royal symbol. It's a way to signal to the viewer that she is aware that, as she once said, she has

the body of 'a weak and feeble woman'. Unlike a dagger, a sieve can't be used to stab anyone. Then again, when you command the whole of England and Ireland, perhaps you don't really need to hold your own weapon. Looking at the Siena Sieve Portrait, you are left in no doubt that the person holding the sieve is extremely powerful, but there's a subtlety to the way she wields her power.

In this painting, the queen is wearing an austere black dress with white lace detailing. She has a translucent string of pearls round her neck and an ornate brooch pinned to her dress. Her red hair is studded with jewels and her fingers are white and tapering. Behind her, through a doorway, we can glimpse a group of male courtiers bearing halberds (a combined pike and axe). This mysterious group does not feature in any of the queen's other sieve portraits and it is one of the elements that makes the Siena version so much the most memorable of the series.

At the front of the group of men, two courtiers with well-shaped calves stare intensely into each other's eyes. These men are wearing the tightest, brightest stockings you've ever seen. Are they about to fight, kiss each other, or simply compete ineffectually for the queen's favour? It isn't clear. One of the men is dressed in red, the other in yellow. Behind them is another man in less colourful attire with the badge of a white hind (a female deer) on his cloak. His own shapely legs are encased in hose of a darker hue. The queen pays no attention to this scene unfolding behind her. Her black eyes gaze in the opposite direction as she delicately holds her sieve between her left-hand thumb and forefinger.

In Tudor households, sieves were essential. They were not just tools for straining and washing ingredients but performed many of the jobs that a modern cook might use an electric blender or food processor for. In an era before ready-ground spices and flours and sugars, you could eat almost nothing smooth if you did not have a sieve. Tudor recipes, especially those for sweet dishes, are full of instructions to sift, to strain, to sieve and to searce (another word for sifting dry ingredients). 'Take a pound of double refined sugar, searce it through a tiffany sieve' reads a recipe for 'sugar puffs' from the late seventeenth century. Tiffany was a kind of semi-transparent muslin. There were also sieves made of silk, cotton, linen and horse hair, each of which offered different degrees of fineness. In addition to sieves there were 'cullenders' made of metal for draining food (much as we still use them today) and 'mazarines', which were like colanders but shallower.

Outside the kitchen, sieves served a still more vital role as tools for rendering grain edible by sifting the good parts from the bad after threshing: sorting the wheat from the chaff. Grain sieves have been used since Neolithic times and they are huge, commonly as large as one metre across. Across the grain-eating peoples of the world, sieving it was seen as women's work and it was back-breaking labour. Women would take the threshed grain and shake it several times in the sieve in a jerky motion to bring any chaff and pebbles to the surface before picking out the impurities one by one.

The sieve in Elizabeth's hand is definitely a real kitchen sieve. It is not made of gold or silver but of latten, a pale-yellow alloy of copper and tin much used for kitchenware at the time. This is an everyday, practical item, not a royal trinket. The equivalent today might be a cheap stainless-steel strainer. Judging from her rich dress and aloof demeanour, Elizabeth is not planning to use her sieve for any kind of labour, back-breaking or otherwise.

The purpose of her sieve is purely symbolic. But of what?

Going back to ancient times, sieves have been associated with wisdom, which is easy enough to understand when you consider what sieves actually do. They are tools for sorting wanted items from unwanted ones. In Renaissance mythology, the figure of Prudence (one of the four cardinal virtues) carried a sieve to underline the fact that she can sift out good from evil. On the edge of the sieve in Elizabeth's Siena portrait there is a motto which reads: *A terra il ben, mal dimora in sella*: 'down goes the good and the bad remains in the saddle'. By carrying a sieve, Elizabeth is reminding her subjects that she is the arbiter of right and wrong. It's a power display disguised as a humble utensil. To her left there is a globe to remind us of her naval conquests.

Yet sieves would also have had a whole other meaning for Elizabeth: at the time, they were a well-worn motif for chastity, which is a little odd given that sieves are riddled with holes. In the misogynist humour of Tudor comedies, 'cheap' women were depicted as 'leaky vessels'. The male authors of Tudor plays often characterised women as oozing with bodily liquids, whether breast milk and tears or blood and sexual fluids. A sieve, you might think, would be the leakiest vessel of them all. But no.

The link between sieves and chastity goes back to a Roman story told about one of the Vestal Virgins – priestesses who were charged with maintaining ritual purity in the temple. As with Catholic priests, the chastity of the Vestal Virgins was considered essential to maintaining the purity of the place of worship. The city of Rome itself would have been cursed if any of the Vestal Virgins had been less than virginal. According to Valerius Maximus, a Vestal Virgin called Tuccia was charged with 'the crime of unchastity'. To prove her innocence, she prayed to the goddess Vesta and then filled a sieve with water from the River Tiber. She carried it all the way back to the temple without spilling a drop. And thus her chastity was proved! When I told my son Leo this story, he rolled his eyes and commented sarcastically that he was sure it was a 'perfectly normal sieve' and that 'no one had plugged any of the holes'.

It isn't hard to see why the idea of an impermeable sieve of chastity might have appealed to Elizabeth, the Virgin Queen. Throughout her reign she enhanced her authority with the notion that she had rejected worldly love in favour of her stately duties (while frequently dangling the idea that she might actually marry, whether for the sake of a useful alliance or to produce an heir). In the Siena portrait the queen's virginity is emphasised not just by the sieve in her hand but by the pillar behind her, depicting the Roman story of Dido and Aeneas, a parable of chaste love.

This emphasis on Elizabeth's chastity was a piece of propaganda. The backdrop to the Siena Sieve Portrait was that it looked for a while as if she might finally change her mind about remaining unmarried. From 1579 to 1581, Elizabeth was being actively courted by François, Duke of Anjou. François was twenty-four to her forty-six and her nickname for him was 'the frog'.

Among members of the queen's court, her possible marriage to the French nobleman was controversial. Some supported it on the grounds that a stronger union between England and France would help to counter the power of Spain. Other courtiers, equally vehemently, opposed the match. One of those in the anti-marriage camp was Christopher Hatton, a courtier in Elizabeth's favour who almost certainly commissioned the Siena portrait. Hatton is thought to be the shadowy figure in the background with the hind on his cloak. Looking more closely at the picture, the Hatton figure seems to be on the point of making some kind of objection to the men in the colourful stockings. Perhaps they are scheming to marry the queen off and he is coming to stop them.

When you know that Hatton was probably the painting's patron, it takes on new, more interesting connotations. A tall and handsome man, Hatton (who became Member of Parliament for Northamptonshire) was one of the queen's favourites. Many observers (including Mary, Queen of Scots) said he was Elizabeth's lover. She was known to have admired Hatton's dancing. In 1577 he became vice-chamberlain of the royal household. The explorer Francis Drake's ship was named the *Golden Hinde*, in honour of Hatton's coat of arms. In letters between them, the queen called Hatton her 'mutton' and he called himself her 'sheep'. She was sometimes observed to wear a jewel shaped like bagpipes close to her neck, on her ruff, given to her by Hatton. Shepherds traditionally play bagpipes so this was another allusion to her being his shepherd and him being her sheep.

Thanks to the queen's favours, Hatton grew so wealthy that he was able to build the largest privately owned house in England, as large as Hampton Court Palace, with 123 glass windows. This fact alone suggests that he had the queen's heart. Work on the mansion was completed in 1583, the same year that the Siena Sieve Portrait was painted. Hatton said he would not sleep in the house until the queen did so. Like Elizabeth, Hatton never married.

All of the imagery about Elizabeth's chastity in the painting seems much more ambiguous when you think of Hatton being the person responsible for it. Yes, Hatton surely wanted his beloved queen not to marry, least of all a French duke. But being unmarried was not necessarily the same as being chaste. Perhaps the most striking detail in the painting is the brooch on the queen's dress, which almost went unremarked until 2014 when two art historians, Christine Kimbriel and Henrietta McBurney Ryan, analysed it. They noticed that the brooch was very similar to one given to Elizabeth's sister Mary by her husband, except that Elizabeth's brooch displays a naked man and woman, touching hands. At the base of the brooch is a pear-shaped pearl and the head of a ram (remember that Hatton called himself the queen's 'sheep'). The sexiness of the brooch is quite at odds with the queen's all-encompassing black dress. Kimbriel and McBurney Ryan suggest that the piece of jewellery may have been a very 'deliberate and personal' comment by Hatton about his true, hidden relationship with the queen.

Seen in this light, the queen's sieve becomes an even more multi-layered symbol. Assuming that Hatton and the queen were lovers – not that we will ever really know – the sieve is not only a public declaration of purity but also a kind of coded love token. By holding it, the queen is maintaining her pledge not to marry any of the noble Europeans who have courted her, and – perhaps – keeping herself free to continue seeing Hatton. Public chastity could be a veil for private love.

After the end of my marriage, I sometimes Googled 'telltale signs secret love'. Some of the articles I found spoke of the phenomenon whereby two people having an affair (emotional or physical) develop new shared reference points, whether it's the same taste in music or a signature drink. In an essay on the subject, the writer and critic Janet Malcolm described how, at the apartment where they met, she and her lover ate off plates with a 'faux folk-art' flower design with sprigs of red and green and pink which were quite unlike her usual plain and minimalist style of china. 'Adultery takes one out of one's usual life, sometimes in unusual ways,' Malcolm wrote.

I looked again at a reproduction of the queen's portrait. Her expression now seemed less the haughty gaze of a monarch than the stunned look of someone who knows that her lover is standing right behind her in a public space where they cannot be as intimate as they wish. The fact that she is wearing his brooch speaks of a secret life behind closed doors. Maybe the metal sieve that the queen is fingering so pensively is, among other things, a giant golden ring, an absurdly oversized gesture of love from Hatton to his royal mistress.

The Vegetable Corers

'One day honey, one day onions.'

Arabic saying meaning that there are good days and bad

We all carry pieces of our childhood homes around inside us. But for a refugee, the dream of home is a heavier kind of ache because of the impossibility of return. Any possessions you manage to retrieve from the old life become potent emblems of a whole culture. For Faraj Alnasser, nothing symbolises his former home in Syria as strongly as two vegetable corers designed for removing the flesh from courgettes and aubergines so that they can be stuffed. These corers look like 'nothing', Faraj says, but to him they are essential: a gateway to an Aleppo that no longer exists.

I first became aware of Faraj – a chef – in February 2021, when the UK was in yet another long COVID-19 lockdown. My mood was low just then. My daughter and youngest son and I were all stuck at home and we were running out of ploys to keep our spirits up on the cold, grey evenings. Someone mentioned that there was a young Syrian chef nearby doing home delivery of the most delicate vegetarian food. That dinner we ordered from Faraj still shines in my memory. We ate *baba ganoush* (a smoky aubergine puree); a gloriously fresh winter *tabbouleh* made with blood oranges; and a vegetarian version of *kibbeh* made with mushrooms and pine nuts instead of the traditional lamb. Most comforting of all was a loaf of yolk-rich plaited bread with a shiny top. We ate the rest for breakfast the next day.

Faraj's cooking reminded me of the food at the Lebanese restaurant my mother had been so fond of, although this was lighter and fresher. It tasted of life. It had nothing in common with what I had read in the news of the horrors of civil war in Syria. I did not fully understand at the time that the intense brightness and care of Faraj's food was his way to reclaim a little of his childhood home after all that he had suffered and lost.

A few months later we met for coffee and Faraj gave me a small jar of apricot jam, made according to his mother's recipe. Back in Syria she would cook the apricots with the heat of the sun, but here in England Faraj uses a low oven to cook the jam instead, combining the fresh fruit with a mixture of sugar and lemon juice. It was the best apricot jam I had ever tasted. He told me more about the long and terrifying journey from Syria to Britain, during which he nearly died several times and suffered hunger, thirst and torture. It started with the day in 2012 after the start of the civil war when his family woke up hearing bombs and realised that they had to leave Syria straight away, relocating to Cairo.

Life in Cairo was not easy. He told me he 'left our beloved Aleppo behind for an unknown future. We fled to face new challenges, adapting to life in Cairo while leaving everything behind – our home, town, relatives, grandparents, friends, and other loved ones.' Although Faraj loved his mother deeply, he found life in the family difficult, partly because he had known from a young age that he was gay.

Sometimes he was so lonely that he talked to trees. He left Egypt for Turkey when he was just seventeen, hoping for freedom, but instead he experienced homelessness and hunger. As he travelled through various European countries, his experiences went from bad to worse. In Hungary, in a jail for refugees, he and others were given dirty water to drink and forced to eat pork ('knowing that we were Muslims', Faraj tells me). He briefly returned to Syria and ran through sniper fire. After two years of near-death experiences he travelled to the UK from France in the back of a refrigerated truck. The driver slammed the door on the fourteen people in the truck and he lost consciousness through lack of oxygen. He was one of only two people to survive. On regaining consciousness, he was in England.

Faraj's situation finally improved after finding a new life in Cambridge when he was nineteen. Through an organisation called Refugees at Home, an English host family who had a spare room welcomed him in. When his host, Shoshana Goldhill, first met Faraj at the train station she told him slightly nervously that they were a Jewish family. In Shoshana's telling (in a TED-x talk they did together), Faraj's face lit up and he said, 'That's fantastic! I've never really met any Jews.' They walked on a bit further before he turned to her anxiously and said, 'Shoshana, I'm gay.' Her reply was, 'Well, that's fantastic!' The Goldhills introduced Faraj to their friends as a brother for their grown-up daughter and son; Faraj felt the same. An added bonus to living with the Goldhills was that Shoshana's husband Simon was an extraordinary cook and he and Faraj experimented together at the stove.

After everything he had been through, Faraj was still homesick and traumatised. He desperately missed his mother in Egypt but knew that he could not visit her again until his British citizenship was confirmed. Another trauma was the knowledge that returning to the Aleppo of his childhood would never be an option. Even if the war ended, he could not bear to return and see so much of the beautiful old town ravaged and gone. 'It got so much worse after I left,' he says. He would rather hang on to his old memories than go back and see the city in its current sad state.

The one activity that consistently made him feel at home again was cooking, because it reminded him that 'Aleppo is inside of me'. He studied at a cookery school in London and found work in several restaurants before the pandemic hit. That was when he had the idea of making his own Syrian food and delivering it around Cambridge, with Shoshana's help. Cooking and sharing the food of home with others was the remedy he had been searching for.

There were still many treasures that he could not recreate from home, however. One of them was stuffed vegetables. For the first few years he was in England, Faraj felt unable to cook a single stuffed vegetable because he didn't have the right tools. This might sound trivial, but as the Lebanese food writer Anissa Helou has written, no special meal in the Levant would be complete without at least one kind of stuffed vegetable on the table. In the Middle East stuffed vegetables – *mahshi* in Arabic – are not a single dish but a way of life, representing celebration and hospitality. Because of the time and skill required to make them, *mahshi* started off as 'court cuisine' for the rich but eventually became a favourite food for all classes in society.

During the pandemic, pining for home, Faraj developed an unquenchable craving for his mother's stuffed vegetables. Unlike Paola White, who found a new way to make the stuffed vegetables of her Tuscan home in England using a pressure cooker, Faraj only wanted to make stuffed vegetables with the exact tool his mother had always used. The slowness of the process was part of what he was craving.

In the spring of 2021, there was suddenly a chance for Faraj to get his vegetable corers when his mother returned to Aleppo from Egypt for the first time since the family had left Syria. She brought back two vegetable corers for Faraj, along with a huge bag of pistachios and a bottle of fresh Syrian pomegranate molasses. Back in Egypt, she gave this care package to a friend of Faraj's, who carried it to England for him.

As soon as Faraj held the two coring tools in his hands he felt a surge of happiness. At last he could make stuffed vegetables again. I mentioned to him that some English recipes I've seen for stuffed courgettes suggest that you can core them using a spoon, an apple corer or a small paring knife, but Faraj found all of these suggestions funny: like saying that you can drink water from a plate – yes, it would be possible, but why bother when there is a better way? He suspects that the basic design of metal corers in Syria has not changed in more than a century but cannot imagine a more efficient implement for removing most of a vegetable's flesh without damaging its structure.

I asked if we could meet for coffee so that he could show me the corers. We met in the courtyard of a café on an unexpectedly hot late summer day. Faraj was holding in his hand two long, narrow devices of a dull-grey metal. The body of the blade was an open curved shape, like a tube cut in half. Faraj looked so proud as he held them: like a little boy holding trophies. 'Seeing these tools, I feel really safe,' he said.

There are many quicker and easier ways to eat a courgette than to stuff it in the Syrian style. You could simply slice it and sauté it in a pan in some oil for five minutes and it would be perfectly tasty, especially if you spritz it with lemon at the end. But it wouldn't give you the sense of festivity and care that you would get from an Aleppine dish of slow-cooked stuffed courgettes, filled with spiced meat or grains and herbs and spices and cooked slowly for many hours. One of the most special stuffed vegetable dishes Faraj's mother makes consists of a whole shoulder of lamb topped with lamb-stuffed vine leaves. She puts it in to cook before the family goes to bed, and twelve hours later it is ready for lunch. In England Faraj follows a vegetarian diet, but the memory of this lamb dish still makes him dreamy. 'It's fatty, it's lamby, it's sweet,' he says.

Slow cooking seems like a chore to many people, but back in

Syria stuffed vegetables symbolised happiness for Faraj precisely because they took so long to make, which forced the women in the house to stop and chat. 'All these fun things happened around the house at the time of the coring,' he recalls. The mood in the house lightened. His mother and grandmother and aunts and various friends would gather on the balcony and gossip. Sometimes they would core as many as 50 kilos of aubergines or courgettes, talking all the time. In Aleppo, before the war, food was intensely seasonal. Aubergines and courgettes were only eaten fresh in the summer. To preserve the harvest for the winter, most of the crop was cored, blanched and dried and left in the family's store room, where it stayed good for months on end. Tomatoes, meanwhile, were cooked down into home-made tomato paste. When he handles his corers, Faraj is back in a peaceful Aleppo, watching his mother and grandmother cook.

When someone yearns for a Syrian vegetable corer, it is a very specific yearning. It can't be satisfied with some other random vegetable corer off the internet. A few weeks after our coffee, I showed Faraj an Italian zucchini corer I had just bought, inspired by him. The blade was stainless steel and it had a cheap wooden handle. When Faraj looked at it, he called it 'fancy'. I could tell he thought it was no match for his own two corers from Syria.

The great difficulty with coring a courgette or an aubergine is that you must dig deep to extract the flesh but not too deep, otherwise you make a hole in the end and the filling spills out. To avoid this Faraj measures each vegetable against his knuckles before he cores it so that he can see where to stop. His grandmother (his mother's mother) had no need of such visual aids. She was famous in the family for the speed and accuracy of her coring. She prepared vegetable after vegetable without even looking, never making a mistake. She then took the leftover vegetable flesh and used it to make soups or dressings. 'Nothing is wasted,' Faraj says.

Faraj's two corers are subtly different from one another. He describes one of them as a 'beginner' version because it has a hook on the end to protect the finger as you core. To use this one is like riding a bike with stabilisers (the hook can also be used to hang it up). The other tool is an advanced corer with no hook. This is the kind his grandmother used.

As soon as Faraj had the special tools in his hands, he set about recreating the stuffed vegetables he remembered. He ordered a box of baby aubergines from his local Turkish food shop to make one of the dishes he had been craving: small aubergines stuffed with bulgur wheat. Unlike many of the stuffed vegetable dishes he grew up with, this traditional aubergine dish is '100 per cent vegan'. The hollowed-out aubergines are stuffed with a mixture of tomatoes, bulgur, chilli pepper, garlic, olive oil and chickpeas, plus plenty of parsley (in Damascus cooks use a lot of coriander leaf, whereas in Aleppo the green herb of choice is parsley). After eating the aubergines, the tradition is to drink the cooking broth with a little lemon juice.

Once the aubergines were all stuffed, Faraj cooked them over a very low heat in a mixture of water, oil, lemon juice and tomato paste. The dish smelled and tasted divine: just as Faraj remembered. It took him back to being in Aleppo again up on the balcony with his mother and aunts. 'I was over the moon,' he says, 'but I was sad as well. Nobody ever makes this dish alone.'

When Faraj looks at his vegetable corers, he thinks about the strength of the women in his family, especially his mother and grandmother. Looking back, he sees that they suffered immense hardship – 'they were going through such a lot' – and yet he can hardly remember a time when they were not smiling. He wonders now whether all the communal cooking they did was the main way they coped with 'dark thoughts'. He can picture his mother looking overwhelmed, only to run to the kitchen and cook a meal with great care. She learned this cooking instinct from her mother.

At home in Syria, Faraj's grandmother owned a whole assortment of vegetable corers – like a knife collection for a Western cook. She needed different sizes for different vegetables. Apart from the corers, she owned very few cooking tools: just some pots and pans, a knife, a grater, bowls and other bits and pieces. Faraj describes his grandmother – a farmer – as a person of uncommon resilience. She raised her six younger sisters like a parent after their mother died in her forties. Her sisters all learned to read and write but she never got the chance to do so because she was working so hard to support the rest of them.

For many years after most of the family had left, Faraj's grandmother stayed in Aleppo. She survived intense and brutal years of bombing in the city and only moved to Cairo to be with the rest of the family in 2023. She brought nothing with her except for her clothes, her medicines and her cooking tools, including her entire collection of vegetable corers.

And then, on 8th December 2024, the Assad regime fell and everything changed for Syrians, Faraj's family included. He sent me an ecstatic message a week later to say it took him three days to believe it was true. He was back in Cairo where the whole family had celebrated with a big feast. His grandmother – who had lived under the rule of Assad and his father before him for 53 years – said that Faraj's grandpa would have been 'dancing in the street' if only he had 'witnessed this day'.

To Faraj, his precious vegetable corers are a symbol of home and of the strength it takes to recreate it in an entirely different country. And then he pauses and remarks that if his grandma were here with us, she would laugh at us for 'going too deep' on the subject of kitchen implements. He reflects that he is in a 'privileged' position to be able to see his possessions in symbolic terms, whereas his grandmother 'doesn't have the time or the energy' for such lofty thoughts. Yet she would agree with him that without these corers, there is no home.

Bruce Lee Drinking Horns

'In almost every culture, objects are chosen to represent the power of the bearer.'

Mihaly Csikszentmihalyi and Eugene Rochberg-Halton, 1981

My oven was on its last legs and I was shopping for a new one online when I came across an appliance website with the strapline 'Create kitchen envy'. It made me wonder. Was generating envy really what I sought from an oven? I thought I was just looking for a heat source which could brown food evenly without wasting too much energy.

Yet kitchen envy is certainly an emotion I have felt in other people's homes. We once tried (and failed) to buy a house mainly because there was a blackboard in the kitchen on which the owner had scribbled the words 'fennel seeds'. I wanted the whole house just because of that blackboard. I have also envied other people's steam ovens and Thermomixes; wine coolers and pizza ovens; pantry cupboards and breakfast nooks; shelving units and skylights.

Some modern kitchens are full of trophies, whether it's a state-of-the-art espresso machine, a cute Staub casserole dish or one of those big-name stand mixers which retail for hundreds of pounds. It is far from essential to buy a brightly coloured stand mixer when you can get a hand-held electric one which does most of the same work for a fraction the price. The value of the mixer is mainly in how it makes you feel. As Amanda Mull wrote in an essay in *The*

Atlantic, KitchenAid mixers 'aren't just culinary workhorses; they've become small markers of stability and sophistication, coveted by young people for whom traditional indicators of both often remain out of reach'.

Then again, it is not new to treat eating and cooking objects as status symbols. Think of the most enviable item in a modern kitchenware shop and you will still not get close to the prestige that has long been attached to certain traditional drinking horns in the Grassfields of Cameroon. In this area of northern Cameroon near Nigeria, buffalo-horn cups are highly coveted articles. To own and drink from one is somewhat like owning an expensive car or designer trainers in the West, but with a greater sense of awe about it. Owning a buffalo horn was for many generations a way for men to demonstrate their power and importance to other men.

In Bambui – a village in the Grassfields of around 16,000 people – a man's drinking horn is not a commodity he can just stroll into a shop and buy, like a ceramic mug or a wine glass. He has to earn the right to drink from one, particularly the 'title cups' made from buffalo horn. The title cup is a special drinking vessel which can only be owned by 'titleholders' – a position that can be conferred either through inheritance or through long service to the royal elite. It is said that the title cup – the most precious of all heirlooms – carries the secret of each family because it contains the breath of the elders inside it. When the *fon* (king) or the head of the family dies, his successor will inherit the title cup but first the deceased person's cup must be placed on his forehead to transfer all of their power into it. It is believed that the success of every titled family in Bambui depends on the wisdom with which the cup holder treats his cup. Drinking palm wine from the title cup – shared among the men – is a crucial element in family meetings. The horn is also drunk from when forming alliances or doing business deals. A business alliance forged with plastic cups would be worthless.

For decades it was understood in Bambui that if you were not a titleholder you were less worthy than other men. A man without a buffalo horn might receive jibes for being little better than a woman or a child. (This remains a patriarchal society and only men may use a buffalo-horn cup. When women are titleholders, their cups are made from gourd or calabash.) Commoners – whether men or women – were only allowed to use plain undecorated drinking cups made from cow horn. A traditional buffalo horn carver commented that cow-horn drinking cups were as worthless as a bird's toenail.

What makes the title cup in Cameroon so special? In the first place, it was traditionally made from buffalo horn, the most prestigious of all animal horns. These horns have become all the rarer since the buffalo became endangered in the Grassfields (any new ones have been made from buffalo horn stolen by poachers and then sold on to carvers through a black market). They are carved by hand – the process may take as much as thirty days – and decorated with symbolic motifs which have specific meaning for the owner. Some buffalo horns are chiselled with pythons – showing the ability of the titleholder to protect his family – or an elephant to symbolise dignity, wealth and majesty. There are lion cups and leopard cups (for power); frog cups for fertility; spider cups for knowledge and wisdom; or palm tree cups for prosperity.

The more status and prestige a possession is given, the more demeaning and humiliating it feels not to own one, assuming that you buy into the values of the prevailing culture. This is as true of granite countertops and fancy coffee makers as it is of drinking horns. The advertisers of luxury watches in the West try to make us feel that their products confer a special aura on people rich enough to buy them. 'I always judge a man by his watch,' said someone I met at a lunch party. The man I had come to the lunch with held up his own naked wrist and laughed.

Then again, the symbolism of possessions can change in remarkable ways. Starting in the early 2000s, the young men of Bambui – aged roughly eighteen to thirty-five – started to fight back against the old ways and commission their own distinctive drinking horns as a way to give themselves the status they had been denied by their elders. These horns were made from cheap and common cow horn, but instead of being undecorated they were painted with a very famous face.

It was 2009 when Dr Mathias Alubafi Fubah, a Cameroonian academic then working in England, first became aware of new drinking horns being used by young men. Fubah had travelled home for a family meeting when he noticed that his cousin had a new one decorated with a man's face. 'What is this image?', Fubah asked when he saw his cousin taking an unfamiliar drinking horn out of a cupboard. 'Bruce Lee, of course, the youth favourite actor' was his reply. When Fubah asked his cousin what he was planning to do with it, he replied: 'That is my drinking horn – I do not want to be ridiculed in the village because I don't have a drinking horn.'

Fubah's cousin was far from being the only young man in this part of Cameroon with a Bruce Lee drinking horn. Fubah discovered that over a short period of time, the Bruce Lee cow-horn version had become all the rage, to the extent that buffalo horns lost some of their former prestige. He interviewed a horn carver called Pa Mandzi, who claimed to have made the very first Bruce Lee cup out of cow horn. Why was it Bruce Lee who became the ubiquitous decoration on the drinking horns? The martial arts actor was not African. On the other hand, his appeal among the youth of Bambui society is immense. Bruce Lee drinking horns – which are often giant in size – are a means by which men can project an image of strength and power, even if they never attain the traditional title-holder status. Kung-fu is popular among young people in the Grassfields. Like the traditional lions, spiders and elephants on the old buffalo horns, Bruce Lee, the master of combat, carries many positive connotations. He is a symbol of force and speed; of wisdom and grace; of succeeding on his own terms in a white man's world; and of winning through defensive tactics. To drink from such a cup gives its owner a certain self-confidence.

Fubah began researching the new phenomenon of Bruce Lee drinking horns in rural Cameroon after he realised how easy it was for young men to be 'belittled' for lacking an acceptable drinking horn. One of his cousins told him that any young man who turned up to a meeting without a drinking horn would be treated 'as a child'.

The Bruce Lee drinking horn is a way for the youth of Bambui (the male ones, anyway) to pay their respects to the old hierarchies while subverting them. This is what makes it such a subtle and clever innovation. 'Absorb what is useful, discard what is not, add what is uniquely your own' is one of Bruce Lee's most famous sayings. Unlike a Western glass or mug, the cow horn is still very recognisably an African artifact. Fubah observed that 'most Bambui youth see the cow-horn drinking cup as an affirmation of their ethnic background'. At the same time, it is a way to resist the old values of the titleholders. While doing his fieldwork, Fubah met young men who no longer respected the old prestige of the traditional elite and who questioned whether it was even worth being a titleholder with a buffalo cup when it did not automatically lead to riches.

The Bruce Lee cow-horn drinking cups have the added advantage of being much easier to use than the old buffalo horns. The problem with drinking from a horn is that – like an ice cream cone – the end is so sharp and pointy that you can never put it down, unless you have a person who is prepared to act as a cup holder for you. (I was a frequent cone holder for my children when they ate ice cream.) Because these buffalo horns are so bound up with tradition, the design could not be changed without altering their value. By contrast, the carvers of the Bruce Lee horns thought to add little coiled snakes at the bottom to make them stand up easily on a flat surface. This design modification proved hugely popular. Pa Mandzie told Fubah that he believed these standable bottoms were the main reason he had increased his sales of drinking horns from 750 in 2006 to 1,200 in 2010. In addition to the Bruce Lee horns, Pa Mandzie crafts cow-horn cups carved with flowers or messages such as 'Happy birthday', which make them useful as gifts.

The appeal of the Bruce Lee cow drinking horn is now so great that even some of those entitled to use a buffalo version prefer to drink from one. Given that buffalo are so rare they are now only found in conservation areas, the rising prestige of cow horns – which are obtained as a by-product of the beef industry – has wider ecological benefits. Fubah spoke to another of his cousins, who confided that he had actually sold his once-valuable buffalo drinking horn several years earlier. He said that the aesthetic was 'outdated'. Instead he used a Bruce Lee horn because it was 'the pride of youth and commoners' to drink from such a vessel.

I can't imagine a world in which a drinking horn was the thing I most cared about. But it isn't hard to relate to the notion that certain tools and utensils can make you feel more powerful than others. I don't have a spear. But what I do have is a couple of my mother's old wooden spoons, and when I hold them I stand up taller and feel safer. When I stir with one of these spoons I remember how brave she was and how patient. She did not mind waiting for a white sauce to thicken or for a stew to tenderise. She cooked for us every day even when our father mocked her cooking. These spoons are shields, not swords, and they make me feel I can take on the world, even if all I am doing is making soup.

The Mushroom Canisters

> 'You do not mock people's things any more than you
> mock their weight or accent or sexual orientation.'

> Janet Malcolm, 2017

When I started writing about food, a long time ago, I naively thought that there might be such a thing as 'good taste' in kitchen tools which everyone would agree upon. But I came to see that tastes in kitchenware varied even more wildly than tastes in food. From plastic egg poachers to avocado slicers, there was no item of culinary design so outmoded that it lacked defenders. After a few of these conversations, I realised that expressing even a mild disapproval of any particular food preparation device was a surprisingly quick way to cause offence. It was like being inadvertently rude about someone's mother.

One person's symbol of bad taste may be another person's fond image of home. This was a lesson that the American political broadcaster Rachel Maddow learned in 2014 when she assumed her audience would agree with her that a certain set of canisters was a symbol of bad taste. Maddow made fun of a Republican candidate called Sharron Angle for posing with a cup of coffee in her hand in a 'folksy kitchen scene' with 'a really hideous, complete set of kitchen canisters' decorated with mushrooms. Maddow doubled down on her mockery of the canisters, describing them as 'a full set of mushroom-ornamented, baby-poop-coloured, made-in-China ugly canisters'.

Maddow's wider point was nothing to do with kitchenware. The overall thrust of her critique of Angle was about some wild remarks Angle had made about guns during an unsuccessful campaign to become Senator of Nevada. Angle had stated that if the vote didn't go her way and the Democrat candidate won, the people might look to 'Second Amendment remedies'. The Second Amendment is the right to bear arms. A couple of months after losing the race, Angle posed in the kitchen with the canisters. By mocking the mushroom canisters, what Maddow was really trying to do was point out the chutzpah of a politician using folksy ceramics to rebrand herself so soon after calling for American voters to resort to guns when a vote didn't go her way. To much of Maddow's audience, however, what came through loudest was that she was being mean about their cherished mushroom canisters.

Still more than beauty, ugliness is in the eye of the beholder. On the next night's show, Maddow offered a full-blown apology and correction for having gone 'a little too far' about the canisters. In the twenty-four hours since the first show had aired, her producers had been inundated with 'mushroom love and appreciation'. Maddow read out some of the tweets and letters. People wrote angrily to say that these canisters were not ugly but 'cute', 'adorable' and 'awesome'. They reminisced about family members who owned a complete matching set.

In a brilliant analysis in *The New Yorker* of Maddow's drama with the mushroom canisters, Janet Malcolm observed that the incident 'betrayed [Maddow's] youth' because she had not yet learned that it wasn't done to be rude about other people's stuff. Malcolm went on: ' "Have nothing in your houses that you do not know to be useful, or believe to be beautiful," William Morris wrote in his

famous dictum. Morris knew very well what was hideous. But he knew enough about human nature to insert that "believe".'

Maddow herself made a slightly different distinction at the end of her apology, suggesting that a canister might be ugly in one context but beautiful in another:

> Yes, I once believed that those mushroom canisters were
> hideous . . . I also do still kind of think they're hideous here at
> my office, but in real life on your shelf on your kitchen counter,
> in the recesses of your childhood memories, the Merry
> Mushroom canisters your mom bought at Sears in the 1970s
> which also happen to match your Merry Mushroom curtains?
> Those mushroom canisters really aren't hideous. They are lovely.

Mushroom canisters were never a craze in the UK, where I grew up, and from the outside such phenomena are always mystifying. How could a storage jar decorated with cutesy mushrooms inspire such strong emotions (both positive and negative)? I learned that the Merry Mushroom range was sold by Sears from 1970 to 1986. For much of the twentieth century, Sears was a retailer so successful that it was simply 'the place where America shopped', as its own tagline had it. Sears, Roebuck, as it was originally called, started off in the 1880s as a watch company but soon expanded to sell everything from ovens to guitars.

Along with canister sets, the Merry Mushroom range would eventually swell to more than 250 products including a bacon rack, a popcorn popper, a cheese board in three variations, a sprinkling can, a slow cooker in eight variations and two variations of fondue set. The Merry Mushroom range is so adored by some Americans that items change hands for huge amounts. In 2023, a Merry Mushroom ice cooler was advertised at an online marketplace for more than $1,000. I managed to find a pair of small Merry Mushroom salt and pepper shakers online; almost everything else I saw for sale was too expensive. I tried to see their charms but lacking any personal associations with the design, I drew a blank.

I was wondering why mushrooms, of all things, should briefly have become one of the most popular emblems for kitchenware among Americans when a friend mentioned she knew someone called Maeve Sheridan, whose mother had owned a set of Merry Mushroom canisters when Maeve was growing up in the 1980s. I emailed Maeve and asked if she would tell me more about them. She explained that for anyone of her age or older in the USA (she was born in 1977), the canisters were so ubiquitous that they were just 'a part of your life'. She couldn't think of a single school friend in the suburbs of Washington DC, where she grew up, who didn't have a set of the canisters on their counters in the mid-1980s. They were so much part of the scenery, it was as if the very idea of canisters was inextricably linked with mushrooms. 'I feel like we all had them and then suddenly they just weren't there,' Maeve said. She remembered that at some point in the 1980s there was a sudden lurch away from the lurid browns and swirling patterns of 1970s fashions. 'The styles shifted pretty dramatically and people put [the canisters] away.'

Maeve is a prop stylist in New York City, mostly working on cookbooks and other food shoots. She therefore has a better sense than most people of how fast styles in kitchenware can change. If you don't know what a prop stylist does, consider the props department on a film and imagine someone doing the same for a cookbook. Next time you see a professional photo of a tomato salad on an especially beautiful oval metal platter or some wontons artfully arranged half on a plate and half on a floury board, know that the platter and the plate and the board will all have been chosen by someone like Maeve.

When I asked Maeve what the mushroom canisters meant to her when she was a child, she says that she found them 'cartoonish' and that they reminded her of the Smurfs. They had a forest feel, which she found 'comforting'. Now, when she looks back, the canisters mostly remind her of her mother. Maeve's mother was unusual in that she bought the melamine version of the canisters, which were much sleeker and flatter than the classic ceramic ones that most of her friends had. Maeve's mother used hers for baking goods such as flour, sugar and oats, but the bigger ceramic canisters of her friends' mothers functioned as cookie jars. With a touch of pride in her voice at her mother's choice, Maeve calls the melamine variation 'more contemporary' than the more ubiquitous ceramic ones.

The original ceramic mushroom canisters came in sets of four, of varying sizes. The body of the container curved like a mushroom stalk and the lid was a brown mushroom cap, topped with a neon-orange mushroom for a handle. Bulging out in bas-relief on the side of the canister were a cluster of toadstool-like mushrooms in tones of brown, yellow and orange on an off-white background. Selling points for the Merry Mushroom range in the Spring/Summer Sears catalogue of 1973 were that 'it SPARKLES because it's kiln-glazed' and that 'all ceramic pieces are imported from Japan' (so much for Maddow's 'made-in-China' jibe).

Part of the appeal of the Merry Mushroom is that it is a hippie-ish design made over into something cosier for Middle America. When the Merry Mushroom kitchen sets were first launched, the bosses at Sears had no idea how popular this would be. The design was dreamed up by Jack Buchanan, the firm's homewares buyer. His boss told him to devise a new ceramic pattern to ring the changes from the usual fruit and flowers. According to Buchanan himself in a talk he gave to a local library when he was in his nineties, he went into his backyard, where he suddenly pictured a mushroom talking to him. He told the mushroom it wasn't pretty enough to be on his canisters, at which the mushroom supposedly replied, in a squeaky voice: 'If you would just take me out of this dark corner I would become beautiful.' Buchanan searched for other mushrooms in popular culture for inspiration before settling on the psychedelic mushroom stickers that were popular at the time among Volkswagen drivers. Buchanan took the groovy VW mushroom and sent it to the manufacturer in Japan, asking them to do 'an extreme makeover'.

Buchanan's boss liked the mushroom design well enough but did not see much sales potential. He refused Buchanan's plea for Merry Mushroom to have a double-page spread in the Sears catalogue. Instead it was given just one page, with the other side featuring a similar range of ceramic canisters featuring blue butterflies: still kitsch but a much more conventionally 'pretty' image.

Pretty doesn't always win. The brown mushroom canisters outsold the blue butterfly ones four to one and Merry Mushrooms would go on to become 'the largest single [homewares] design' that Sears ever did, according to Buchanan. The first year the Merry Mushroom range was produced (at which point there were twenty product lines), Sears received orders for 50,000 units. There were only 10,000 in circulation. Buchanan asked the manufacturer in Japan to produce and ship the rest as fast as they could. Americans couldn't get enough of cute mushrooms. Jessica Sawinski Couch is a Chicago-based historian who runs a website devoted to Merry Mushrooms and who even wrote a book on the subject (*A Collector's Guide to Merry Mushrooms*, 2020) listing every example ever included in the Sears catalogue. I asked Jessica to explain the appeal of Merry Mushrooms and she wrote back to say that they were 'well-made, glazed with colors that are mellower than the usual 1970s decor, and have a huge variance of items which triggers the "gotta have them all" mentality many of us collectors have'. She added that, to her, these mushroom-decorated designs had a 'kitsch' joy, describing herself as someone with a love of vintage corduroy bell-bottoms and 1970s trucker movies. Jessica doesn't care whether they are fashionable or despised; she loves them for their own sake.

The heyday of the Merry Mushroom coincided with the final glory years for Sears. In 1974, the Sears Tower in Chicago was completed, becoming the tallest building in the world (110 storeys high). It was an impressive achievement, but business analysts questioned whether it was taking money and focus away from what should have been Sears' core business: its retail operations. James Shrager, a professor at the University of Chicago School of Business, commented in 2018 that from 1969 onwards, 'Sears slowly lost track of its retail business by being fascinated with other things.' Sears failed to keep pace with lower-cost brands such as Walmart and Target, which had moved their largest stores away from shopping malls and into strip malls outside the city centres. Meanwhile, the Merry Mushroom fell out of favour, much to the chagrin of Jack Buchanan, who lamented the fact that 'Sears gave up on it' in 1986 as tastes changed.

It is the way of things for each new generation to reject the aesthetics of the one that came before. We may not have had Merry Mushrooms in the UK, but there were many gems in my mother's kitchen which I callously deemed passé as soon as I left home. She had small blunt knives; I favoured large sharp ones. Her oven gloves were chintzy and patterned; mine were plain. Her lemon squeezer was glass; I bought one that was metal (she found metal too cold and industrial).

One of the great virtues of kitchenware, however, is that some of it is durable enough to have more than one life. Ceramics may lurk in an attic for forty years – like Roopa Gulati's dinner service – only to be reclaimed and loved again. As Jack Buchanan said, 'Merry Mushrooms never die, they just show up on eBay.' A lot of the items feature at garage sales, where they find surprising new love from teenagers, some of whom see mushroom designs as so uncool that they are cool again. Jessica Sawinksi Couch tells me that the new cult of Merry Mushrooms is part of the 'cyclical' nature of homeware trends, comparing their new popularity to the way in which 1960s sofas with exposed wooden arms covered in 'scratchy' fabric are now celebrated as 'Grandma couches' though they were once denounced as ugly.

When we spoke in 2024, Maeve Sheridan told me that recently, for the very first time, she had used the Merry Mushroom as a prop in one of her photoshoots, for a new baking book. The author had told Maeve she was interested in an aesthetic called 'cottagecore', which has been in style among some young people since around 2018: a mix of a foresty vibe with something chintzy, cosy and old-fashioned. Cottagecore celebrates a slightly kitsch and fairy-tale version of country living: a look which might once have been condemned as cutesy or twee. Cottagecore is related to other movements such as 'gnomecore' and 'grandmacore'. Mushrooms are one of the main motifs in 'cottagecore' because of their nostalgic associations with foraging and folklore. The mushroom canister felt like a perfect fit, and as a backdrop to one of the bakes Maeve included a Merry Mushrooms canister 'peeking in', ready to prove once more that not everyone found them hideous.

Gifts

The Glory Box

'The three obligations: To give, to receive,
to make a return.'

Marcel Mauss, 1925

Although I knew that weddings and presents go together, I was
still startled, when the time came, by how much stuff people gave us
simply because we were getting married. Most of it arrived a week
before the actual wedding, at a big pre-wedding party we'd agreed
to in deference to my ex's mother, who felt that the wedding itself
was going to be too small. After the party, I remember sitting on
the floor in the home we had only just started sharing, surrounded
by boxes, feeling as celebrated and adored as I imagined the most
popular child in the class must feel after his or her birthday party.
There was another emotion, too. I felt mildly undeserving of this
mass of carefully chosen offerings – most of them from his parents'
friends and distant relations, people I had never met; and some
from friends of my parents whom I scarcely knew.

A generous hoard of brand-new treasures now surrounded me,
tokens of my new existence as a wife. A terracotta chicken brick, a
knife sharpener, silver photograph frames, a food processor, multiple
pans and serving bowls, several handsome cookbooks, beautiful
glasses (sadly long since smashed). Despite my gratitude, I couldn't
shake the feeling that it was all too much; and misdirected. We were
the lucky ones – if presents had to be given, shouldn't they have gone

to people who would have benefited more? Why don't we give deluxe drinking glasses to the lovesick and the lonely rather than to couples so wrapped up in each other that they would happily drink from an old shoe?

I now see that I didn't understand much about gifts back then, especially in relation to weddings. I had made the mistake of thinking that the friends of my fiancé's parents were giving us these domestic riches freely and spontaneously, purely out of kindness. In fact, they were playing their part in a patchwork of social obligations which had only a little to do with us personally. We were obliged to accept these items in order to maintain relations between our parents and their circles of friends. This is not to deny the thoughtfulness of the people who gave us gifts but to suggest that their personal acts of generosity took place in a wider social structure.

Giving gifts – unlike paying taxes – looks voluntary. But it can actually be a costly duty, not least at weddings. In his groundbreaking work *The Gift*, the French theorist Marcel Mauss laid out the ways in which ceremonial gift-giving, particularly in Polynesia, becomes part of a vast cycle of social exchange which places strong obligations both on those who receive as well as those who give. Mauss writes of 'The three obligations: To give, to receive, to make a return.'

The name Mauss gives to this system of giving and receiving is the 'potlatch'. When it comes to the ritual gift-giving of the potlatch, there are no free gifts. In Mauss's observation there was something almost 'magical' about a gift, because the giver is actually donating a part of themselves, an act which creates a social bond with strong obligations to reciprocate. Through the gift, the giver retains a 'hold over the recipient'. In numerous societies, Mauss found that to refuse either to give or to receive a gift was 'tantamount to declaring war' because it was a rejection of 'the bond of alliance and communality'.

My fiancé and I wouldn't have minded in the slightest if people had come to our party without a present. But in Mauss's terms, a wedding gift is not about what the couple themselves want as individuals. It is about the givers maintaining and burnishing their honour, sometimes from one generation unto the next. In modern-day Japan, writes anthropologist Katherine Rupp, it is 'not uncommon' for 'close friends to agree not to invite each other to their children's weddings' as an act of kindness to spare them the sheer burden of 'their giving obligations'.

The boxes of lovely artifacts that arrived during the week of my wedding in the 1990s were a very toned-down version of the exchange rituals that have accompanied weddings since ancient times. Among the Polynesian and Melanesian tribes studied by Mauss, gift-giving morphed into a form of crazed rivalry: 'a competition to see who is the richest and also the most madly extravagant', in Mauss's words. An unreciprocated present would make the person who accepted it 'inferior'. To be the most generous one was a mark of power, honour and superiority.

Among the tribes of the Solomon Islands in the early twentieth century, wedding presents were the most highly ritualised of all offerings, as observed through fieldwork by the Australian anthropologist Ian Hogbin. If you were the bride, your family was expected to give *taro* pudding (*taro* being a starchy vegetable) and receive coconuts in return. For the groom's family, it was reversed: they gave dried fish and coconuts and in return the bride's family would give them *taro* pudding, in a proportionate amount to the coconuts. Unfairly, the man's gift counted for more than the woman's, regardless of how delicious or large the *taro* pudding might be. A father who gave his daughter-in-law's family a particularly large amount of coconuts could gain prestige, but the bride's parents' donation of *taro* pudding could never win prestige and was never remarked upon.

These rituals may seem a world away from how we go about weddings – or indeed, gift-giving – in the West. But although the

rules of Western 'potlatches' may be different from those of traditional Polynesian societies, a wedding is still an occasion when the
usual rules of giving become vastly inflated.

Of all the staging points of a human life, a wedding is the most
universally associated with gifts; and specifically with kitchen
items. The Mass-Observation archive in Britain – a social research
project based at the University of Sussex designed to document
everyday life – shows that from the late 1930s to the late 1990s, gift-
giving was a central feature of British weddings. As historian
Louise Purbrick writes, 'With almost no exceptions, whatever the
type of wedding, civil or religious, large or small, there was a gift.'
One Glasgow couple got married with just two witnesses and
asked the witnesses not to give them anything, but they still did:
two crystal glasses.

One of the functions of a gift is to make the object given more
valued than it would otherwise be. A wedding gift is doubly hallowed, because it is associated with what is supposed to be 'the
happiest day of your life'. Until the mid-twentieth century, a staple of
life in Australia was something called the 'glory box': a chest-like
container kept by young women in anticipation of their marriage.
(The phrase seems to have been naively unconnected with the term
'glory hole', another phrase in use at the time, which could either
mean an untidy drawer or a vagina.) A 'glory box' – sometimes
called a 'trousseau' – would contain an assortment of goods that the
woman had made herself, such as hand-embroidered tablecloths,
and donations from others, such as kitchenware or cutlery. It might
also contain beautiful nightgowns and underwear, in anticipation of
the wedding night, suggesting that silverware and lacy underwear
were all part of a single feminine package. The glory box was a
throwback to the centuries-old European tradition of the dowry,
according to which a bride's father was expected to contribute a certain number of goods to the marriage.

A typical glory box might contain gifts of cake forks and crystal bowls; tea sets and enamel pie dishes. Women – and their female relatives – spent a long time collecting many of these items for themselves, sometimes from childhood onwards. As for the box itself, it could be anything from a fancy wooden chest or veneer sideboard to an old cardboard carton. Some of the specially made glory boxes for sale in Australian department stores bore the names of film stars: the 'Ginger Rogers' glory box or the 'Judy Garland'. The glory box was supposed to contain a capsule of the household possessions a woman might need as she embarked on married life. In America, the glory box was aptly named the 'hope chest'. These boxes illustrate the extent to which kitchenware can become a repository of a person's hopes and dreams.

One glory box belonging to a woman who got married in the 1940s contained:

Linen, glass dishes, tea set of six cups, saucers and plates (all items bought by the woman herself)

Supper cloth, set of six canisters, enamel pie dishes and plates, salt and pepper shakers (all items given to her by others)

In 2009, an Australian academic called Moya McFadzean interviewed a group of seventeen women in Melbourne, many of them immigrants, who had received or created glory boxes for their weddings between the 1930s and the 1950s. McFadzean found that for many of them the glory box became a box of emotions as well as things. Many of the women (who came from working- or lower-middle-class families) spoke of using the glory box to get exactly the household accessories they wanted for their future lives. A woman called Betty Phillips had always wanted a kitchen decorated in cream and cherry colours and was thrilled when her fiancé gave her a cream-and-cherry-coloured biscuit barrel.

'A trousseau to last a lifetime' was the strapline of an advert for Irish linen in *The Australian Women's Weekly* in 1954. The idea of a glory box was that everything in it – from flour sieves to doilies and pillowcases – should be special. Sometimes the contents of the glory box – like Roopa Gulati's parents' dinner service – were almost too special to use. A woman called Val told McFadzean that she had a beautiful damask tablecloth as one of the 'luxuries' in her glory box, but it did her no good because she never had the right occasion to use it personally – she just loaned it out to friends to use at their weddings.

Many of the women interviewed by McFadzean described the great lengths their mothers and grandmothers went to in order to ensure that the contents of their boxes were of the finest quality. Carmel Tata came from an Italian family and her mother travelled 'to the cities' to purchase the pots and pans for her box because those on sale in her village were not of the same quality.

Eventually, the tradition of the glory box died out in Australia, along with the vision of femininity it embodied. Feminists of the 1960s questioned the idea that the ultimate goal of a woman's life should be to marry. McFadzean writes that for her own mother in the 1970s, a glory box symbolised all the 'constrictions' she was working to throw off. Meanwhile, the growth of mass-produced domestic goods meant that it no longer made as much sense to spend years meticulously assembling a box of household items. You don't need to hoard salt and pepper shakers in a veneer box when you can buy them for a dollar or two anytime you like.

For Australian women of an earlier generation, however, the contents of a glory box could represent not constriction but a rare fragment of riches in lives that were hemmed in on all sides. When speaking of their glory boxes, the women interviewed by McFadzean, all of whom were married to men on modest incomes, repeatedly spoke of them containing 'nice things'. They told her that getting pieces for the glory box – whether they were given to them by others or collected by themselves – felt like the only chance they might ever have to get nice things: a window of opportunity between financial dependence on their parents as a child and financial dependence on their husband as a wife.

To Kath Davis, an Australian woman who was born in 1921 and married in 1944, the glory box represented freedom. She remembered thinking that she 'wanted to escape' life at home and how marvellous it would be to 'use all my own things' when she did. Kath's marriage ended in divorce, yet her attachment to her glory box remained and she continued to care for the wooden box and the items it contained long afterwards. These included beautiful crystal glasses, a dinner service decorated with flowers, a fluffy tea cosy and a sweet blue and white scone holder which she had made for herself.

Sometimes, just knowing that an object is a gift is enough to make it feel precious, which may in turn make the recipient feel precious. I felt a little of this while sitting on the floor surrounded by boxes, about to commit myself to another person for the rest of my life. The psychologist Susan Isaacs observed in the 1930s that among young children, being offered a gift makes the recipient feel 'loveworthy'. When I met my ex-husband aged nineteen, my self-esteem was low. Often I felt inadequate, self-loathing and ugly. I excelled at schoolwork but felt hollow inside. Maybe this was connected to the fact that my father had left when I was fourteen. He remarried when I was seventeen and I never felt at home in his new house.

More than my previous boyfriends, my ex-husband helped me to feel better about myself. It was a balm to eat meals together and to feel that I wasn't being judged for what I ate or didn't eat; to know that he thought I was beautiful regardless. Getting married at twenty-three was crazily young, I now think. As much as I pretended I didn't need any presents and spoke of being a feminist, it actually gave me a boost to be using my new food processor, drinking from my sparkling-new glasses. At some level, these offerings felt like proof of my worth. I thought that getting married would make everything all right. And for so many years, it really did. His arms felt as safe and solid as the kitchen table.

A fifty-year-old female factory worker from Lowestoft in the east of England who got married in 1968 told the Mass-Observation project that she had kept and cherished every gift she received at her wedding. She commented that 'Some of the Pyrex dishes I have yet to use. But I still keep them. I wouldn't part with them for the world.'

Burial Plates

> 'they accustomed to burn or bury with them things
> wherein they excelled, delighted, or which were dear
> unto them'
>
> Thomas Browne, 1658

If there are gifts to the living, there are also gifts to the dead. Throughout history, the dead have been buried with 'grave goods': assets to take with them to the next life. Many of these have taken the form of pottery or other food-related utensils or indeed of actual food. In his classic 1658 book on urn burial, the doctor Thomas Browne wrote of the 'lasting pieces and toys' contained in tombs: the intimate treasures given to the dead by the living. A grave good is a very curious and self-sacrificing type of offering: the recipient can never thank the giver or use the object, no matter how carefully chosen it is.

In eighteenth- and nineteenth-century England, the dead were sometimes buried with a blue and white plate: a piece of home in a place of death. We know this because of the construction of HS2, a new high-speed rail line due to run between London and Birmingham. In 2017, teams of archaeologists began to dig up thousands of bodies from several Victorian burial grounds in England on land where the new rail lines would go. The displacement and reburial of these bodies is just one of the reasons why HS2 has been such a controversial project. For British archaeologists, however, this ambitious rail project has been a valuable chance to discover things about the past that would otherwise have remained hidden, including the surprising discovery of blue and white plates in some of the coffins.

'It is rare to find objects of any type with eighteenth- and nineteenth-century burials,' writes Beth Richardson, one of the archaeologists analysing the HS2 burial grounds. It is rarer still to find any artifacts buried with the poor. Yet at St James's Gardens in London alone, where the burials date from 1788 to 1853, there were around 5,200 'finds': things belonging to people of humble backgrounds as well as wealthier people. All kinds of personal possessions were found inside these coffins. Some were part of the outfit of the person who died, such as wedding rings, brooches, necklaces and gold pocket watches. There were also articles related to a person's interests and occupation in life, such as a hammer, a glass paperweight, thimbles, knives, scissors, a pestle and mortar or a child's spinning top. And then there were goods of a different nature, such as figurines and crucifixes, as well as ceramic vessels and plates.

Twelve blue and white ceramic plates were found in graves in London and Birmingham (as well as a blue plate in a 'Verona' pattern also found by HS2 archaeologists in a coffin in Blackburn in Lancashire). Some of the plates were decorated with Willow Pattern – a traditional and hugely popular British design which was a cheapened Western pastiche of Chinese porcelain. These plates were called 'china', in recognition of their Asian origins; and they leaned heavily on traditional Japanese and Chinese imagery. But there was nothing Chinese about them.

Willow Pattern plates were first produced by the Spode factory in Staffordshire in the north of England in 1790, but were eventually copied by all of Spode's rivals such as Wedgwood, Worcester and Derby and became as much a feature of British life as eating marmalade for breakfast. What became the standard version of the pattern

depicts three figures on a bridge, one figure on a boat, two flying birds, a far-off island, a pagoda-like house and a weeping willow tree. Behind the pagoda is a giant orange tree, laden with fruits so fat and round they could be balloons. When I was a child eating my dinner off Willow Pattern, this orange tree with its joyous fruits was the part that always caught my eye. It looked so luscious.

Many people know the story behind the Willow Pattern plate. It is a tale of forbidden love between a poor man and the daughter of a wealthy mandarin. The mandarin has arranged for his daughter to marry a duke, in exchange for some jewels, but she doesn't love him. The poor man (Chang) steals the jewels and runs off with the girl to a far-off island. When the mandarin finds out where the couple have gone he sends three of his henchmen to kill them – the henchmen are the three men on the bridge. After their deaths the gods turn the two lovers into doves – these are the birds on the plate, who look as if they are moving in to kiss each other.

Unfortunately, this Willow Pattern story – which was first published in *Family Friend* in 1849 – is a total fake. I don't just mean that it's fiction, but that it was invented decades after the original Spode Willow Pattern plate was designed. The bridge on which the henchmen were supposed to be pursuing the couple was not even there in the original 1790 china design (it was only added by Spode in 1810). The love story attached to the design is not so much a backstory as a spin-off, which is notable mainly for its title: 'The Story of the Common Willow Pattern Plate'. The most important word here is common. The most remarkable thing about Willow Pattern – and other forms of blue and white china – is that by 1849 it had stopped being an aspirational luxury good, as it had been for hundreds of years, and had become common, among the most everyday and universal of all possessions in Britain.

When blue and white ceramics were first made in China

during the Tang dynasty (618–906), each piece was hand-crafted and hand-painted. The cobalt ore needed to make the blue pigment under the glaze was extremely expensive because at the time it could only be sourced from Central Asia. In medieval times, blue and white wares were prestige objects in China, associated with the imperial palace – certainly not a cheap purchase that a poor person could afford to toss into a grave.

Over the centuries, the price of blue and white china came down as the Chinese learned how to produce lower-quality 'export porcelain' for a European market. Meanwhile, in the seventeenth century, Dutch and English potters made 'Delftware': an affordable imitation of Chinese blue and white pottery glazed with tin. These cheaper ceramics found many willing buyers in Britain, not least because of the nation's love of tea and coffee. Classic Delftware pieces included coffee pots, teapots and cocoa pots.

As early as the mid-eighteenth century, when most ceramics were still being imported either from China or the Netherlands, nearly a third of all people in the city of Bristol, rich and poor, owned some form of china. But mass ownership of blue and white plates (and teacups and jugs and all the rest) only took off in England after the rise of the Staffordshire potteries in the late eighteenth century.

From the 1750s onwards, a technique called 'transferware' meant that beautiful blue and white china plates could be produced far more quickly and cheaply than ever before. What the printing press did for books, transferware did for pottery. Instead of each plate being hand-painted it could be batch-made, using an engraved metal plate to add pigment to a piece of paper, which then transferred the pattern onto the ceramic before it was fired. Thanks to transferware, a design as intricate as a Willow Pattern plate was no longer the preserve of the wealthy. Almost anyone could now afford one (which partly explains why wealthier customers started to shun

Willow Pattern and move on to other, less familiar designs). The author of the 1849 article wrote that Willow Pattern was 'mingled with our earliest recollections; it is like the picture of an old friend and companion whose portrait we see everywhere, but of whose likeness we never grow weary'.

The puzzle remains: why would someone put one of these blue and white plates on top of a dead person in a coffin? Scholars have long brooded over the meaning of grave goods and why they are placed among the dead. Archaeologists have come up with a whole range of reasons. Depending on the culture the dead person was part of, and their place in it, these grave gifts might be:

Marks of rank or prestige (the Frankish leader Childeric was buried with a golden sword, two hundred rubies and three hundred golden bees)

A piece of bodily decoration (such as jewellery, fine clothes or shells)

Things for personal use (such as tweezers or a knife; Cardinal Farnese was buried with two spoons)

A protective charm to keep the person safe from evil (think of the amulets with which Egyptian mummies were buried)

Something to help the person travel to the afterlife (Anglo-Saxons were sometimes buried with footwear or small model boats)

A magical substance to promote rebirth (such as white pebbles, red ochre or phallic symbols of various kinds)

Equipment for the afterlife (things to help the dead to cook and eat and keep warm, such as flints and knives and various pieces of food; there is a long Yorkshire tradition of being buried with ham)

Broken objects to set the spirit free

Since ancient times, there was a persistent belief that the spirit of the dead person could only be set free through breaking some of their possessions. As late as 1890, a Lincolnshire widow said that she had to 'dead' her husband's jug and mug to 'release their spirits' and allow them to go with him. Pieces of ceramics, carefully arranged round a gravestone, were a regular feature of slave funerals in nineteenth-century America. The art historian Robert Farris Thompson noted that whereas white graves in South Carolina were covered with 'stark plots of grass', Black graves would often be ornately decorated with 'bleached sea-shells, broken glassware, soap dishes, coffee cups'. Thompson saw this as 'art for the dead'. The use of fragments of ceramics echoed the funeral practices of the Bakongo people of modern West Africa, where many of the slaves of South Carolina had been taken from. An ex-slave from Georgia, Jane Lewis, said that the reason for decorating a grave with dishes and bottles was to help 'the spirit to feel at home'. For Thompson, the purpose of arranging beautiful museums of broken things round a person's grave was as the 'distillation of a life'.

Some of this same sense of care for the dead seems to have been at work in the blue and white plates placed in those coffins in London and Birmingham. Archaeologist Beth Richardson notes that the plates most likely held salt, as a deterrent against the devil. There was a tradition dating back at least to the seventeenth century of placing a plate of salt over the chest of a dead person to keep them safe but also, as the antiquarian John Brand wrote in 1795, as 'an emblem of the immortal spirit'. As James Frazer noted, this custom was widespread 'amongst the poorest classes'. Usually the plate of salt would be removed before the coffin was closed, but sometimes it was left there, either accidentally or on purpose. Beth Richardson notes that many of the blue and white plates have been found 'with children and young women', and possibly the mourners forgot to remove them because 'their untimely deaths were so deeply mourned'.

Giving a dead person a blue and white plate to protect them makes perfect sense, if you ask me. My mother died in October 2022. I was lucky enough to be there with her in the room of her care home, holding her hand when her breathing finally stopped, a moment for which I will always be grateful. Minutes before our mother died, I put her on the phone to my sister in the States and she smiled at hearing her voice. I rang my sister back to tell her the news. Even though we both knew it was coming, and even though it was a mercy to know that she was finally liberated from dementia, we both found it a shock to realise that this was the end. There were to be no loopholes, no changing her mind, no going back to the shop and asking to exchange it. 'This is a very extreme thing she has done,' my sister said. 'So unlike her.'

The nurse who had been looking after her at the end asked me to choose an outfit for the funeral home to dress her in before she was cremated. I picked out a green corduroy dress and her favourite necklace and some underwear. Something was missing. 'She needs thick tights!' I said to the nurse. 'She always gets so cold.' That was when I broke down, realising that she would never be cold again. Or rather, that she would always be cold.

My sister and I spent ages choosing the bouquet of flowers to go on top of the coffin when she was cremated. Like Marianne Dashwood in *Sense and Sensibility*, she preferred wild flowers to anything too showy or artificial. I found a florist who made her a bouquet of locally grown English blooms in subtle pinks and whites. If only I'd thought of it, I would have asked the funeral home to put one of her beloved blue and white plates with her in the coffin – she favoured Spode Blue Italian over Willow Pattern – in the hope of keeping her safe for whatever would come next.

The Unwanted Tureen

'Parents spend years and years demanding from
their offspring the saying of "thank you".'

Margaret Visser, 2008

For more years than I can remember, I had two Wedgwood lidded
vegetable tureens in a Kutani Crane design. They took up a substantial section of one of my kitchen cupboards even though I
never served anything from them. I longed to use that cupboard
space for something else. Yet somehow I could neither persuade
myself to use these tureens nor get rid of them.

The Kutani Crane range – which was produced for twenty-
seven years from 1971 to 1998 – is made of fine bone china. The
word 'Kutani' means Nine Valleys and refers to an area in Japan.
The pattern echoes the Imari designs of nineteenth-century Japan.
It features a delicate bird (a crane) with turquoise and purple feathers surrounded by multicoloured floral arrangements with a peony
elegance. It's all done in muted hues of greens, pinks, browns and
blues against a white backdrop.

Kutani Crane is one of Wedgwood's most distinctive late-
twentieth-century designs and second-hand pieces still sell well. A
print advert for it from 1986 showed a plate of smoked salmon (still
a luxury food back then) and a bowl containing wedges of lemon.
'When your boat comes in' was the strapline. 'When it does, you'll
be able to treat yourself to Kutani Crane fine bone china.'

My Kutani Crane tureens came to me from my father, who in turn received them from his parents. As I've mentioned, his own father, Norman Wilson, was the works manager and later production director at Wedgwood from 1927 onwards. Although Norman had retired from Wedgwood by the time the Kutani Crane pattern was launched in 1971, he had a passion for this particular design and bought a lot of it to give to his three children (my father, uncle and aunt) and well as for himself. By the time Norman died in 1985 there were a huge number of Kutani Crane plates, cups, saucers, teapots, tureens and serving dishes in the family.

Many people consider Kutani Crane to be some of the loveliest china you can eat your dinner off. The problem is that these people do not include my father, uncle or aunt. After my grandmother died in 2003, my father gave me some of his unwanted Kutani Crane plates, cups and saucers, as well as the two tureens and various serving platters. Around the same time, my mother gave me the Kutani Crane plates that my father had left behind after the divorce. A few years later, my uncle and aunt gave me still more of it. I became known as the person in the family who really liked Kutani Crane. But perhaps I was just the person incapable of voicing her true desires.

As a child, I had an eccentric passion for patterned china. I grew up in Oxford and at weekends I regularly went by myself to the Ashmolean Museum specifically to look at the ceramics. These rooms were usually deserted, because most visitors to the museum felt that china was boring compared to paintings or Egyptian artefacts. To me it was never boring because each set of china represented its own little universe. There were cream boats and butter dishes; pickle plates and sweetmeat dishes. Many of the plates with Chinese designs featured people: a mandarin with a bowl of giant citrus fruits; a woman breastfeeding her baby; a traveller carrying a bundle on a stick. Other plates were pure colour and texture.

There was a cake plate in a deep azure blue with an uneven orange-peel surface and a gilt edge which I loved to look at. I would stare at all the different tea and dinner services and fantasise about which one I would choose if I were a rich person in the eighteenth century. There was a sulphur-yellow 'cabaret' set from 1770–72 decorated with sprays of blue flowers with which I was particularly taken. A cabaret is a tea or coffee set which comes with its own porcelain tray. If there are two cups it is called a 'tête-à-tête'; a one-cup cabaret is a 'solitaire'.

I especially loved the Marshall Collection: a vast collection of hand-painted Worcester porcelain. It was donated to the museum by Mr and Mrs Henry Marshall in memory of their son, who died in the Second World War, on the condition that the collection should always be displayed in its entirety. After his son's death, Henry Marshall threw himself into collecting Worcester porcelain as a 'distraction and solace' from his son's death, according to his wife. His collection consists of more than 1,000 pieces of eighteenth-century porcelain. Like Kutani Crane, many of the Worcester designs feature birds and flowers, but to my eyes these Worcester birds had far more character and life. There were quails and finches; owls and geese; cockerels and extravagantly plumed pheasants.

Some objects become more lovable the longer you own them. Others become more tedious and less special with each use until eventually you outgrow them. I felt this way about the Kutani Crane plates. We all ate off them for years and years, yet the repetition only made them dull. This was partly my fault: I put some of the plates in the dishwasher and the pattern faded. But even the pristine vegetable tureens on which the pattern was still perfect did not delight me.

My ex-husband didn't have any opinion on these plates, positive or negative. When we got married he said that all he wanted was some ordinary white plates from Habitat. I was so in love with him that I stifled my former passion for patterned pottery and adopted his way of thinking. When choosing furnishings for the house, he would always say it didn't really matter either way. He didn't set much store by possessions; and I respected him for being so ungrasping and easy-going. But sometimes I looked around and wondered why we seemed to have so many items that neither of us particularly liked. We ended up with a lot of beigey-grey furniture and walls painted in magnolia. Our cupboards were full of stuff we'd been given by his family or by mine, including the Kutani Crane tureens.

'If you don't mind me saying so,' said a friend, 'those plates don't really suit you. They are too fussy.' I realised it was true. Did my Kutani Crane china 'spark joy', to use Marie Kondo's phrase? It did not. It wasn't that there was anything wrong with it. Yet when I looked at these pieces, I saw something dreary rather than cherished. Roopa Gulati's father had taught her that the Braemar plates were the most special thing in the world, whereas my father had taught me that Kutani Crane was unwanted. He left it behind when he left my mother.

It's strange how a piece of china, even one that you don't especially like, can make you feel guilty. Every time I opened the cupboard that contained the Kutani Crane vegetable tureens they made me feel faintly strangled. These dishes had been handed down to me not just by my own father but by his father. When I looked at them I felt weighted down by two generations of filial obligation. I couldn't deny that they were beautifully made. The tureens' handles were scrolled like the edges of a fancy sofa. Many people would have been only too willing to serve their vegetables from them. I must therefore keep them because to do otherwise would be horribly ungrateful.

Unwanted gifts can carry just as much emotional charge as those that are loved; perhaps more so. An unused present invades our space and gives us feelings of resentment, yet it can be strangely hard to give away. An unwanted household gift may not be quite as dramatic as the fatal gifts of Germanic folklore, such as Hagen's cup, which sapped the power of anyone who drank from it. But it can still feel lowering to open a cupboard and see something you never really wanted but which you are reluctant to dispose of lest the giver's imagined feelings be hurt.

The philosopher Jean-Paul Sartre believed that all giving was a form of control, because the recipient had not chosen the thing they were given. Some people deal with this potential loss of control by issuing 'wish-lists' to their loved ones when a birthday comes round. Does this wish-list approach ruin the spirit of gift-giving? You tell me. What I do know is that the loss of control that comes from accepting a present is never felt as acutely as when you never actually wanted the thing you were given.

The problem of unwanted presents is probably nowhere greater than in Japan, which has a culture of gift-giving more extensive than any other advanced capitalist society. Life-cycle events such as births, weddings and funerals come with an expectation not just that the guests should give a gift but that the recipients should immediately reciprocate with a return-gift (*oiwai no okaeshi*), often a household item such as a set of glasses or towels, which may be roughly half the value of the original offering, although sometimes the return-gift is worth even more than the original, which increases the general sense of gifting escalating out of control. The anthropologist Katherine Rupp spent eighteen months of field-work among sixteen Japanese households. One of her interviewees was a Japanese woman called Mrs Ueda, who reported that when the son of some neighbours got married she gave him 30,000 yen. After the marriage, the son brought round a bag containing 30,000 yen worth of gift certificates plus a set of fancy plates. Mrs Ueda was shocked. 'I thought to myself, exactly the same amount of money that I gave to them came back to me, plus a set of plates! What meaning, then, did it have for me to even try to give a gift in the first place?'

In Japan there is an expectation of exchanging items at all manner of seasonal occasions (as well as for no occasion at all). As of 2003, a full 60 per cent of the annual profits of Tokyo department stores was accounted for by purchases of summer and winter gifts: *ochugen* and *oseibo*. Every season has its own allotted gifts. New Year's Day leads in to Coming of Age Day on 15 January and on to Valentine's Day in February and Girl's Day and White Day in March. Boy's Day and Mother's Day are in May, with Father's Day in June and Old People's Day in September.

Nor are these special days the only occasions requiring gifts. A person's obligations to give are so great that parents will often help their children out with the cost of buying all the gifts they will need to give in order to get along at work, well into their twenties and thirties. Presents may be required from a patient to a doctor or between employees and bosses. Mrs Ueda observed that she also received and gave what she called 'meaningless' gifts every day: offerings between friends and neighbours for no discernible reason at all except to oil the wheels of everyday life. These ranged from freshly dug bamboo shoots and other vegetables to bottles of sake and wine and Japanese sweets to household items such as cooking pots and aprons.

The endless exchange of goods in Japan means that many people have houses cluttered with superfluous items which they would dearly love to dispose of but feel they can't. For this reason, many people in Japan prefer to give and receive perishable foodstuffs – premium treats such as perfect melons or luxury seafood – because once they are eaten they are gone. But even food may feel burdensome when it is not wanted. A stockbroker called Mr Tanabe told Katherine Rupp that he had developed an intense dislike of gift-giving and tried to opt out of the whole elaborate exchange. He had invested some stocks for the owner of a bar where he sometimes went after work. Every winter and summer the bar owner sent Mr Tanabe gifts, although he did not reciprocate. Once, writes Katherine Rupp, when the stocks were doing badly, the bar owner sent him a winter gift of some live shrimp. Mr Tanabe refused the shrimp and asked the delivery person to return it to the sender. A day later the package was redelivered to Mr Tanabe; it had not been possible to return it to the sender. Now all the shrimp were dead.

Many of the more durable gifts in Japan take the form of household articles, such as forks or placemats or cups or plates, given in sets of three or five (the number four is considered inauspicious). But how many plates can one household really use? Mrs Tanaka was a housewife in her mid-thirties who lived with her daughter and husband in a new-build house in the city of Nara. Mrs Tanaka complained to Inge Daniels – another anthropologist studying Japanese gift-giving – that she was stuck with a set of ceramic plates passed on by a former teacher of her husband. The teacher had some plates which were not to his taste and he thrust them upon Mr Tanaka, telling him that since he had got married he would now need plates. Mrs Tanaka's husband, she said, was 'in no position to refuse'. His wife was left feeling that these wretched plates were 'something one would want to throw away, but difficult to throw away'.

I could understand how Mrs Tanaka felt. My Kutani Crane tureens were also something I wanted to give away yet felt that I couldn't. In the months after my husband left, I did a lot of thinking about what it means to be a good fit with someone or something. There are many wonderful things and people in this world, but that does not mean that all of them can be *your* things or *your* people. We each have to choose what to let into our little corner of life.

A new thought crept into my head. What if *I* had become the

Kutani Crane in the marriage – something he still valued and felt a duty towards, but not quite enough to keep? Suddenly, I almost admired him for his decisiveness in making the break.

'It's only plates,' I told myself as I finally packed up all of the Kutani Crane, including the tureens, to give it away to a charity shop. 'I can do this.' Once the Kutani Crane was out of the way, I instantly felt better about that cupboard. From now on we were free to eat off china that I actually liked, an assorted mish-mash of vintage plates and mint-green plates and bowls with a glaze I really loved from a modern homeware shop.

To be unwanted by one person is not the same as being universally despised. I had moved the boxes of Kutani Crane into the hallway ready to give away when my fifteen year-old son asked me what I was doing and protested that he really liked these plates. They were what he had always eaten off, he said; and they were nice. I put them away in the attic for when he leaves home, lightened by the thought that the tureens would eventually be valued again, even if not by me.

Sasha's *Budare* Pan

> 'Fewer and fewer Americans possess objects that have a patina, old furniture, grandparents' pots and pans – the used things, warm with generations of human touch, essential to a human landscape.'
>
> Susan Sontag, 1977

One of the strangest parts of dealing with my mother's stuff after she moved to the care home was finding various presents that I had once given to her, things which she now had neither need nor memory of. One year, she had asked me to get her some candlesticks for Christmas. I spent ages weighing the options, before settling on some weighty black ones from a Nordic design company with a minimalist look that I hoped she would like.

When I saw these candlesticks again in her house while clearing it, they looked as lifeless as dust. What was the point of this stupid present if she couldn't be there to use it? My gift had boomeranged back to me and the sight of the candlesticks made me feel annoyance and despair. When she unwrapped them on Christmas morning, she had reacted with pleasure, but was she just being polite? My mind played on self-punishing loops, thinking of other candlesticks she might have found more pleasing. The sombre black was more my taste than hers. Why hadn't I given her some jollier candlesticks made from coloured glass or some nice wooden ones to match her wooden spoons? Now it was too late.

Gifts between a parent and a child are in a category all of their own. They matter both more and less than other presents. Based on Russell Belk's research among seventy-three people in Philadelphia in 1973, such offerings do not come with the usual obligation to return the favour. In most cases, the act of giving is a way of solidifying a relationship, which is why it is so important to reciprocate. But from the first day a parent and a child are already so entwined that, as Belk writes, 'reciprocal gifts' are not necessary for the cycle to continue. Another way of looking at it, Belk suggests, is that when a parent gives something to a child, they pay the parent back with their joy. 'The smile on our child's face puts a heart-felt smile on our own face.'

Kitchenware seems to be one of the main forms of currency between grown-up family members, whether given by a child to a parent or the other way round. What is really being exchanged is an idealised memory of the family dinner table. When a child leaves home, giving them something for the kitchen can be a way to connect them with the meals they have left behind and a rite of passage acknowledging that they are in charge of their own cooking now.

When Sasha Correa left her home in Venezuela for a new life in Spain in 2013, there was one thing her father wanted to give her. He said, 'OK, you are leaving Venezuela, you need a *budare*'. A *budare*, for those who have never seen one, is a flat metal griddle pan. Its main function is for making *arepas*, puffy corn patties which are the staple bread of Venezuela, an accompaniment to any and every meal. I have tried making *arepas* in an ordinary cast-iron pan and they came out pretty well, with a pleasing airiness, like a squishier version of an English muffin. Some modern cooks on the internet say that the air fryer is the perfect thing for making *arepas*. For traditionalists, however, only the *budare* will do.

I already told you about Sasha in the chapter on the 'Casserole

Protests', where I explained that she left Venezuela out of sheer despair about the political system during the era of Chávez and then Maduro: the repression, the corruption, the absence of press freedom, the food shortages and black market economy. The Correas are a close-knit family and Sasha was agonised to leave her mother and father and sisters and nieces, especially since she knew she was leaving them in more difficult life circumstances than the ones she would experience in Spain. Her father's *budare* became an essential link with life at home.

The *budare* that Sasha's father gave her, she told me, was 'a very perfect one, very light [in tone], the colour of scissors', but through daily use it became as black as squid ink and as shiny as marble. It was made of iron and, like other iron pans, only develops its slippery non-stick surface through repeated use, as the oils and fats used for cooking 'polymerise' with the metal. Such a pan gets better the more you use it, assuming you wash it gently. Once you start using a *budare*, Sasha said, 'you can't imagine using anything else'. She uses it not just for making her staple *arepas* but for making corn tortillas and tacos from scratch and sometimes reheating pizza or flatbreads when she is in a hurry.

Sasha is by no means the only person to feel attached to her *budare*. Colombian coffee expert Karen Attman, who has lived in Colombia for twenty years (where *arepas* are also part of the culture), has written about her affection for her *budare*, which over years of use has become 'blackened' and 'bent' like 'the ones you'll see in any other house in Colombia or Venezuela'. Sasha's *budare* meant even more because she was no longer in Venezuela and because her father still was. She was so attached to this particular *budare* that, despite its hefty weight, when she went on holiday she would travel with it in her bag, like a very heavy comfort blanket.

Of all the reasons to cherish a kitchen object – the way it feels in our hand, the way it cuts or cooks or grates, the way it looks on our countertop – perhaps the most powerful is because it was given to us by someone we love. Ruminating again about the black candlesticks, I consoled myself that even if they were not my mother's taste, perhaps it was enough that they came from me. I thought of all the gifts my own children had given me, starting with the misshapen and glittery artworks of toddlerdom. Not long ago, my daughter gave me a mug decorated with a dog, in honour of our family pet. It doesn't match any of our other mugs in size, shape, colour or design. That is why I love it so much. It is a piece of her.

Among the 300 Chicago families studied by Eugene Rochberg-Halton in the late 1970s, 80 per cent of all those interviewed, of all ages, cherished at least one possession 'because it reminded them of a close relative'. One Chicago woman described how important her cups and saucers were to her because they were her mother's wedding gifts, which she had brought with her from England in 1905.

A gift is not just special purely because of what it is. It matters very much *who* gave it to us. As well as being a form of social exchange, gift-giving can clarify how we feel about someone. Almost all of us, whether as giver or as recipient, have had the awkward experience of realising that the thing given was too much for the situation. A girl at school once presented me with a very expensive doll, the kind which a collector rather than a child would buy. It gave me a squirmy feeling. I hadn't realised she thought of me as such a close friend and couldn't begin to think what she expected in return. The next term, she started bullying me.

How much we love a gift (or not) may reflect the quality of our bond with the person who gave it to us. The word 'belonging' has a double meaning. A belonging is a possession, but belonging also refers to close and intimate relationships with people or places. When Sasha Correa talked to me about her *budare*, which she sometimes referred to as her 'precious', two things were clear. First, that she really loved making the *arepas* of her homeland and second, that she really loved her father.

When you love someone, to see a possession associated with them get damaged can feel as if they themselves have been attacked. Sasha warned me that the story of her *budare* was about to become sad. It was about 'when I split up with my Catalan boyfriend', she said. Sasha and this boyfriend had been together for eight years; things were getting serious. His parents were due to visit them in San Sebastián and he paid 'a lady to help with the cleaning' to prepare for their visit while Sasha was out at work. When she returned to the flat, she found that her precious *budare* had been scrubbed back to its original pale-grey state, losing all of its seasoning. Her boyfriend told her proudly that the lady had spent four hours scrubbing the 'dirt' out of it. 'Of course the relationship ended,' Sasha commented in a matter-of-fact way.

Happily, Sasha soon met someone else. Her new boyfriend was Basque, not Catalan, and 'an amazing man', Sasha said. When we talked, they were expecting their first baby together. Unlike the Catalan boyfriend, Sasha's new man understood how much the *budare* meant to her. And yet, despite this, he made an even worse mistake with it.

You can tell how you really feel about an object when it is lost or stolen. In one study of bicycle theft, some of the owners said they felt losing their bike was like losing something more precious than money. Burglary victims may describe feelings of personal violation and people who lose all of their possessions in natural disasters such as floods or mudslides go through a process akin to searing grief. In January 2025, thousands of families in Los Angeles lost their homes and most of the contents as wildfires raged through the city. The scale of loss is unimaginable. A reporter for *The New York Times* spoke to a sixty-three-year-old woman who was searching for her silver cutlery outside the wreckage of her mobile home in the Pacific Palisades. The machine beeped and she found a lump of metal: 'her forks, knives and spoons had melted together'.

Not every belonging that is lost is mourned equally. In the summer of 1986, Russell Belk interviewed flood victims about their losses and spoke to one man who said that the things he really lamented having lost were his record collection, a book collection and various things associated with his father: the tools that his father had used in his job as a cabinet maker, the stereo cabinet that his father had made for him and the ceiling of the basement which his father had helped to install. All of these things felt irreplaceable because they were not just part of the flood victim himself but part of his father.

Sasha always used to store her father's *budare* in the oven. Having it there made her feel safe, she told me. Her new Basque boyfriend had arranged for builders to come and refit the kitchen. The day they came to take the old oven away, Sasha was out at work. Her boyfriend forgot to remove the *budare* and it was dumped, along with the oven. When Sasha found out, she was furious. Her boyfriend tried to make it up to her by buying her a new *budare*, but he made the mistake of ordering it online from Amazon, which made it impersonal and valueless in Sasha's view. 'It's embarrassing. It's awful.' She showed me the new *budare* as we chatted via Zoom and I could see that while this might be a decent enough *budare* for someone else, it was no substitute for her old 'precious' from her father. She did admit, however, that her boyfriend surprised her by teaching himself to make *arepas* with this embarrassing pan and that they were actually very tasty.

Four months later, I emailed Sasha to see how she was doing. She reported that it would still be three months until the baby was born. Meanwhile, she had good news. She had gone on a long trip home to Venezuela and her father greeted her at the door, posing with a new *budare* in his hands in a mock-heroic fashion ('he is a comedian'). During her months at home, she and her parents cooked everything they could using the *budare* because her dad wanted her to come home with a well-seasoned pan. But when she got back to San Sebastián the new pan didn't work at all on her induction stove ('we didn't even think about this possibility'). She couldn't bear to tell her father this, after all the trouble he had gone to. 'He thinks it works perfectly.'

When someone doesn't like a gift they say, 'It's the thought that counts.' But it can take immense thought to be the recipient of a not-quite-right gift who honours the giver by making them feel that whatever they chose was perfect. After her baby is born, one of Sasha's sisters will come from Venezuela to help her and she will bring Sasha 'a proper *budare* for induction without my parents knowing' so they can believe that this new pan was the one they gave her if they glimpse it when they video-call her and the baby. After everything her father had given her, Sasha wanted him to think that every batch of *arepas* she made was thanks to him.

A Red Washing-up Bowl

'One must be a friend to one's friend,
And give present for present; One must have
Laughter for laughter
And sorrow for lies'

The Hávamál, tenth century

Six months or so into my separation, my next-door neighbour Jane, a retired doctor, dropped something round. It was a red washing-up bowl and a beechwood washing-up brush with natural bristles. She had bought it from a Scandinavian design shop. Like Jane herself, this gift was both level-headed and very generous.

A new washing-up bowl was exactly what my household needed right then, for both practical and emotional reasons. One of the many small changes I was adjusting to in my new life was washing all the dishes every day and loading and unloading the dishwasher. Before my husband left, he had done most of the washing-up and I had almost always cooked. Now it was all on me, though my daughter, then seventeen, chipped in. I decided to turn washing-up into a communal activity, one we could do after dinner while listening to music. I washed, my daughter dried and my younger son (in theory) cleaned the surfaces, though he seemed to spend an awful lot of time not so much cleaning as fiddling with my phone to queue up the next song. My aim was for washing-up to become something that none of us resented, just a daily routine like eating breakfast.

The red washing-up bowl was a genuine help. Every time I looked at it and filled it with hot sudsy water, several times a day, I felt that washing-up might actually be cool and Danish rather than tedious and mildly oppressive. When I looked at the bowl I thought of Jane and her kindness. I had known her for seventeen years, ever since my daughter was a baby, and in all that time she had been unfailingly nice. Our older sons were the same age and they used to play together when we first moved into the house.

This cheery rubber bowl seemed to project a quiet faith in my abilities. As a gift it pleased me more than any 'pampering' luxury item could have done. When Jane dropped it round I was at my wobbliest, lowest point. Sometimes I woke in the night with my teeth chattering, but this bowl made me feel sturdier.

Unlike weddings, divorces are not generally associated with gifts. Indeed, in some cultures a separation will see a woman actively being stripped of the wedding gifts she received on getting married. In Tajikistan, a bride's family is expected to supply her with an expensive dowry when she marries. A typical dowry might consist of household appliances and furniture; multiple tea sets and pots and pans; mattresses, pillows and slippers. In addition, like the Australian brides of yesteryear, she would have her own trousseau of clothes and gold jewellery. When a woman is divorced she may lose everything. Some French anthropologists interviewed fifty women in Tajikistan in 2011 and found that many of them got a rough deal, gift-wise, on separation. The women's comments included:

'With everything I brought, I didn't get anything back!'
'When I went to get my chests [*sanduq*] my mother-in-law had taken half of what was in it.'
'I left and left everything. I thought about going back but I didn't have the courage.'

'Of course it's mine, but how can I get it back? It's all in their house.'

Compared to these women, I knew I was lucky. Preposterously lucky. I still had work, freedom and my own stuff. My ex did not want anything from the kitchen we had shared all these years and he would not have dreamed of stripping me of my share of the wedding presents. He had already taken his clothes and books when he left and he hardly wanted anything else.

The small gifts I was given after my separation by some of my friends and relatives were completely different from wedding presents: less showy and more casual. I appreciated them all the more for it. My sister-in-law gave me a sleep spray for my pillow. After a pipe near the water tank in my house sprung a leak and our electricity went off, my sister bought me some portable USB chargeable lights. A couple of weeks before my ex remarried, an old friend from university gave me and three other friends matching mugs, in a gesture of team spirit. Sometimes we posted photos of ourselves on our WhatsApp group, drinking coffee from our special mugs. A friend from down the road sometimes left packages of cake by my side door with a little note saying she suspected my blood sugar was low.

One afternoon, someone I'd been friendly with at the school gates years earlier turned up on my doorstep with a basket full of beautiful produce from her allotment and a jar of blackberry jelly which she had made herself. With a slight air of awkwardness, she said that the basket was just because she had far too many vegetables and flowers and she hoped I could help her out. I later learned that there is a Japanese category of gifts called *susowake*, used to describe items that one has such an overabundance of that it is necessary to share. In Japan, calling something *susowake* is a kind way to tell the recipient that they have no obligation to reciprocate.

As we chatted, this friend didn't mention my separation until I brought it up, although this was quite clearly the reason she had appeared at my door. I'm not sure which I loved more: the basket of vegetables or her deep tact in pretending that this was not a pity gift.

There is a fierce debate among anthropologists over whether there can ever be such a thing as a 'pure gift': a present given without any expectation of an offering in return. Marcel Mauss's book *The Gift* rejected the idea of pure gifts without any ulterior motive. The very rationale of giving, for Mauss, was to enhance either status or solidarity. Even gifts which do not come with an expectation of a return may be calculated to change the way the recipient feels and behaves. Another anthropologist called Bronisław Malinowski had claimed that the presents regularly given by husbands to their wives in the Trobriand Islands were examples of pure gifts. Mauss disagreed. Far from being pure, Mauss argued that they were in fact payment to the wives for their 'sexual favours'.

And yet despite everything, people do sometimes behave with great kindness and without any expectation of personal gain. In *The Gift Relationship* (1970), Richard Titmuss argued that voluntary blood donation should be viewed as a pure gift because there is no possibility – never mind expectation – that the stranger who receives your blood can ever reciprocate. The offerings I was given by friends after my separation felt the closest thing I've ever had to pure gifts: small tokens of real kindness (although a cynic would point out that the fact that they made me feel so warmly towards my friends was itself a kind of return).

Apparently, the 'divorce shower' – like a baby shower – is now a thing. You could if you wished buy your divorced friend a scented candle whose label reads 'Smells Like Freshly Signed Divorce Papers'. The idea of holding a divorce shower gives me mixed feelings. I wouldn't have wanted my children to have felt that I was celebrating their dad moving out. Clearly, some people figure out a way to make a divorce shower work, though. There was an article in *The New York Times* in 2012 featuring a Manhattan graphic designer who had been given an 'unbridled shower' in order 'to replace the stuff that my ex had taken from the house'. The loss of this man's set of nesting bowls had 'really hurt', but friends gave him a replacement set. They also gave him knives, a chopping board and other basic utensils, along with a collection of foolproof recipes that he could cook for his teenager.

For me, the real prize my friends gave me was the realisation that, given time, I could build myself a new life. I never would have left my husband – it was unthinkable; or rather, it was a thought I never allowed myself. But the reality of his absence, sudden as it was, created space as well as sorrow. Without him to chat to, I had time to read novels again and to consider the fact that despite the settled life we had built together, despite all the shared meals and mutual support, the days of conversation and the nights of love, I had often felt lonely. He must have felt lonely too, as he stood and did the washing-up all those nights. *Poor man*, I thought.

A friend came round with a bunch of tulips. She knew that when I was married we could never have flowers in the house because they gave him instant hay fever. Her bouquet inspired me to start planting roses in the garden. I had previously dismissed rose gardens as boring and middle-aged, but now (perhaps because I was now middle-aged), they entranced me: the ornate names, the colours, the different formations of petals. Thanks to the red washing-up bowl, I could recycle some of the dishwater by giving it to the roses. The next time I met my ex, to discuss the children over a tense cup of coffee, I told him about my new interest in gardening. 'You have given me the gift of flowers,' I said, and I wasn't being sarcastic.

Treasure

The Elephant Plate

> 'But by sacred things one must not understand simply those personal beings which are called gods or spirits; a rock, a tree, a spring, a pebble, a piece of wood, a house, in a word, anything can be sacred.'
>
> Émile Durkheim, 1915

When the nights of feeding still drag and the days creep along like a slug, people will warn you with a knowing air that your baby's life will 'go so fast'. But they don't tell you that the time will come when you stare into the cupboard where the Elmer the Elephant plate used to be kept and feel a small but insistent stab of loss. They don't say that you will mourn this garish and ugly melamine plate – which you rashly gave away during a clear-out – as if it were a dead pet. They don't tell you that – missing this plate and other related accessories of toddlerdom – you too will become someone who meets new parents and feels an urge to warn them that it all goes so fast, as if the warning could somehow stop the onward rush of time.

You can spend a long time obsessing about a baby's first spoon, plate, bowl (we also had various utensils involving Miffy the Bunny Rabbit). These items are receptacles of love and apple sauce. The particular choice of pattern or cartoon character for that first plate is a decision that feels weighty but pleasurable. It is an easy act of courtship, like buying flowers for a lover, but one whose love you already feel secure in.

I considered the options for my son's first plate. I discounted princess plates (although now I wonder if I was just imposing my own ideas of what a boy 'should' like). I was tempted by farm animals and dinosaurs and space (would it perhaps be wise to plant the idea of being an astronaut in his head as early as possible?). In the end, Elmer the patchwork elephant seemed the friendliest, least controversial decision. With its many colours it had a 'be whatever you want to be' kind of vibe.

During early parenthood you are always buying for the next stage. When I got that Elmer plate, the idea that my son could ever actually be advanced enough to understand the words in one of the Elmer board books felt like a wondrous dream. It seemed enough just to be looking together at this creature on the plate and trying and failing to say 'elephant'. And then, suddenly, he was old enough for me to read him the Elmer books. The one we read the most was *Elmer's Colours*. Through Elmer, we considered the white of snowmen and the purple of scarves; the pink of strawberry ice lollies and the red of sunsets. There was a page where Elmer balances an orange and a lemon on his trunk – 'Don't drop them, Elmer!' We could relate to this. We were habitually dropping things, including the Elmer plate itself. Melamine may not be the most elegant material, but I was grateful for the fact that, no matter how violently a one-year-old dropped that plate, it would bounce and not shatter (the same could not be said for the food).

I couldn't count the times I took that plate and lined things up on it, things my son could eat with his fingers or a fork if we were lucky: tiny florets of broccoli that looked like trees, *farfalle* with pesto (oily moss-soaked butterflies), tiny meatballs, tiny fishcakes, fragments of chicken, cubes of roast potato and roast sweet potato – things which I hoped would please him and give him a balanced diet, whatever that is. He was easy to feed but struggled with sleep, and by teatime we were often both exhausted, hence the endless dropping of things.

Over time, the Elmer plate lost most of its original sense of excitement. It became just another thing that went in and out of the dishwasher on a daily basis. We were still using it long after my son had moved on to Spiderman and The Hulk. It was only after his sister was born and became old enough for solid food that the Elmer plate stopped being his and became hers. All over again, I was lining things up on its smooth and colourful melamine surface. She was a fan of hard-boiled eggs and slices of fresh avocado, and she too loved to read about the pink of strawberry ice lollies and the red of sunsets and the orange of oranges. Someone gave her a plate with purple flowers on it, but the Elmer one was her old familiar until it got passed on to her younger brother.

And then one day, no one in the family needed it – they had all graduated to china – and I gave it away. I didn't understand then that it is possible to hanker deeply after something which is neither pretty nor useful, just because of the person who once used it. The fact that no one needs it anymore is exactly what makes the wanting so fierce, because it reminds you of a time when you were needed too. Children change and grow but the left-behind plate stays the same.

It is the nature of childhood possessions that the child is always outgrowing them, and this is how things are meant to be. We are constantly being weaned or weaning ourselves from one thing to another and this means leaving other things behind: from liquids to solids, from toy trains to Nintendo, from Harry Potter to *Lord of the Flies*. As a parent, you wouldn't want your child to be stuck forever wearing a onesie and drinking from a sippy cup. The boy for whom I bought that Elmer plate is now in his twenties and going to work each day in a much more challenging job than I have ever done without any help from me. He is so many stages beyond the phase of life when I would speak to him in a sing-song voice about patchwork elephants that it is laughable even to think of it. He has a beard, for goodness' sake.

But there is part of you that never forgets the sweet, sweaty way a toddler's head used to smell after a nap; and how he hesitated quizzically after he dropped something to see if you would mind, because sometimes you were so tired that you *did* mind and couldn't quite summon up the energy to hide it. And you remember how something in his expression made you laugh involuntarily, even though by this point of the day you just wanted dinnertime to be over already and for this person – much as you loved them – to be asleep and out of your life for a few hours, and you picked the Elmer plate up off the floor and started again.

The Corkscrew Collection

> 'Collections are essentially a narrative of experience.'
>
> Susan M. Pearce, 1995

At first, I only went to Zoltan Bogathy's shop to buy gifts for other people. A kind of deli and grocer, it seemed to stock almost every delicious thing imaginable, from French cheeses to Sardinian artichokes, from fresh cinnamon rolls to miso paste. When it opened up a few streets away from where I live, I saw it as a fairyland of delights. I learned from a friend who also frequented the shop that Zoltan grew up in Hungary and that this Cambridge food store was based on a similar one he had in Budapest.

When I went to the shop, I would choose such things as tins of tea, little jars of jam made from rare fruits, special spices in tiny silver canisters, fine chocolates which I had never seen outside of France and elegant bottles of Sicilian olive oil. I always felt happy after I had chosen someone a treat from there. But then I started popping in more regularly to pick up things for myself too: risotto rice, Japanese soy sauce flavoured with shitake mushrooms, excellent mustard, exquisite blood oranges and the best goat's cheese I ever tasted.

Sometimes, when I knew that my son would be away for dinner at his dad's house, I would buy myself a single luscious thing to make me feel less lonely at the table: a few slices of cured meat, an unusual shape of pasta or some smoked cod's roe for making taramasalata.

Cheaper than therapy, I told myself (although I was also having therapy and it helped). I was mesmerised by the abundance and variety of the products for sale on the neatly arranged shelves. It was like being inside a carefully curated museum where you could actually buy and eat the exhibits.

Once, when I was in the shop, Zoltan mentioned casually that he collected corkscrews. I asked if we could have coffee and talk more about it. We met at a Greek café down the road where he told me about the 'fixation' he had with vintage corkscrews, most of them from the nineteenth and early twentieth centuries. Back in his apartment in Hungary, he said he had whole boxes of corkscrews.

Why would someone choose to devote time and money to collecting corkscrews (or nutmeg graters or ice cream scoops or jelly moulds, as the case may be)? An 'obsession organised' is how the writer Nikolai Aristides once defined the act of collecting. Zoltan told me straight out that he was 'pretty self-aware' about the fact that his interest in corkscrews had become a 'fixation'.

No one *needs* dozens and dozens of vintage corkscrews, least of all someone like Zoltan who recently purchased a pricey new gadget called the Coravin wine preservation system. This miraculous gizmo can siphon off a glass of wine at a time using argon gas, leaving the rest of the bottle as fresh as before. When he has an excellent bottle of wine, Zoltan appreciates being able to drink it a few glasses at a time without wasting a drop. The downside, as he concedes, is that owning the Coravin makes his whole collection of corkscrews 'obsolete'. And yet, when he finds himself at a flea market selling old corkscrews, he generally can't resist buying just a few more.

It has been estimated that one in three Americans has a collection of some kind or other, making it a far more mainstream pursuit than you might guess from the cruel laughter with which collectors are sometimes greeted. The question is why some of us become collectors while others don't. In describing the origins of their collection, a collector will often attribute it to some kind of fortunate accident. Perhaps it started when a parent gave them a fossil as a birthday present or a kindly relative brought them back a beautiful teapot from China and the interest escalated from there. But this only gets to 'the edge of the question', as the scholar of collecting Susan Pearce observes, because most of us are given random gifts but we don't all end up collecting them. 'We are left wondering', Pearce writes, whether an essential feature of the collector is a predisposition to collect.

Zoltan certainly recognises collector-like traits in himself. Corkscrews are far from being his only obsession. 'Fruit is another of my interests,' he told me one time when I came into the shop and he offered me a taste of a wild strawberry from a punnet he had stashed for personal use under the counter. He says that his beautiful food shop partly came about as a way to manage his own 'hoarding' tendencies. After training as an electrical engineer in Hungary, he worked in the newspaper industry for a while and then ran his own graphic design business. The food shop in Budapest was the first line of work in which he could fully channel his obsessive desire to collect. 'Grocery helped me a lot,' he says. In his new shop in England he is able to amass and arrange beautiful things but the food must be disposed of before it goes off, thus forcing him to stop hoarding it at a certain point. 'I remind my staff we actually have to sell this stuff!' he tells me.

As to why Zoltan got hooked on corkscrews as opposed to anything else, he has a few different answers. One reason is that, as a young man, he took a trip to Portugal to see how corks were produced. Standing in the ancient cork forests, he was struck by what a 'magical product' cork is. His obsession with corkscrews, as opposed to corks, is a little more mysterious. Corkscrews were not something he grew up with. In the old Soviet-era Hungary his grandfather used to make his own 'terrible'-tasting wine. It was stored in large demijohns like home-brewed beer, and so there was no reason for anyone to use a corkscrew. 'Nobody had bottles then,' Zoltan says. The first time he handled a corkscrew was during his student days in Budapest, when he worked as a bartender while studying Science at university. 'We all drank red wine mixed with Coke,' he recalls. This wine-and-Coke combo was a continuation of the old Hungarian custom of mixing wine with sparkling water. (Fizzy water is called 'wine water' in Hungary.) Working behind the bar, Zoltan had to open bottle after bottle of ropey red wine and he noticed that the corkscrew the bar supplied really hurt his hand because it was so badly made.

Until 1989 Hungary was still under Communist rule, which affected corkscrew design, along with almost everything else about everyday life. The corkscrews at the bar where Zoltan worked were made from 'cheap plated metal' and 'mass-produced to a standard that was deemed sufficient'. So far as Zoltan was concerned, these Communist bottle openers were 'nasty' to use and felt flimsy, but in this, as in other matters, 'the consumer didn't have a say'.

The first time Zoltan found a corkscrew he really liked was sometime in 1990–91, after the fall of the Berlin Wall, when it became possible to trade freely again. Suddenly, the flea markets of Budapest started to sell lots of old items from the pre-Communist era. Many restaurants were sold off and people found storage rooms from the 1940s which were just as they had been back then – like a 'time capsule', according to Zoltan. Perusing the flea markets, Zoltan bought a corkscrew from the 1920s. It was in a compact lever design known in Hungary as a 'lemonade' because the lever at the end is used to open bottles of lemonade or beer. In much of the world, the folding lever design is called the 'waiter's friend'; this is the one an early-twentieth-century waiter kept in his apron as he bustled from table to table opening bottles. The basic formula was established in 1883 by a German called Carl Wienke, who figured out that a folding corkscrew could combine with a knife-like handle plus a grippy lever to attach to the bottle's rim and take much of the grunt work out of pulling the cork. In later designs the lever doubled up as a cap lifter, and sometimes a small folding knife was added for cutting the foil from the wine bottle to reveal the cork. The first corkscrew Zoltan found in the flea market was one of these.

Not all corkscrews are made alike. Technically, the Communist corkscrews that Zoltan had used up to now were very similar in design to this 'lemonade' corkscrew from the 1920s. But the two tools felt entirely different in his hands. The 1920s corkscrew was heavier – it was made of pleasingly solid steel, not plated metal – and he was gratified to find that it didn't hurt to use it. Plus, it did a much better job of opening bottles. When he took it back to the bar to use, 'Everyone was like "Oh My God!" It's so efficient! So fast!' It was a thrill to realise that the older corkscrew was actually more effective than the modern one. The next stage of Zoltan's corkscrew obsession was that he fell in love with good wine (as opposed to the wine-and-Coke kind) on a trip to France with a French girlfriend. He found himself buying half a dozen more vintage corkscrews. The collection was now becoming serious.

Before my conversation with Zoltan, I had never paid much attention to corkscrews, old or otherwise, but he made me see how easily they could become an object of desire. The question of how to extract a firmly lodged cork from a bottle without damaging either the cork or your hand is far from obvious. A perfect corkscrew has a combination of brute force and delicacy, and there are whole subcultures of corkscrew collectors who know the difference between a good corkscrew and a great one. In 1974, two corkscrew connoisseurs called Bernard Watney and Timothy Diener founded 'The International Correspondence of Corkscrew Addicts', a society with fifty members all crazy about old corkscrews.

I say 'old', but in truth there is no such thing as a very old corkscrew. Wine is an ancient drink but the corkscrew is not. The first patent for a corkscrew (with a button added to the shank) was issued to one Samuel Henshall of Edinburgh as late as 1795. 'Bottle screws', as they were first known, had been around for longer than this, but not much. There is a very simple explanation: for most of its history, wine was stored not in cork-stopped bottles but in large clay jars, from which wine was transferred to smaller pitchers for consumption. In the ancient world wine jars were often only loosely sealed because the wine was consumed fresh, almost as soon as it was made. The ancient terracotta amphora or wine jar, as used in Greece, Rome and Egypt, was stoppered with various bungs made from such things as cork, clay, wood or wadded leaves or cloth, sealed over with something like beeswax or resin. How these bungs were extracted from wine jars is not known, although archaeologists in Egypt have found some ingenious 'pop-top' clay seals with strings at the sides for lifting out the seal: the screwcap openings of their day.

Technologies are not born one at a time but in clusters. Cork-topped glass bottles only became standardised in size and shape in the eighteenth century, meaning that for the first time wine could be aged in the bottle. But this gave rise to a new problem: how to extract the cork and get to the precious liquid inside. Hands, nails, skewers and teeth would all have been used in the days before the corkscrew was a common device. We have no idea who invented the first twisting metal screw for pulling corks – the technical term for the screw part of a corkscrew is the 'worm'. What we do know is that something very similar had been used for extracting bullets from guns since the 1630s, so it is possible that the corkscrew has military origins.

Every corkscrew has roughly the same anatomy: a worm, a shank and a handle. But from this basic pattern they have been beautified and improved in countless ways, which is part of what

makes them so collectable. The worm itself may take one of three different forms: the classic helical worm (like DNA), the centre worm (with a steel core round which a ridge spirals) and the Archimedean worm, in which the screw looks like wool wound round a knitting needle. As for the handle, it could be anything from basic to ornate: from wood to silver; from bone to horn; from patterned to plain. Nineteenth-century corkscrew handles might be decorated with advertising messages like a mini billboard, or encrusted with precious metals and ornamentation like a Fabergé egg. In Germany in the 1890s there were a whole series of corkscrews – more or less obscene – made to mimic the human anatomy. In some of the most popular designs, the worm emerged from a pair of jauntily folding legs or out of the breasts of a mermaid.

I have not even begun to discuss all the ways in which the basic mechanism of the corkscrew was elaborated over the years: the various shafts and levers and racks and concertinas, each of which claimed to make the job of opening a bottle easier (although some of them were little improvements on the basic twist-and-pull model). Zoltan told me that he was a fan of the classic French 'winged' corkscrew, with two large levers attached to oversized gears. This design is sometimes called the 'de Gaulle', because when the wings are up it calls to mind the French politician Charles de Gaulle, who gesticulated with his arms in the air when giving speeches. The 'de Gaulle' has a satisfying and reliable mechanism which takes most of the jeopardy out of opening a bottle of wine, although some of us still find it tricky to use.

It is not clear what the future is for corkscrews – or indeed for corks – in an era of climate change. On the one hand, cork is a renewable and biodegradable product. Moreover, the cork trees of Portugal are a carbon sink: they actually capture CO_2 from the atmosphere, thus offsetting the carbon emissions involved in producing a bottle of wine. On the other hand, cork trees are at risk from drought and wildfire as average summer temperatures rise in the Mediterranean. Meanwhile, many wineries have switched to screwcaps, not least because they are so much cheaper to produce than corks.

And yet the corkscrew endures. When I first asked Zoltan why corkscrews meant so much to him, the first answer he gave me was a sensory one. Nothing, he said, could replace the delicate popping sound – quieter but no less exciting than a champagne cork bursting – that happens when the worm has managed to free the cork from the bottle, enabling you to smell its contents at last. It is a sound associated for most wine drinkers with the anticipation of happy times with friends.

Enjoying the popping sound of a wine bottle is a fine reason to own *one* corkscrew. But why amass a whole collection of them? When I asked Zoltan this question for a second time a couple of weeks later, his answer went deeper. It was about a 'connection', he said, with previous generations. British people like me had no idea how lucky we were to have lived through so many years with 'no invasion, no camps, no wars'. In the Eastern Europe of his youth, by contrast, 'the change has been relentless'. His own family was testimony to the number of times that borders had changed in the region after the fall of the Austro-Hungarian Empire in 1918, after the end of the First World War. 'I could have five passports,' Zoltan told me. His great-grandfather was a prisoner of war until 1917 in what is modern-day Ukraine. Zoltan still owns a metal teapot which belonged to him and sleeps with it near his bed. This teapot, he says, is actually more precious to him than any of the corkscrews.

Among other things, Zoltan's corkscrew collection was a way to bypass the Communist Hungary he grew up in and return to an earlier and freer Europe in which there were waiters opening bottles of wine and lemonade in lovely cafés. He had long been haunted, he told me, by the thought that we can never know what the food of the past really tasted like. 'We didn't taste it. We can't smell it.' By contrast, a tool such as a corkscrew can offer continuity with the human beings who handled it before us because it is still the same piece of metal.

Zoltan loves to imagine an archetypal waiter in Paris during the Belle Époque using a corkscrew just like the ones in his collection. 'He was opening the same bottles. I have a connection with that. Everything else is perishable.'

The Oil Dispenser

> 'Giving a first gift breaks into somebody else's life; it decisively changes a relationship between the two people involved.'
>
> Margaret Visser, 2009

I did not think I liked oil dispensers much until you gave me one. You brought it back from a holiday in Italy with your children, along with two kinds of *panforte* (the sticky Sienese sweetmeat made from dried fruits, crystallised peel and almonds) and a beautiful turquoise-blue notebook. I had been on a separate holiday with my own children and I brought you back: exactly nothing! This left me poised between gratitude for your perfectly chosen presents and awkwardness that I had failed to get you anything in return. I had wrongly thought we weren't doing gifts.

For the first Christmas we knew each other, we agreed to take each other out for dinner instead of exchanging presents, to avoid the pressure of expectation that comes with gift-giving. But we also kept giving each other stuff, for no particular reason, so perhaps the no-gifts rule was not as strict as I thought. You gave me a book about the art of Siena; I gave you wine. You gave me a pale bronze canister of tea; I gave you flowers. I gave you a Microplane grater, but I didn't see this as a present as such; just something you really needed for grating the ginger for your morning turmeric drink (your one crucial daily fad). You gave me cold medicine when I had flu – another present that wasn't a present. I gave your children a box of chocolates; you gave my children a different box of chocolates. We went to Rome together and bought each other plates of artichokes and pasta.

The oil dispenser was made of pottery with a white glaze. It was decorated with black olives and primitive leaves of dark forest-green. In the neck of the bottle was a cork fitted with a metal pourer. It was exactly the kind of utensil I used to think was completely pointless: something that kitchenware designers made just so they could sell us more gear we didn't need. I remember years ago talking to my ex-husband about the fussiness of decanting olive oil into a separate container. What was wrong with pouring oil straight from the bottle, I asked. He heartily agreed with me that oil drizzlers were silly. Back in the 1990s, TV chefs were forever talking about 'drizzling' oil into a pan and it used to make me irrationally annoyed. The word drizzle, I felt, should be reserved for rain.

The moment you gave me the oil dispenser, I saw what a fool I had been and wondered how I could have lived without such a vessel all these years. At first sight, this drizzler became the loveliest and most essential kitchen item I owned. I admired its curves and the way its neck felt when I clasped it. It seemed to shine with memories of you and the meals we had cooked together, almost all of which involved abundant quantities of olive oil. From your Lebanese father you had learned to think of olive oil as one of the rudiments of life, along with tahini and aubergines. I wished I could redesign my whole kitchen so that it matched better with the black of the olives and the green of the leaves on the dispenser.

Far from being fussy, an oil pourer dispenses the oil in a much more even stream than a bottle, whether at the table or the stove. What's more, it protects the oil from sunlight, which helps keep it good for longer. This pottery bottle was not merely decorative and charming; it was practical! (I could have said the same about you.)

When making mayonnaise, I could now add the oil drop by steady drop, meaning that it was much less likely to split.

Oil cruets, as they are sometimes known, are not a modern affectation of chefs of the 1990s. On the contrary, this kind of small receptacle for oil is of ancient origin. The Bible refers to a 'cruse' or jar of oil. The word cruet comes from the old French word for a pot. Later, a 'cruet' came to mean a small set of matching containers for oil, vinegar, salt and pepper and other condiments, to be placed at the table. At Wedgwood, my grandfather designed a beautiful cruet set in Summer Sky consisting of a mustard pot, a salt shaker and a pepper pot. The three utensils sit on a special plate with small round indents.

Little oil dispensers with pourers to let the oil flow in a more controlled manner have been in use for close to 1,000 years, as Corinne Myatt explains in her book *Tools for Food* (2021). Until modern times, olive oil was not sold in bottles but in giant pigskins and terracotta jars; or later, in the nineteenth and early twentieth centuries, in large tins. To decant some of the oil into a smaller vessel for pouring was the only way it could easily be used, whether by cooks or by eaters.

The Spanish version of these oil vessels – known as *aceitera* – probably originated in Arab communities. They may be made from glass, stainless steel or ceramic and the spout may either be at the side – as with an Asian *kendi* – or at the top. In 1961 a Catalan architect called Rafael Marquina designed a new and improved glass oil dispenser – still on sale – to deal with the problem of drips. As Mynatt writes, 'a central spout protrudes upwards from the middle of the vessel like a submarine periscope, and after pouring the oil returns back into the central cone which catches any excess fluid'.

There was nothing new and improved about the oil dispenser you gave me. It seemed to belong to a rustic Tuscany of the 1950s and I loved it all the more for this. It was not the kind of flashy and uber-stylish coloured-glass oil dispenser you sometimes see in kitchenware shops. It was something solid and almost grandmotherly. You told me that when your Irish mother wanted to praise a meal, she described it as 'full of goodness'. All my senses told me that this oil drizzler, too, was full of goodness. When I came downstairs in the mornings, its gentle presence on the counter was proof of your generosity and taste. We did not manage to see each other every day – you worked such crazy hours and I was often busy with my son – but even when we didn't meet, the oil dispenser was there to greet me.

A month or so after we met, I had an urge to re-read *Love* (1822) – a treatise on falling in love by the French novelist Stendhal. I had a vague memory that Stendhal had written about something called 'crystallisation', which happens when people fall in love. I wanted to check what crystallisation really meant because I was pretty sure that it had happened to me. It didn't take me long to find the passage I remembered:

> At the salt mines of Salzburg, they throw a leafless wintry bough into one of the abandoned workings. Two or three months later they haul it out covered with a shining deposit of crystals. The smallest twig . . . is studded with a galaxy of scintillating diamonds. The original branch is no longer recognisable.

Stendhal's point is that the act of falling in love is a 'mental process' which is constantly seeking 'new proofs of the perfection of the loved one'. It is as if every object associated with them sparkles with crystals until, as Stendhal writes, 'the original naked branch is no longer recognisable by indifferent eyes, because it now sparkles with perfections, or diamonds'.

Many mundane objects in my life started to sparkle in curious ways after you arrived in it. You showed me how to use my AeroPress coffee maker by the upside-down method, and this nondescript contraption of black plastic became a thing of wonder (even though a few months later you abandoned your own AeroPress for a fancy new coffee machine). To a person in love, Stendhal writes, anything can be beautiful.

This process of crystallisation didn't happen straight away. We were set up by kind friends who knew that we had got divorced at roughly the same time and that neither of us was much enjoying online dating. About a month before my ex-husband left, I had heard you sing in an impromptu concert on my street and remembered you as a handsome man with a powerful bass voice. You sang 'Night and Day' and I had never heard it sung so well. I didn't harbour romantic thoughts for you, though, not even after my friend told me about you and said we should meet. Frankly, when has a set-up ever worked? Even the friend who gave me your number – the same fierce friend who never uses paper cups – seemed to have low expectations of our meeting leading to anything. She told me I should not think of it as a date, just a chance to grumble about single life with another divorced person.

After the first cup of coffee, I could see you were very nice but couldn't feel any chemistry, either from you or from me. I was starting to think that I might be too old to fall in love and that, in any case, life without a romantic relationship was not too bad, as long as I had friends and interesting books to read. Having lost the person I had clung to as my soulmate, I felt that the best I could hope for a second time round might be a mild form of companionship to ward off loneliness, and I wasn't sure if this was any improvement on being alone.

We went for a walk with my dog and spent much of the time talking about growing roses, my new specialist subject, something you were better versed in than me. You told me about your pruning technique and which blooms had a disappointing tendency to drop. You laid out the advantages and disadvantages of different types of pink rose. It was all handy info, and I was glad to have it, but it didn't seem like the start of anything. On our next walk, the conversation turned still more prosaic. We discussed paint colours and you told me about the virtues of brown rice. This was clearly just a friendship, I decided. Two weeks later, I woke up with a strange fluttering feeling in my chest and bright crystals in my eyes.

An object can change its meaning in an instant, but perhaps this is no surprise given that we were the ones who gave the object its meaning in the first place. The pavements and trees and sky now felt infused with you. Stendhal writes that 'the habit of listening to music and the state of reverie connected with it prepare you for falling in love', and this was true for me. Snatches of music I had listened to decades before we met had simply been distant groundwork for meeting you. The Fred Astaire CD I bought in Paris when I was a student now only existed for me in relation to your voice singing 'Night and Day'.

It didn't seem possible that we could have been living a five-minute bike ride away from each other for more than twenty years without once meeting. We had children of the same age at the same school. You used to do concerts at my local coffee shop and somehow I had managed to miss every performance. You said you had cycled past my house many times. Years earlier, you and your family had regularly frequented my mother's favourite Lebanese restaurant on the street where I grew up. Had we ever been there at the same time? I couldn't see how I could have been so stupid as not to have noticed you. Your face was unforgettable and yet, if I had ever seen it, I had no memory of it. And this was just as well. We met – finally! – at the only time in our respective lives when we could possibly have been together.

All sorts of things became like holy relics to me, because you touched them or approved of them. Yellow soap. Vermicelli. Orange flower water. My old satin dressing gown, which I had been on the verge of giving away. The colour blue. I cooked you a dish of pasta with oyster mushrooms and onions softened in butter with caraway seeds and lots of green dill – an Ixta Belfrage recipe – and because you liked it, this was promoted in my mind to the best pasta I ever made.

Stendhal writes that 'from the moment he falls in love even the wisest man no longer sees anything *as it really is*'. Even my washing-up gloves developed a glow about them because of the way that you would jump up and put them on after you had dinner at our house. When the children and I played songs on Spotify while washing the dishes, you actually danced.

Seven weeks after we met you sang at my mother's funeral. My son thought your voice had broken the recording equipment because he noticed that the volume dial maxed out when you started to sing.

Most of the time, we avoid talking about the future. Too many things have smashed or died; so much in this world is uncertain. And yet there on my kitchen counter is the oil drizzler you gave me. It doesn't matter what kind of olive oil I put in it; every drop that comes out of it is treasure.

Broken Cups

'I have been bent and broken but – I hope – into a
better shape.'

Charles Dickens, 1861

Like people, ceramics can break: some more easily than others.
But, unlike a person, a bowl cannot heal itself. The question, then,
is what we do with the precious things in our lives after they
break. Do we shove them to the back of a cupboard? Give them
away? Or do we try to mend them and make them useful again
while we can?

On a rainy morning in Tokyo, I booked us into a 'kintsugi
workshop' to learn about the Japanese art of mending smashed
crockery with seams of precious metals. We were in Japan together;
you were there for work and I flew out for a week to be with you.
For our kintsugi repairs you picked a plain black cup; I went for a
blue and white one decorated with grapes and vines. You decorated
your cup in gold powder; I chose silver.

We sat side by side, slowly applying urushi – the sap of the lacquer tree – to our broken cups using tiny paintbrushes before
sticking the sections back together like a jigsaw puzzle. Your technique was far neater and more meticulous than mine. I failed to
make my brush follow the lines of the crack exactly and some of the
lacquer oozed out messily in places. Still, it was soothing to spend
the morning fixing something together. The day before, I had been

jetlagged and on edge, but now, sitting at this orderly wooden bench surrounded by tools, I felt so grateful to be there with you.

Once the lacquer had dried, we filed it to make it smooth and applied a fresh layer of lacquer before sweeping over silver and gold powder with a soft piece of silk wadding. It was remarkable to see how quickly the cracks in my cup started to gleam as the silver stuck to the lacquer. Technically, my cup was *gintsugi*, not *kintsugi*, because it was silver not gold. *Kin* is gold and *gin* is silver. *Tsugi* means to join together, so the meaning of *kintsugi* is 'joining with gold'.

It was hard to avoid the feeling that the act of patching something up might have a wider significance for us as two divorced people. Without the cracks in our past we never could have met. I sometimes felt you were piecing me back together into a new and better shape, even if it occasionally felt tender at the joins.

In the West, the goal of ceramic repair has generally been to make something as 'good as new', so that the cracks don't show: to pretend that what is broken isn't actually broken. In modern Western museum repair the approach is slightly different. Ceramic restorers follow the six/six rule: the fix should be invisible at a distance of six feet, but visible from six inches away. This was my mother's way when things went wrong: plaster over the breaks and hope that from a distance no one will notice. After my father left, I once found her at her desk in floods of tears. I tried to comfort her but she acted as if I were making a fuss and told me it was only a little hay fever making her eyes water.

Kintsugi is another matter altogether. It turns the cracks into something precious and thus gives the repaired utensil more value than it had before. *Kintsugi* highlights the cracks rather than concealing them.

In the West, *kintsugi* has become an obsession in recent years and its meaning has stretched far beyond tableware. It even found its way into one of the *Star Wars* movies. In *The Rise of Skywalker*

(2019), Kylo Ren's broken mask is mended *kintsugi*-style with glowing red crystalline glue. *Kintsugi* has been turned into a branch of 'wellness', whatever that term means. There are *kintsugi* self-help podcasts and *kintsugi* blogs. 'Embrace your imperfections and find happiness – the Japanese way' is the subtitle of a book about *kintsugi* by the psychologist Tomás Navarro.

Accepting our individual human imperfections and learning resilience is certainly a good way to live. But is this philosophy of living – helpful and kind as it is – really *kintsugi*? The Western version of *kintsugi* is all about the self. In Japan, however, the art of *kintusgi* is linked to a reverence for objects as something larger than the individual. The word *tsugi* has social connotations. As well as meaning to join or patch together, it has associations with family, meaning to inherit or follow on from another person.

Aya Oguma, the delightful young woman who led our *kintsugi* workshop in Tokyo, told us that *kintsugi* was 'not seen by the Japanese as spiritual', at least not in the Western sense. When we met Aya in the summer of 2024, she had been working as a *kintsugi* restorer for eighteen months. Before that she had worked in IT for a while and later ran her own business making and selling a special kind of Japanese dumpling made from rice flour. Aya's interest in *kintsugi* started several years ago, when she was living in Vietnam with her ex-husband, but she had no way to pursue it until she was back in Japan.

Like so many of us, Aya is attracted to tableware because it reminds her of her mother, a talented cook who died twenty years ago. Starting her current job in *kintsugi* repair felt like a return to her roots, she says, after the end of her marriage. On her return to Japan, Aya trained in *kintsugi* techniques with a master craftsman and learned the basics of pottery from the owner of the high-end pottery shop where she now works (and where our workshop took place), which supplies a range of fine china to restaurants. During the short time she has been working there, Aya says that demand for their *kintsugi* services has soared among their Japanese customers. Her theory is that the craze for *kintsugi* outside Japan has given the Japanese themselves a renewed appreciation for it.

Kintsugi in Japan goes back a long way, although no one can say exactly how long. Japanese craftsmen have been repairing ceramics with *urushi* for at least 4,000 years, since the Jōmon era. These *urushi* repairs would originally have been done in a frugal spirit, simply as a way to fix broken things: make do and mend. The main downside of *urushi* is that in its liquid form it can cause severe skin reactions, although by the time it has fully set and cured it is non-toxic. (A less risky and cheaper modern alternative is a glue made from cashew shells.) Nevertheless, *urushi* is an excellent form of natural glue because after it has dried and cured it develops an exceptionally strong polymer structure. The mystery is when the *urushi* used for mending broken tableware started to be embellished with expensive powders of gold and silver.

If you look for the origins of *kintsugi* on the internet, you will find many legends. The most common origin story – tinged with anti-Chinese sentiment – is about a fifteenth-century shogun (Ashikaga Yoshimasa), who was supposedly unhappy with the way his favourite Chinese bowl had been mended by clumsy Chinese craftsmen. He asked Japanese repairers to do a better job and they allegedly then invented *kintsugi*. This is definitely *not* how *kintsugi* was invented, not least because Yoshimasa's mended tea bowl still exists and it has no *kintsugi* mends anywhere on it; it is mended instead with locust-like staples. This gorgeous celadon bowl – so delicate it looks translucent – is a very famous one, known as Bakōhan, and it belongs to the Tokyo National Museum.

It is more likely that the craft of *kintsugi* emerged a century or two later, under the influence of two contradictory movements. The first was that some tea masters developed a philosophy of the imperfect called *wabi-sabi*. The second movement was an aesthetic one: a new vogue for the use of gold in art, architecture and furniture called *maki-e*.

Traditionally in Japan it was considered poor form to use broken china, particularly when serving guests. The person who did the most to reverse this belief and raise the status of cracked ceramics was the tea master Sen No Rikyu (1522–91). Rikyu actively championed tea vessels with cracks and other signs of damage as part of a frugal and beautiful way of life. These ideas were continued by his disciple Furuta Oribe (1543–1611), who once said that 'perfect tea bowls are dull ones'. In Zen Buddhism, the concept of *wabi* (or *wabi-sabi*) is an acknowledgement of the ephemerality of life and an acceptance that everything is imperfect and transient.

The broken dishes praised by these early tea masters were mended with plain *urushi* rather than *urushi* plus gold. The idea of adding precious metals to the lacquer emerged out of a new branch of art, *maki-e*, whose literal meaning is 'sprinkled pictures'. A classic *maki-e* work of art would consist of a design painted in *urushi* with gold or silver powder sprinkled over the top in various gorgeous patterns, whether leaves or flowers or golden cranes. The lavishness of *maki-e* first grew popular during the Momoyama era (1573–1600), when it became fashionable for those who could afford it to add gold to almost anything, from buildings to furniture to plates. A prominent lord called Toyotomi Hideyoshi commissioned an entire portable tea room in which everything was gold, except for the bamboo whisks for whisking the tea. If gold made everything better, it was an obvious next step to add it to broken pots.

But why does *kintsugi* endure? Almost everything about Japanese culture has changed radically since 1600. Much of my time in Tokyo was spent walking in crowds in the summer heat through busy metro stations. On the trains, people stared vacantly at their phones and iPads, just as they did in London, and they bought plastic bento boxes of food for lunch.

Some have explained the undimmed appeal of *kintsugi* in Japan through the country's history of earthquakes. In her book *Kintsugi: The Poetic Mend* (2021), artist Bonnie Kemske notes the Japanese saying: 'Everything that has a shape, breaks.' Cracks and fault lines are part of the scenery in Japan in a way that is not true in most other countries.

In 2011 Japan suffered the most powerful earthquake ever recorded in the country, triggering a tsunami in which around 20,000 people died and thousands more lost their homes and all their possessions. A *kintsugi* teacher called Nakamua Kunio started holding *kintsugi* workshops in the worst-affected areas of the country. 'I realised we needed to repair ourselves, to remake things,' he said. He used a mixture of silver and brass powder, rather than gold, to make his *kintsugi* workshops more affordable.

The mainstream Western interpretation of *kintsugi* is a kind of 'go-with-the-flow' attitude to breakage. There are '*kintsugi*' repair kits for sale on the internet which are basically a tube of superglue with some fake gold powder to mix in. The kits also provide cheap bowls to smash so that they can be fixed with the superglue and fake gold.

These kits are a world away from *kintsugi* as Aya demonstrated it to us. Traditional *kintsugi* is a process that can take many months to complete as the *urushi* is carefully applied multiple times, with many days of setting and curing in between. Aya told us that for most Japanese people *kintsugi* was underpinned by the idea of *mottainai*, which implies frugality and a desire to waste nothing. But I was still a little puzzled as to how *kintsugi* fulfils this idea.

If frugality is the goal, wouldn't simple glue suffice? Why go to the length and expense of gold? *Mottainai*, Aya explained, is a much heavier and more collective idea than the Western word 'sustainability'. It carries with it a sense of regret and sadness for objects which have not been handled correctly and given their due. In the Shinto religion, the gods are found everywhere, in homeware as in living things. To break something without making proper amends is not just wasteful, it potentially offends the gods.

As I was trying to puzzle my way through what *kintsugi* really meant, I went to a friend's party in London where, quite unexpectedly, I met the Japanese-British writer Kazuo Ishiguro. I didn't mention to Ishiguro that I was writing a book about kitchen objects; he was the one who randomly brought up the subject as part of a conversation about children's books. Ishiguro told me that while trying to teach himself written Japanese in the 1970s, he came across a children's story which induced guilt at the very idea of breaking something, although it was really a story about friendship. The story's title was 'The Broken Rice Bowl'. It began by asking 'Who broke the bowl?'. Before the bowl was broken it had a picture of a cat and dog on it who happily danced together. But then a careless child broke the bowl and it got chucked in the rubbish. The cat and dog found themselves separated in two broken halves, yearning to be reunited. Missing the dog, the cat tried to make friends with a real dog but the real dog was only interested in finding food, not friendship. The picture dog had the same experience with a real cat. The picture dog and cat called out to each other from far away, saying how much they preferred each other to real cats and dogs. Over time, the two fragments got rained on and the picture dog and the cat vanished altogether. At the end of the story, Ishiguro told me that the question of who broke the bowl was repeated. I said how crushingly sad I found this story and he agreed.

The story that Ishiguro told me about the broken bowl made me think again that we have got *kintsugi* wrong in the West. Far from being relaxed about damaged ceramics, Japanese culture seems to be almost neurotically distressed by them. Bonnie Kemske interviewed a woman called Raku Fujiko who was married to a famous Japanese potter called Raku. One day, a cat broke Raku's favourite tea bowl (*chawan*). He was so devastated, according to his wife, that he 'left the studio and couldn't work for three days'. She kept the shards in a box for a year before sending them to a *kintsugi* restorer, who needed another year to complete the repairs. Raku was surprised when he saw the gold-mended *chawan* back again, two years after it had been broken.

Mending something with gold is a kind of overkill, reflecting the torrent of emotion that can be unleashed when a treasured possession breaks – or, in the case of the 2011 earthquake in Japan, when thousands of people lost every last thing in their house. When the quake happened, some people died in the process of trying to retrieve personal belongings such as photographs, documents and family heirlooms, rushing towards danger rather than away from it for the sake of their possessions. Many people were deeply distressed to find that their prized ceramics had broken in the earthquake. The *kintsugi* repairer Kunio Nakamura has said that in Japan certain pieces of pottery are like family members: 'We cannot just throw them away.'

Most of the things that we lose or break are beyond our control to resurrect. But to mend a pot or a cup and make it shinier and stronger than before is a small, possible action. Aya told me that the most special moment so far of her career as a *kintsugi* repairer was restoring some pottery that had belonged to a widower's wife. Aya said that when she returned the pottery to the man with its new golden seams she was 'so moved' to see the look on his face. It was as if she had restored part of his wife to him. The *kintsugi* pottery gave him a new way to honour her spirit and bring back memories, while acknowledging the weight of his grief. It was a glowing shrine that he could hold.

Epilogue: The Heart-shaped Tin (Again)

'I saw grief drinking a cup of sorrow and called out,
"It tastes sweet, does it not?"'

Rumi

Mother. You taught us to call you that: such a formal word. I wished I could call you 'Mum' instead. When I finally used the heart-shaped tin to make another cake, it felt wrong that you weren't there.

Your spectre, far more than my ex-husband's, was the one that hung over my kitchen; he had chosen to leave but you had gone unwillingly. You were the one who taught me to make cakes in the first place, with a rotary whisk for the eggs and a wooden spoon for the batter. It was you who made me love cake tins when I was a child. You would hand me and my sister empty butter wrappers and tell us to use the remnants of butter to grease every inch of the tin so that the batter didn't stick.

The tin was smaller than I remembered, when I felt brave enough to pick it up again. In my memory, the tin was vast enough to make a cake for dozens and dozens of people. But as I held it in my hand to scrub off the rust and bake with it, it didn't look so very large. I was reminded of how people always say that their old school or childhood home has shrunk in size when they go back later in life. Of course this is because, as children, we are so much smaller; but I think there's another, more emotional reason too. Things that matter to us loom larger in the mind.

It was three and a half years on from my separation and my fiftieth birthday was coming up. I didn't feel like having a huge celebration. Not because I was sad; not most of the time. My days were fuller than I ever thought they could be – full of holding hands, of cups of tea drunk from the Summer Sky teapot, of music – such a lot of music. Much as you would have lamented the end of my marriage, you would have adored this surge of music in my life and the person who had brought it about. As I switched my cream-coloured radio on to Radio 3 each morning while emptying the dishwasher and cleaning the surfaces, I sometimes felt I was turning into you. This was odd; for years, I swore we were nothing alike.

All I wanted for my birthday was to see all three of my children (two of whom were not living at home anymore) and to have some cake. Vanilla or chocolate? The obvious answer was both: vanilla cake with chocolate frosting. I decided that I would make the Nigella Lawson buttermilk birthday cake I had baked for almost all their early childhood birthdays. It's a classic yellow vanilla sponge, but the added buttermilk makes it extra moist. To go on top, I made the same glossy chocolate ganache with which I frosted my oldest son's very first birthday cake in our old house by the river (probably eaten off his Elmer the Elephant plate).

I had become so daunted by the tin and its meaning that I was convinced it would require an unfeasibly large amount of mixture. 'We will be eating the cake for days and days,' I told my youngest son. 'We will never manage to finish it.' My brain had glorified the tin into something monumental, fit for kings or giants. But it was really not so big or so impressive. I only had to double the quantities in the Nigella recipe to make enough mixture. It was a six-egg cake: large but not insanely so. After scrubbing the tin clean I buttered it and cut out a heart-shaped section of baking parchment to line it before pouring in the cake mix. My dog hovered nearby, his nose in the air, hoping for a morsel.

As the cake baked, the top of it developed a pleasing crack, like a Madeira cake. You would have loved the cake best then, before the addition of icing; you had a fear of food that was too sweet or too salty (Marmite aside) and preferred baked goods without too much adornment. I had recently had a conversation with Subha about sponge cakes in Kolkata and how her mother's favourite cake always had one of these cracks; the crack was how she knew the cake was good. I was reminded of the Leonard Cohen line about how there is 'a crack in everything' and 'that's how the light gets in'. The light was not going to have much chance to shine through the crack in my cake, however. I smothered it in a thick layer of ganache as dark as night.

The only constant in life is change, as the saying goes, and the older you get (or so I find), the harder it is to accept that just because something was true a year ago or five years ago, it doesn't mean it still applies. I assumed that when they tasted it, the children would all instantly recognise the cake as their signature birthday cake. With my slow middle-aged mind, I'd forgotten that it had been ten years since I had actually made this particular cake for any of them.

So I was the only one at the table who consciously remembered the buttermilk cake, although the children did recall that I had once made them big vanilla cakes decorated with cartoon characters or Barbie or football pitches, as the case may be. For the last few years, post-pandemic, I had made a much smaller traybake cake for birthdays, an Edd Kimber recipe for a light chocolate sponge topped with a burnt caramel ganache. Before that, my daughter had switched over to lemon or carrot cakes for her birthdays and my older son had a predeliction for maple syrup cake with a meringue-like frosting and pecan nuts on top (another Nigella recipe).

Even when we think we have forgotten a certain detail, the memory may still be lodged somewhere in our brains, like the toast rack at the back of the cupboard. When they tasted the heart-shaped cake, the children all responded with such pleasure that I felt the flavour or texture must have triggered deep memories for them, even if they denied it. A Norwegian scientist of smell and memory called Trygg Engen once said that our sense of smell (and, by implication, flavour) is a system 'designed not to forget'.

I sliced the heart in two and then into long slabs, divided into smaller squarish hunks. The golden sponge inside seemed to sigh with vanilla and butter. There was still a breath of warmth on it from the oven, and where the ganache touched the cake the chocolate had softened slightly. We ate it with raspberries scented like violets, each berry tickling with tiny hairs. 'I wonder if the ganache makes it too rich?' I asked, pouring another cup of tea from the Summer Sky teapot, but their mouths were too full of cake to answer. My youngest son shook his head vigorously and took another slice.

It was a relief to be able to look at the tin again without wincing. As with Roopa and her dinner service, I was happy that this object had the chance of a second chapter and new associations. What's more, I was managing to look back at my own past more kindly. In the early days of separation, all the years of my marriage became polluted in my mind. If our relationship could end like this, I felt, it must *never* have been good.

Lately, though, it was as if a new portal had opened and I could once again access shared times in the past without forcing them into an unhappy narrative arc. I could picture myself picking up my oldest son from nursery when he was one, pushing his blue pushchair down the trafficky, ugly main road that ran near his nursery, on our way home. I remember thinking that at this moment no one could possibly be happier than I was because I had two people I loved so much. After our son was born, anytime my ex-husband saw a child on screen who was hurt, he exhibited intense sorrow and pity, as if his love for our baby radiated outwards to all babies.

Hearts can change; do change. Love can and does take a million forms. There are some people who manage to bring the joy and tenderness of a wedding to everyday life. I sometimes think the single greatest act of love I have ever witnessed was that of a friend making an apple pie for her children with what seemed like infinite care. She gave each stage its due, not hurrying the peeling and coring of the apples. As someone who is mostly in too much of a rush, I watched her slowness in awe. Her fingers caressed the rolled-out pastry as she crimped the edges and cut leaf shapes to go on top. Her love for her children had transferred itself into the way she touched the pastry and the pie dish.

When I began searching to see whether tins like my heart-shaped one still existed, I found a similar version online made from 'traditional tin plate with steel edges' and a fixed base. It was advertised as 'ideal for weddings and Valentine's Day'. I suddenly felt what a crazily limited view of love this was. Why should heart-shaped cakes only be for people in the grip of romantic coupledom? Frank Trentmann, a historian of things, has written that products have 'ideas of how they will be used designed into them'. A cake tin's purpose is scripted to some degree by manufacturers and kitchenware shops, which send the message that hearts are only for grand gestures of love. But we could pretend that we never got the memo.

The great unspoken truth of objects is that we can invent our own uses and meanings for them. It follows that a heart-shaped tin can be used for moods and occasions other than romance. That tin could also be used to express affection for one of the dozens of people in our life deserving of non-romantic but heartfelt love: friends, parents, colleagues, cousins, dog-walking chums, neighbours, in-laws, aunts, siblings. Or for ourselves. I have mixed feelings about the emojis that have taken over so much of modern communication, but one of the points I like about them is the way they have broadened out the meaning of a heart as an expression of feeling between human beings. As well as the red heart of romantic love there is the purple heart of compassion, the yellow heart of friendship, the blue heart of trust and loyalty (or autism awareness, depending on context), the white heart of unchanging love after death, the orange heart of encouragement and support.

Sometimes, from your care home, when we were separated during the pandemic, you sent me funny nonsensical text messages strewn with various unicorn stickers, oblivious to their sexual connotations. Your words were muddled but contained a weird poetry, full of passionate expressions of love for your relatives, intermingled with worries that we might fall into a dangerous river or that we might already be dead. Even in the jumble of these messages, you retained your appetite for toast. One of your messages read: 'Toast? Wine. Wine too? Hurrah!!'

We only get one life and it is often cruelly short. As your beloved Shakespeare wrote, 'our little life is rounded with a sleep'. But the magic of things is that they can live more than once, passing faithfully through many pairs of hands, gaining different meanings each time. Our most significant kitchen objects can keep us connected with the dead and the absent, so no wonder we sometimes act as if they were charmed. A mother's vegetable corer can bring the distant flavours of Syria to England. A chocolate bottle can lie undiscovered for thousands of years, only to be found and bring with it news of a whole forgotten civilisation. A father's gift of a pan may feel more precious than gold, especially when he is a continent away.

The meaning of objects is never fixed; it can change in a heartbeat. And this is just as well. In a world of finite and dwindling resources, our ability to change the meaning of the many material goods in our environment is one of the greatest powers we have. Rusty as it is, an old metal cake tin may one day far in the future find another life and another meaning, unimagined at the moment of purchase. In their 1982 book *The Meaning of Things*, Eugene Rochberg-Halton and Mihaly Csikszentmihalyi argued that the human ability to create meaning from everything around us was the 'only hope' we had against 'this vast expenditure of the earth's resources'. They wrote:

> The world is not made just of fuel, it contains things that can make us grow and change our natures – change our needs. Things can have meanings that may transform the very world in which we live. But things by themselves cannot help us; only in the way we relate to them is their symbolic energy released.

We could stop seeing so many of the objects in our lives as individual possessions and start to envisage them as something shared, not just within families but across streets and cities and countries. When belongings are shared, you don't need to buy so many of them. We could try to change our values and see second-hand things as more beautiful and special than the shiny and new (there are already signs of this happening with the rise of apps for selling second-hand possessions, from clothes to forks). The technology to make it happen may have changed but these ideas are not new. You were ahead of the game in this – another thing I didn't give you credit for. Like other wartime babies, you always loved the idea of 'make do and mend' and took great delight in vintage bookshops and jumble sales and borrowing and lending books among your friends.

A few months after my fiftieth birthday I had a second celebration with some friends, old and new. I realised I didn't have enough glasses in the house and went to a second-hand shop, where I found a set of sparkling Waterford crystal champagne glasses going for a song. The glasses made me think of those brides in the mid-twentieth century with their hope chests. These were the kind of special crystal our grandparents kept locked away in cabinets but now they were cheaper than new wine glasses made from ordinary glass. The autumn light glinted through them.

Faraj came to cook dinner and Subha was also there. Faraj made beetroot falafel and the most incredible cheese scones seasoned with dill and za'atar. Then there was hummus ('I've never tasted hummus like this,' said one of my friends), and *muhammara* (a roasted red pepper dip seasoned with walnuts and pomegranate molasses and coffee), and peach salad with tahini and lime, and vegetarian *kibbeh* filled with oyster mushrooms and served on a warm yoghurt sauce with dried Iranian mint, and a cucumber salad with fine strands of Syrian cheese and herbs.

We were looking for plates to put the cucumber salad on when I showed Faraj your Matsumai platters – the oval second-hand ones you bought but never used. 'Yes!' he said. 'These are perfect.' Cucumber was your favourite vegetable and you would have been so cheered to see the green of the cucumber against the blue-black of the plate.

At the crematorium nearly two years earlier, I had watched your poor little coffin taken away. 'Fear No More the Heat of The Sun' from *Cymbeline* was one of the songs at your funeral. 'Fear no more the lightning flash, Nor the all-dreaded thunder stone'. You would never again feel the warmth of the sun on your face but you were also free at last from the distress of dementia, which had made you so frightened.

Yet looking down at the pale cucumber on the dark ceramic, I had the strangest feeling that you hadn't really left after all. You were still vividly there in the pattern of that old plate, which had once caught and pleased your eye as it now pleased mine. This is the power of objects; they keep those we miss in the room with us. A plate is something to hold onto when hands are gone.

Suddenly, eating that fresh green cucumber salad, you were at the table with me, as real as spring. I could feel your presence in the chair where you once sat and ate Thanksgiving pies the last time. Do you remember that night, when both your daughters were still happy in love and we ate stuffing and mashed potatoes and cranberry sauce on Kutani Crane plates? Your youngest grand-daughter had gaps in her smile where her milk teeth had fallen out, and the candles shone in our old metal candle holder which wasn't yet broken, back when we were all alive.

Acknowledgements

Some of my books were mostly written in libraries but this one owes as much to the kitchen table. Most of all, I need to thank the many people who generously agreed to speak to me about some of their own most beloved objects or those belonging to family members. Special thanks to Faraj Alnasser, Kristina Awatsu, Zoltan Bogathy, Gloria Chaim, Shoshana Chaim, Sasha Correa, Roopa Gulati, Kate McDermott, Subha Mukherji, Aya Oguma, Jessica Sawinski Couch, Avra Selick, Maeve Sheridan, Bonnie Slotnick, Paola White, Chris White, Barry Yourgrau.

I am also so grateful to the academics and other experts who answered questions about their research including Russell Belk, Julie Franklin, Mathias Alubafi Fubah, Paul Rozin, Francisco Valdez, Sonia Zarrillo. Thank you to Kazuo Ishiguro for telling me about 'The Broken Rice Bowl'.

I am so grateful to everyone at my publishers in the UK, especially my extraordinary editor, Louise Haines (what a joy to work on another book with you), as well as Patrick Hargadon (ditto), Vic Pullen (for so many things, especially your notes on Symbols), Alex Gingell (who worked so hard to make everything come together), Matt Clacher, Linden Lawson (to whom so many thanks are due for sparing me some mistakes, though any that remain are my own) and the rest of the Fourth Estate team. Special thanks to Ethan Humphries and Julian Humphries for the superb photography and cover design.

Huge thanks too to my US publishers Norton, especially my wonderful editor Melanie Tortoroli, whose encouragement and ideas made it a better book, as well as Huneeya Siddiqui (for countless things: thank you), the amazing Steve Attardo, Erin Sinesky Lovett, Meredith McGinnis and the rest of the Norton team.

I am so lucky to have Zoë Pagnamenta and Georgia Garrett as my agents; with huge thanks, too, to Jess Hoare and Ivy Pottinger-Glass.

I could not have written this book without the support and conversation of friends and family, including (but not limited to) Deirdre Black, Catherine Blyth, Freya Brackett, Psyche Brackett, Catherine Carr, Miranda Carter, Emily Charkin, Rachael Claye, Menna Clatworthy, Theo Fairley, David Foreman, Shoshana and Simon Goldhill, Nicola Holton, Ingrid Kopp, Henrietta Lake, Miranda Landgraf (you will never know how much I owe you), John Lanchester, Annabel Lee, Jane Lockie, Liz McDermott, Anne Malcolm, Miriam Manook, Jeannie and Philip Milward, Jason and Elspeth O'Rourke, Ranjita Rajan, Sarah Ray, Imogen Roth, Miri Rubin, Cathy Runciman, Leo Runciman, Lisa Runciman, Tash Runciman, Tom Runciman, Abby Scott, Ruth Scurr, Liz McDermott, Gareth Stedman Jones, Sylvana Tomaselli, Alison and Martin Trowell, Jo Vincent, Chris Wallace, Jackie Watson, Andrew Wilson, Emily Wilson, Sharon Wilson, Stephen Wilson. Thank you to Tom for telling me about the Merry Mushrooms and for all the meals, from the elephant plate onwards. Thank you to Tash for giving me so many ideas and for making any table that you sit at feel like my favourite home. Thank you to Leo for forcing me to stick to my deadline. Thank you to Charlie for more than I can ever say.

List of Illustrations

Background Reading

There were certain sources I returned to many times while writing the book and two in particular, even though neither of them has much to say about kitchens. *The Meaning of Things: Domestic Symbols and the Self* by Mihaly Csikszentmihalyi and Eugene Rochberg-Halton was the richest book I found on the subject of ordinary domestic objects and why they mean so much to us; and by far the most useful article on the subject was Russell Belk's 'Possessions and the Extended Self'. Belk created a whole new field of consumer research with his concept of the 'extended self'. If my book had been aimed at academics rather than the general reader, I might have called it 'Kitchen Objects and The Extended Self', in Belk's honour.

Preface: The Heart-shaped Tin

Pearce, Susan M., *On Collecting: An Investigation Into Collecting in the European Tradition*, London: Routledge, 1995

CHARMS

1. The Best China

Epigraph: Csikszentmihalyi, Mihaly, and Rochberg-Halton, Eugene, *The Meaning of Things: Domestic Symbols and the Self*, Cambridge: Cambridge University Press, 1981

Ames, Kenneth L., 'Material Culture as Nonverbal Communication: A Historical Case Study', *Journal of American Culture*, 1980, vol. 3, 619–41

Ewins, Neil, *Ceramics and Globalization: Staffordshire Ceramics, Made in China*, London: Bloomsbury, 2017

2. Our Kitchen Table

Quotation: Jager, Bernd, 'Body, House, City or the Intertwinings of Embodiment in Habitation', in *The Changing Reality of Modern Man*, ed. Dreyer Kruger, Pittsburgh: Duquesne University Press, pp. 51–9, 1983

3. Drinking Glasses and Other Magical Objects

Epigraph: Fallon, April E., Rozin, Paul, and Pliner, Patricia, 'The Child's Conception of Food: The Development of Food Rejections with Special Reference to Disgust and Contamination Sensitivity', *Child Development*, 1984, vol. 55, 566–75

Frazer, James, *The Golden Bough: A Study of Magic and Religion*, London: Macmillan, 1890

Rozin, Paul, Millman, Linda, and Nemeroff, Carol, 'Operation of the Laws of Sympathetic Magic in Disgust and Other Domains', *Journal of Personality and Social Psychology*, vol. 50, 703–12, 1986

Rozin, Paul, and Fallon, April E., 'A Perspective on Disgust', *Psychological Review*, 1987, vol. 94, 23–41

Young, Molly, 'How Disgust Explains Everything', *The New York Times*, 27 December 2021

Wilson, Bee, *First Bite: How We Learn to Eat*, London: Fourth Estate, 2015

4. The Ukrainian Kitchen Cabinet

Epigraph: Belk, Russell, 'Possessions and the Extended Self', *Journal of Consumer Research*, September 1988, vol. 15, 139–68

Bittman, Mark, 'A No-Frills Kitchen Still Cooks', *The New York Times*, 9 May 2007

Sopova, Alisa, ' "Be Strong Like a Kitchen Cabinet": Indestructible Objects as Symbols of Resistance in Ukraine', *American Ethnologist* website, 4 May 2022, https://americanethnologist.org/features/reflections/be-strong-like-a-kitchen-cabinet

Vaughn, Joe, ' "Rooster, Hang On! A Traditional Symbol in the Nowadays Context" ', 6 October 2022, *The Museum of English Rural Life* website, https://merl.reading.ac.uk/blog/2022/10/rooster-hang-on/

5. The Chocolate Pot

Epigraph: Ariosto, Ludovico, *Orlando Furioso*, 1494, trans. William Stewart Rose for Project Gutenberg, 1996

David, Nicholas, Sterner, Judy, and Gavua, Kodzo, 'Why Pots Are Decorated', *Current Anthropology*, 1988, vol. 29, 365–89

Lanaud, C., Vignes, H., Utge, J. et al., 'A Revisited History of Cacao Domestication in Pre-Columbian Times Revealed by Archaeogenomic Approaches', *Scientific Reports*, 2024, vol. 14, article number 2972

Merrifield, Ralph, 'Witch Bottles and Magical Jugs', *Folklore*, 1995, vol. 66, 195–207

Mousa, Deena, 'Why Do Superstitions Persist Among Seemingly Rational People?', *Scientific American*, 3 May 2024

Powis, Terry G. et al., 'Spouted Vessels and Cacao Use Among the Preclassic Maya', *Latin American Antiquity*, 2002, vol. 13, 85–106

Valdez, Francisco, 'The Mayo-Chinchipe-Marañón Complex: The Unexpected Spirits of the Ceja', *The Archaeology of the Upper Amazon*, ed. Ryan Clasby and Jason Nesbitt, 2021, 62–82

Zarrillo, S., Gaikwad, N., Lanaud, C. et al., 'The use and domestication of *Theobroma cacao* during the mid-Holocene in the upper Amazon', *Nature Ecology and Evolution*, 2018, vol. 2, 1879–88

Zarrillo, Sonia, 'Clues to Cacao', 2018, Spinger Nature Research Communities blog, https://communities.springernature.com/posts/clues-to-cacao

MEMENTOS

1. The Mystery of the Silver-plated Toast Rack

Epigraph: *Shakespeare's Sonnets*, ed. Katherine Duncan-Jones, Arden, 1997

'The History and Use of Silver Toast Racks', blog, Dart Silver Ltd. https://dartsilverltd.co.uk/the-history-and-use-of-silver-toast-racks/

2. Subha's Rice Pan

Epigraph: Belk, Russell, 'Possessions and the Extended Self', *Journal of Consumer Research*, September 1988, vol. 15, 139–68

Din-Kariuki, Natalia, Mukherji, Subha, and Williams, Rowan, *Crossings: Migrant Knowledges, Migrant Forms*, Santa Barbara: Punctum Books, 2024

3. The Happy Hands

Epigraph: Romanyshyn, Robert, *Technology as Symptom and Dream*, London: Routledge, 1989

McDermott, Kate, *Art of the Pie: A Practical Guide to Homemade Crusts, Fillings and Life*, Woodstock: Countryman Press, 2016

McDermott, Kate, *Pie Camp: The Skills You Need to Make Any Pie You Want*, Woodstock, Countryman Press, 2020

4. The Rotary Whisk

Epigraph: Morris, Wright, *Time Pieces: Photographs, Writing and Memory*, Lincoln: University of Nebraska Press, 1991

Csikszentmihalyi, Mihaly, and Rochberg-Halton, Eugene, *The Meaning of Things: Domestic Symbols and the Self*, Cambridge: Cambridge University Press, 1981

5. Barry's Pasta Bowl

Epigraph: Dickens, Charles, *Bleak House*, London: Bradbury and Evans, 1853

Borges, Jorge Luis, *Labyrinths: Selected Stories and Other Writings*, trans. James E. Irby, New York: New Directions, 1964

Frost, Randy O., and Steketee, Gail, *Stuff: Compulsive Hoarding and the Meaning of Things*, Boston: Mariner Books, 2011

Steketee, Gail, and Bratiotis, Christina, *Hoarding: What Everyone Needs to Know*, Oxford: Oxford University Press 2020

Yourgrau, Barry, *Mess: One Man's Struggle to Clean Up His House and His Act*, New York: W. W. Norton, 2015

JUNK

1. The Babyfood Scissors

Epigraph: Jarrett, Christian, 'The Psychology of Stuff and Things', blog, *British Psychological Society*, 2013, https://www.bps.org.uk/psychologist/psychology-stuff-and-things

Belk, Russell, 'Possessions and the Extended Self', *Journal of Consumer Research*, September 1988, vol. 15, 139–68

Belk, Russell, 'Why Not Share Rather Than Own?', *Annals of the American Academy of Political and Social Science*, 2007, vol. 611

Börsch-Supan, Axel, 'Housing Market Regulations and Housing Market Performance in the United States, Germany and Japan', in *Social Protection Versus Economic Flexibility: Is There a Trade Off?*, Chicago: University of Chicago Press, 1994

Cox, Madeleine, 'An Inventory of the Goods and Chattels', blog, *Shakespeare Birthplace Trust*, 2016

'Kay', 'Tiny Tot in Tokyo', blog, https://tinytotintokyo.com/, accessed 8 October 2024

2. The Paper Cup

Epigraph: Belk, Russell, 'Sharing', *Journal of Consumer Research*, vol. 36, 715–34 YEAR OF PUBL? 2010

BBC News Website, 'Coffee cup ban: Boston Tea Party's Sales Fall by £250k', 2 April 2019, https://www.bbc.co.uk/news/uk-england-bristol-47629820

House of Commons Environmental Audit Committee, 'Disposable Packaging: Coffee Cups', January 2018

Sukhbir Sandhu, Lodhia, Sumit et al., 'Environment friendly takeaway coffee cup use: Individual and institutional enablers and barriers', *Journal of Cleaner Production*, 2021, vol. 291

3. The Unused Platters

Epigraph: Pushkin, Alexander, *Eugene Onegin*, new translation by James E. Falen, Oxford: Oxford University Press, 1998

Beaglehole, Ernest, *Property: A Study in Social Psychology*, London: George Allen & Unwin, 1931,

Doulton, Michael, *Discovering Royal Doulton*, Shrewsbury: Swan Hill Press, 1993

Eyles, Desmond, *The Story of Royal Doulton*, Stoke-on-Trent: Royal Doulton Tableware, 1983

Royal Doulton 'Our Story', https://www.royaldoulton.com/en-gb/discover/our-story?srsltid=AfmBOopjACNxsWjLiDG7BnV8nwu yzzbskxfdAeUu6HJVtcpWqo9JeWi8

Stoke-on-Trent City Museum and Art Gallery, *Legacy of Sir Henry Doulton: 120 Years Of Royal Doulton*, Stoke-on-Trent, 1997

4. Bonnie's Salt Shaker

Epigraph: Oliphant, Margaret, *A Beleaguered City*, London: Macmillan, 1880

Goldfield, Hannah, 'Bonnie Slotnik, The Downtown Food History Savant', *The New Yorker*, 26 August 2024

Slotnik, Bonnie, 'A Life in Objects', *The Gourmand*, 17 February 2016

5. My Grandfather's Teapot

Epigraph: Landon, Letitia Elizabeth, *Romance and Reality*, London, 1831

Head, Roland, 'British Ceramics of the 1950s', *Antiques Info*, 2011

Reilly, Robin, *Wedgwood*, London: Stockton Press, 1989

Reilly, Robin, *Wedgwood: The New Illustrated Dictionary*, Woodbridge: Antique Collectors' Club, 1995

TOOLS

1. Paola's Pressure Cooker

Epigraph: Belk, Russell, 'Possessions and the Extended Self', *Journal of Consumer Research*, September 1988, vol. 15, 139–68

Chappell, Gweneth M., and Hamilton, Audrey M., 'Effect of Pressure Cooking on Vitamin C Content of Vegetables', *British Medical Journal*, April 1949, vol. 1, 4604, 574–75

Moscardini-Hall, Christine, 'Kook-Kwick Steam Pressure Cooker', Collection Blog, UTSA Institute of Texan Cultures, https://texancultures.utsa.edu/collections-blog/object-pressure-cooker/, accessed October 2024

Wild, Matthew J., 'Eating Spain: National Cuisine Since 1900', PhD dissertation, Hispanic Studies, University of Kentucky, 2015

2. Jacob's Spoon

Epigraph: Goffman, Ernest, *Asylums: Essays on the Social Situation of Mental Patients and Other Inmates*, London: Penguin, 1991

Haitiwaji, Gulbahar, ' "Our Souls Are Dead": How I Survived A

Chinese "Re-Education Camp" for Uyghurs', Montréal Holocaust Museum, 'Jacob Chaim's Spoon', https://museeholocauste. ca/en/objects/jacob-chaims-spoon-camp-dora-mittelbau/, accessed October 2024

Neufeld, Michael J., *The Rocket and the Reich: Peenemünde and the Coming of the Ballistic Missile Era*, Cambridge: Harvard University Press, 1996

Michel, Jean, *Dora*, written in association with Louis Nucera, trans. Jennifer Kidd, London: Weidenfeld & Nicolson, 1979

Mikaberidze, Alexander, *Behind Barbed Wire: An Encyclopedia of Concentration and Prisoner-Of-War Camps*, Santa Barbara: ABC-CLIO, 2019

Visser, Margaret, *The Rituals of Dinner*, London: Viking, 1992

3. The Casserole Protests

Epigraph: Lovett, Lorcan, 'The Nights of Pots and Pans Are Back, On Myanmar's Fearful Streets', *Guardian*, 2 February 2021

Combis, Hélène, 'De la Monarchie de Juillet à Emmanuel Macron, petite histoire de la casserole comme outil politique', radiofrance. com, 3 March 2017

Janetsky, Megan, 'Kitchenware cacophony', *The World*, 26 November 2019

L'Huillier, Nicole, 'Sounding Manifesto', in *Dismantling the Nation: Contemporary Art in Chile*, Amherst: Amherst College Press, 2023

Tarver, H. Michael, with Frederick, Julia C., *The History of Venezuela*, New York: Palgrave Macmillan, 2006

Ulmer, Alexandra, 'Venezuela Revels in Pots-and-Pans Protests After Maduro Humiliation', Reuters.com, 10 September 2016

Ulmer, Alexandra, 'Banging on Empty Pots, Venezuelans Protest Food Shortages', Reuters.com, 3 June 2017

4. Dave's Poetry Jars

Epigraph: James, William, *The Principles of Psychology*, New York: Henry Holt, 1890

Chaney, Michael A. 'The Concatenate Poetics of Slavery and the Articulate Material of Dave the Potter', *African American Review*, 2011, 44, 607–18

Chaney, Michael A. (ed.), *Where Is All My Relation? The Poetics of Dave the Potter*, Oxford: Oxford University Press, 2018

Finkel, Jori, 'The Enslaved Artist Whose Poetry Was An Act of Resistance', *The New York Times*, 17 June 2021

Koverman, Jill, *I Made This Jar: The Life and Works of the Enslaved African-American Potter, Dave*, Columbia: University of South Carolina Press, 1998

Lasser, Ethan W., 'Writing in Clay: The Materiality of Dave's Poetry', in Chaney, Michael A. (ed), *Where Is All My Relation? The Poetics of Dave the Potter*, Oxford: Oxford University Press, 2018

Todd, Leonard, *Carolina Clay: The Life and Legend of the Slave Potter Dave*, New York: W. W. Norton, 2009

5. The Cream-coloured AGA

Epigraph: Tuan, Yu-Fi, 'The Significance of the Artifact', *Geographical Review*, 1980, 70, 462–72

Goodhart, Maud, 'Design Classic: The Aga Range Cooker', *Financial Times*, 25 November 2016

Harding, Julie, 'Mary Berry: "Why I Love My Aga"', *Country Life*, 18 March 2017

SYMBOLS

1. The Melon Baller

Epigraph: Durkheim, Émile, *The Elementary Forms of the Religious Life*, translated from the French by Joseph Ward Swain, London: George Allen & Unwin, 1915

Ong, Marilyn, 'We Love a Melon Baller, And Not Just for Melons', *The New York Times*, 26 June 2024

Wolfe, Burt, Aronson, Emily, and Fabricant, Florence, *The New Cook's Catalogue: The Definitive Guide to Cooking Equipment*, New York: Knopf, 2000

2. The Queen's Sieve

Epigraph: Herbert, George (compiler), *Jacula Prudentum*, London, 1651

Baert, Barbara, *About Sieves and Sieving: Motif, Symbol, Technique, Paradigm*, Berlin: De Gruyter, 2019

Malcolm, Janet, *Still Pictures: On Photography and Memory*, London: Granta, 2023

McBurney, Henrietta, and Slottved Kimbriel, Christine, 'A Newly Discovered Variant at Eton College of the Queen Elizabeth I Sieve Portrait', *Burlington Magazine*, October 2014

3. The Vegetable Corers

Epigraph: Many sources

Helou, Anissa, *Feast: Food of the Islamic World*, London: Ecco, 2018

Roden, Claudia, *A Book of Middle Eastern Food*, Nelson, London: Penguin, 1970

4. Bruce Lee Drinking Horns

Epigraph: Csikszentmihalyi, Mihaly, and Rochberg-Halton, Eugene, *The Meaning of Things: Domestic Symbols and the Self*, Cambridge: Cambridge University Press, 1981

Fubah, Mathias Alubafi, 'Title Cups and People: Relationships and Change in Grassfields Art', *Anthropos*, 2012, 107, 183–95

Fubah, Mathias Alubafi, 'Contemporary Drinking Horns in the Western Grassfields, Cameroon', *Anthropologie*, 2016, 54, 129–39

Fubah, Mathias Alubafi, and Ramphalile, Molemo, 'The Shifting Iconography of Drinking Horns in the Western Grassfields, Cameroon', *Cogent Social Sciences*, 2017, 1-19

Mull, Amanda, 'The New Trophies of Domesticity', *The Atlantic*, 29 January 2020

5. The Mushroom Canister

Epigraph: Malcolm, Janet, 'Rachel Maddow: Trump's Nemesis', *The New Yorker*, 2 October 2017

Howard, Vicki, 'The Rise and Fall of Sears', *The Smithsonian Magazine*, 25 July 2017

Mekouar, Dora, 'Why America Stopped Shopping At Sears', voanews.com, 18 October 2018

Sawinski Couch, Jessica, *A Collector's Guide to Merry Mushrooms*, 7 July 2020

Sawinski Couch, Jessica, 'On The Big Screen: Rachel Maddow & The Canisters', blog with link to video of Rachel Maddow talking about the mushroom canisters, merrymushrooms.weebky.com, 17 August 2020

Sawinski Couch, Jessica, 'Discoveries: Jack Buchanan Talks!', blog with link to Jack Buchanan talking about Sears and The Merry Mushroom, merrymushrooms.weebly.com, 5 February 2021

GIFTS

1. The Glory Box

Epigraph: Mauss, Marcel, *The Gift*, expanded edn, trans. Jane I. Guyer, Chicago: Hau Books, 2016

Hogbin, Ian H., 'Polynesian Ceremonial Gift Exchanges', *Oceania*, September 1932, vol. 3, 13–39

Isaacs, Susan, 'Property and Possessiveness', *British Journal of Medical Psychology*, 1935, vol XV, part I, 69–78

McFadzean, Moya Patricia, 'Glory Boxes: Femininity, Domestic Consumption and Material Culture in Australia, 1930–1960', PhD thesis, University of Melbourne, 2009

Purbrick, Louise, *The Wedding Present: Domestic Life Beyond Consumption*, London: Routledge, 2016

Rupp, Katherine, *Gift-Giving in Japan: Cash, Connections, Cosmologies*, Stanford: Stanford University Press, 2003

2. Burial Plates

Epigraph: Browne, Thomas, *Hydriotaphia, Urne-Buriall, or a Discourse of the Sepulchral Urnes Lately Found in Norfolk*, 1658

Cooper, Anwen, Garrow, Duncan et al., *Grave Goods: Objects and Death in Later Prehistoric Britain*, Oxford: Oxbow Books, 2022

Copeland, Robert, *Spode's Willow Pattern and Other Designs After the Chinese*, New York: Rizzoli, 1980

Drakard, David, and Holdway, Paul, *Spode Transfer Printed Ware 1784–1833*, Woodbridge: Antique Collectors' Club, 2002

Draper, Amanda, 'Story of the Willow Pattern', blog, University of Liverpool, https://vgm.liverpool.ac.uk/blog/2021/willow-pattern/, 15 January 2021

O'Hara, Patricia, '"The Willow Pattern That We Knew": The Victorian Literature of Blue Willow', *Victorian Studies*, 1993, vol. 36, 421–42

Richardson, Beth, 'An Emblem of the Immortal Spirit? Salt Plates from St James's and Park Street Burial Grounds', MOLA headland blog, 24 October 2015, https://molaheadland.com/salt-plates-from-st-james-and-park-street-burial-grounds/, accessed October 2024

Roediger, David R., 'And Die in Dixie: Funerals, Death and Heaven in the Slave Community 1700-1865, *Massachusetts Review*, 1981, vol. 22, 163–83

Thompson, Robert Farris, 'African Influence on the Art of the United States', in *Afro-American Folk Art and Crafts*, ed. William F. Ferris, 1983

3. The Unwanted Tureen

Epigraph: Visser, Margaret, *The Gift of Thanks: The Roots and Rituals of Gratitude*, Boston: Houghton Mifflin Harcourt, 2009

Blake-Roberts, Gaye, and Rawsthorn, Alice, *Wedgwood: A Story of Creation and Innovation*, New York: Rizzoli International Publications, 2017

Daniels, Inge, 'The Social Death of Unused Gifts: Surplus and Value in Contemporary Japan', *Journal of Material Culture*, 2009, vol. 14

Rattner, Steven, '200 Years of Fine Pottery', *The New York Times*, 25 April 1982

Rupp, Katherine, *Gift-Giving in Japan: Cash, Connections, Cosmologies*, Stanford: Stanford University Press, 2003

Sword, Rosalind, *The Marshall Collection of Worcester Porcelain in the Ashmolean Museum, Oxford*, Oxford: Oxford University Press, 2017

4. Sasha's *Budare* Pan

Epigraph: Sontag, Susan, *On Photography*, London: Allen Lane, 1978

Attman, Karen, 'Cooking in Latin America: My Beloved Budare', blog, *Flavors of Bogotá*, https://flavorsofbogota.com/what-is-a-budare/, 2017

Belk, Russell, 'It's the Thought That Counts: A Signed Digraph Analysis of Gift-Giving', *Journal of Consumer Research*, December 1976, vol. 3, 155–62

Belk, Russell, 'Possessions and the Extended Self', *Journal of Consumer Research*, September 1988, vol. 15, 139–68

5. A Red Washing-up Bowl

Epigraph: Orchard, Andy (trans. and ed.), *The Elder Edda: A Book of Viking Lore*, London, Penguin, 2011

Cleuziou, Juliette, and Dufy, Caroline, 'Marriage, Divorce and Mutual Indebtedness: Perspectives from Tajikistan', *Journal of Extreme Anthropology*, 2022, vol. 6, 73–95

Newman, Judith, 'The Unbridled Shower: Celebrating Divorce', *The New York Times*, 14 September 2012

Titmuss, Richard, *The Gift Relationship: From Human Blood to Social Policy*, London: Penguin 1970

TREASURE

1. The Elephant Plate

Epigraph: Durkheim, Émile, *The Elementary Forms of The Religious Life*, translated from the French by Joseph Ward Swain, London: George Allen & Unwin, 1915

2. The Corkscrew Collection

Epigraph: Pearce, Susan M., *On Collecting: An Investigation into Collecting in the European Tradition*, London: Routledge 1995

Gelfman Karp, Marilynn, and Franklin Brooke, Jeremy, *Uncorked: A Corkscrew Collection*, New York: Abbeville Press, 2019

Gendzier, Stephen J., 'The Corkscrew', *Gastronomica*, 2001, vol 1, no. 3, 67–71

Iongone, Jan, and Odom, Susan, 'Jelly Jammer, Pie Birders and Other Passionate Collectors', *Gastronomica*, 2006, vol. 6, no. 4, 87–90

Wallis, Fletcher, *British Corkscrew Patents from 1795*, London: Vernier Press, 1995

Watney, Bernard M., and Babbidge, Homer D. *Corkscrews: For Collectors*, London: Sotheby Parke Bernet, 1981

3. The Oil Dispenser

Epigraph: Visser, Margaret, *The Gift of Thanks: The Roots and Rituals of Gratitude*, Boston: Houghton Mifflin Harcourt, 2009

Mynatt, Corinne, *Tools for Food: The Objects That Influence How and What We Eat*, London: Hardie Grant, 2021

Stendhal, *Love*, trans. Gilbert and Susan Sale, London: Penguin, 1975

Wolfe, Burt, Aronson, Emily, and Fabricant, Florence, *The New Cook's Catalogue: The Definitive Guide to Cooking Equipment*, New York: Knopf, 2000

4. Broken Cups

Epigraph: Dickens, Charles, *Great Expectations*, London: Penguin, 2008

Aiyar, Pallavi, 'A Japanese Ceramic Repair Technique Teaches Us to Embrace Our Scars', online article, *Nikkei Asia*, https://asia.nikkei.com/NAR/Articles/A-Japanese-ceramic-repair-technique-teaches-us-to-embrace-our-scars, 1 December 2016

Sansho, 'Kintsugi: Fact and Fiction', blog, Sansho: Handmade in Japan, https://sansho.com/blogs/news/kintsugi-fact-and-fiction?srsltid=AfmBOord4RZjICsT5xMongoghxkTgzlTyR1wixbQkrKSAV_3w7pjyvX2, 2 December 2021

Kemske, Bonnie, *Kintsugi: The Poetic Mend*, London: Herbert Press, 2021

5. Epilogue: The Heart-shaped Tin (Again)

Epigraph: Rumi, *Selected Poems*, trans. Coleman Banks, London; Penguin, 1995

Csikszentmihalyi, Mihaly, and Rochberg-Halton, Eugene, *The Meaning of Things: Domestic Symbols and the Self*, Cambridge: Cambridge University Press, 1981